Unraveling U.S. Health Care

A Personal Guide

Unraveling U.S. Health Care

A Personal Guide

Roberta E. Winter

ROWMAN & LITTLEFIELD PUBLISHERS, INC.

Lanham • Boulder • New York • Toronto • Plymouth, UK

Published by Rowman & Littlefield Publishers, Inc.
A wholly owned subsidary of The Rowman & Littlefield Publishing Group, Inc.
4501 Forbes Boulevard, Suite 200, Lanham, Maryland 20706
www.rowman.com

10 Thornbury Road, Plymouth PL6 7PP, United Kingdom

British Library Cataloguing in Publication Information Available

Library of Congress Cataloging-in-Publication Data

Winter, Roberta E.
  Unraveling U.S. health care : a personal guide / Roberta E. Winter.
    p. ; cm.
  Unraveling United States health care
  Includes bibliographical references and index.
  ISBN 978-1-4422-2297-7 (cloth : alk. paper) — ISBN 978-1-4422-2298-4 (electronic)
  I. Title. II. Title: Unraveling United States health care.
  [DNLM: 1. Delivery of Health Care—United States. 2. Economics, Medical—
United States. 3. Insurance, Health—United States. 4. Quality of Health Care—
United States. W 84 AA1]
  RA395.A3
  362.10973—dc23

                                                              2013013668

♾️™ The paper used in this publication meets the minimum requirements of
American National Standard for Information Sciences—Permanence of Paper
for Printed Library Materials, ANSI/NISO Z39.48-1992.

Printed in the United States of America

This book represents reference material only. It is not intended as a medical manual,
and the data presented here is meant to assist the reader in making informed choices
regarding wellness. This book is not a replacement for treatment(s) that may have
been suggested by the reader's personal physician. If the reader believes he or she is
experiencing a medical issue, professional medical help is recommended. Mention of
particular products, companies, or authorities in this book does not entail endorsement
by the publisher or author.

This book is dedicated to my son, Nathan,
and all of the other children in America,
for they will surely be our
stewards of tomorrow.

Contents

Part IV. Health Measures: Regional and State Results

Prologue

Why You Need to Read This Book

$\mathcal{A}$ decade ago I was an insurance broker representing corporate clients for benefit planning, including medical insurance—both self-insured and traditionally financed. Over the years I grew frustrated with the minimal impact the insurance business has on improving and distributing health care. The insurance industry's short attention span (most clients renew contracts annually) and the job of overhauling how we, as a nation, allocate, deliver, and finance health care, requires a long-term view (at least fifteen years).

My decision to enter the field of health care advocacy was a protracted one after years of observations and frustrations. During my insurance career, I was horrified to learn that full-time employees were often unable to afford the insurance premiums to enroll their families on their employer's group insurance plan. There were situations where a full-time employee qualified for medical assistance from the state. After nineteen years of researching and advising corporate clients on group benefit plans, regulatory compliance, and administration, I chucked it all to go back to school.

As a graduate student, I researched and wrote policy papers on health care reform initiatives, methods to decrease the uninsured population, ethical considerations for organ transplantation, and health care financing methods. My perspective was different from many of the students because I came from a business background, not a clinical-care perspective. In fact, the reason I chose to go to graduate school was to find a way to synthesize the best of the private sector, along with effective government regulations, to create a better health care system for the country.

After completing my Master's degree in health administration, majoring in health policy analysis, I moved to Austin, Texas, to work for a large nonprofit hospital group. My job was to work with clinical, financial, and operations staff members to identify, develop, and produce value propositions for the organization. This meant the off-budget initiatives would either be money-saving initiatives, like changing drug treatment protocols, or testing new patient services to bring in revenue. The hospital network had devoted a considerable amount of resources to identifying the uninsured and underinsured populations and to figuring out how to serve them appropriately. Even though it wasn't their domain as a critical-care provider, the hospital administration created primary-care disease-management clinics to try to prevent unnecessary emergency-room admissions for the uninsured. One wonders how health care could improve as a nation if we deployed these ideas across the nation, not through the hospital emergency room, but through public health clinics.

Missing the place where the mountains meet the sea, I moved back to the Pacific Northwest to complete my master's degree in public administration, and I subsequently started working as an external consultant for health care entities and nonprofit advocacy groups.

In 2007, I created a health care column called "Straight Talk on Health Care," under the blog name of healthpolicymaven™. After several articles penned on the 2010 health care reforms were published in other media, I decided to write this book.

This book provides a practical view of health care in the United States—everything from tips for choosing the best hospital to the worst state in which to reside for birth-control options. As you know, the healthpolicymaven™ cuts through the bureaucratic red tape to help you avoid pitfalls and get the best health care services.

The year 2010 may have been the most exciting year for health care in U.S. history. With the triad of health care reforms including the Patient Protection and Affordable Care Act, the Health Care Affordability Reconciliation Act, and the Public Health Services Act, there is plenty to write about. However, before the regulatory "yawn-a-thon" overtakes you, if any of these circumstances resonate, I encourage you to read further:

1. Uninsured: You are currently without medical insurance and reside in the United States; learn how to obtain medical care without insurance.
2. Employed but uninsured: You are working and not receiving medical insurance from your employer; learn about federal subsidies to help you obtain health insurance in 2014.
3. Low-income household: You are unable to afford medical insurance for yourself or your family; understand what your state and the federal government offer in terms of health care programs.

4. Cancer diagnosis: You have had breast, ovarian, or prostate cancer; learn about the wide variances in deaths state by state from these diseases.

5. Cardiac or heart trouble: You previously have had a heart attack; learn how your state compares for cardiac deaths.

6. Pregnancy: You have a child or are thinking about having one; read the state health scorecards for children's health and infant mortality.

7. Medical tourism: You are considering obtaining health care outside the United States; learn how to assess health care quality for international facilities.

8. Relocation: You are considering relocation and want to find out about health care facilities and patient safety reporting in another state.

9. Students and other visa holders: You are a new resident or visitor to the United States and need to understand the health care system, such as locating a high-quality hospital.

10. Global health care data: You are becoming an expatriate and want to have an idea of how U.S. health care compares to other countries.

11. Medicare: You will soon become eligible for Medicare and want to understand the options.

12. Holistic health care: You are contemplating holistic or naturopathic treatment and want to find out about provider licensing criteria in your state.

13. Insurance mandates: You want straight talk on insurance and the implementation of the 2014 Affordable Care Act mandates.

14. BFF: You are a friend or relative and are morally obligated to purchase this book.

For a quick reference, just go to the chapters that interest you, and if you are really in a hurry, skip to the healthpolicymaven's™ analysis, or review the state-by-state scorecards.

I

U.S. HEALTH
CARE OVERVIEW

The Truth about U.S. Health Care

$\mathcal{B}$efore embarking on any review of health care quality, let's spend a little time debunking the myths about health care delivery in the United States. The top deceptions most often communicated about the U.S. health care system are:

1. the system is privatized, not socialized medicine;
2. a national health care program would be more expensive;
3. we have the best health care in the world;
4. we can't afford to cover everybody; and
5. everyone gets to choose his or her own doctor in America.

The correct answers are:

1. U.S. health care is a combination of public and private health care resources.
2. A national health care program would not have to be more expensive than what the United States has now; in fact, other industrialized countries with national health care programs spend considerably less than we do per person for health care.
3. The United States has many technologically advanced medical centers, but because it does not effectively deploy health care services to all its citizens, the country is nowhere near the top for basic primary care, infant or maternal mortality, and even healthy life expectancy. And it only gets worse when you look at the data for customer satisfaction and health-system fairness.
4. It could take a minimal investment to provide primary health care for the 48 million people who don't have health insurance, because

we are already paying for their health care—or rather their lack of it—when they show up in the emergency room. Covering everyone for basic primary care is far cheaper than treating end-stage diseases.

5. The ability to choose which doctor you see in America is based on several factors, the most important of which is determined by the dictates of your insurance plan, where you live, and, sadly, your ability to pay. This means you are free to choose a doctor from a limited menu, as long as you have the ability to pay, which typically means the clinic will accept your insurance.

PRIVATE VERSUS PUBLIC
HEALTH CARE IN AMERICA

As of 2009, only 49 percent of all employers in the United States provided health insurance for their employees. This information is based on an annual survey done by a nationally recognized nonprofit health care research group: the Kaiser Foundation. According to the 2009 Kaiser Foundation survey, 5 percent of individuals buy health care on their own.[1] These two groups represent the private-sector insurance contribution, but not the copayments, deductibles, or out-of-network charges that an individual must also pay. So in terms of contributions, 54 percent of the investment to pay for health care for employed adults in the United States comes from the private sector.

It is important to note that medical insurance is only one method of financing health care in the country. The same Kaiser Survey also found that 17 percent of the entire nation had no health insurance at all. The remainder of the population—low-income children, the disabled, retirees, the poor, and, of course, veterans—are all covered on government health care programs, including the Children's Health Insurance Program, Medicare, Medicaid, and the Veterans Health Administration. As so many people have become unemployed since 2007, the proportion of funding from state Medicaid programs has increased considerably.[2]

But wait a minute, just because an employer provides medical insurance for the employee doesn't mean the firm is paying all of the cost. In fact, most plans require an employee to contribute to the cost of the health insurance plan through payroll deductions. About 80 percent of private employers require employees to contribute to the cost of medical insurance for their family coverage. The 2009 national insurance survey by the Kaiser Foundation confirms this and also shows that 20 percent of employers also expect the employee to pay for a portion of their individual insurance regardless of whether or not that person has a family.[3] So the insurance isn't exactly provided by the employer; it's more like a partnership between the employer (who contributes), the government (who provides a tax break), and the employees (who also pay some percent of the cost). Again, it isn't necessarily something the employer is doing for you; it's more like something you are doing together. Cost-sharing has become a greater burden for employees, who now pay as much as $1,000 per month for family medical coverage. The latest Kaiser Foundation Survey indicates the average health insurance cost for a family now exceeds $12,000 per year, and 73 percent of that is paid directly by employees.[4]

PUBLIC-SECTOR HEALTH CARE PROGRAMS

The federal government, through our tax contributions, pays for the following medical care programs: Medicare, which is primarily for senior health care, the Veterans Health Administration for retired service persons, and the Bureau of Indian Affairs for American Indians. Using information from the 2010 federal budget, here is the breakdown of the national health care budget.[5,6]

According to information from the United States Office of Management and Budget, the 2010 federal government allocated 8 percent for Medicaid, which is the medical program for the impoverished. The Medicare program, which is mainly for retirees age sixty-five and older, received 12 percent of the entire budget. The Veterans Affairs allocation was just under 4 percent and includes a health care program. The Bureau of Indian Affairs is part of the Department of the Interior, and the 2010 budget allocation for Indian health services was $4 billion, which is less than 1 percent of the budget. Other government health care programs include: funding for Disproportionate Share Hospitals that serve the urban poor, 340B drug price subsidies for health care facilities covered under the Veterans Affairs Act of 1992, and grants for Federally Qualified Health Centers that serve underrepresented populations. Generally, these programs are funded through the Department of Health and Human Services, which had a federal budget allocation of 5.7 percent. This funding also covers research grants and other agency initiatives. The total federal health care spending in 2010 was 30.7 percent of the entire national budget. If you subtract the Health and Human Services allocation, it still totals 25 percent. These federal payments support private-sector doctors, hospitals, pharmaceutical firms, medical equipment suppliers, and insurance companies. Therefore, as a nation we have deliberately made a significant investment in health care by funneling tax revenue to support the various components. Unfortunately, this is a bifurcated way to support health care.

By comparison, military spending in the same federal budget was 37 percent; 19 percent targeted for defense and 18 percent was discretionary defense spending for things like private military contractors.

GLOBAL COMPARISON OF HEALTH CARE SPENDING

Another argument against a nationally organized health care program is it would cost too much. Let's review current health care spending in the United States, compared to countries that have such national programs.

Here are the 2010 health care costs per person from industrialized countries around the globe[7]:

United States:	$7,538
Norway:	$5,003
Switzerland:	$4,627
Canada:	$4,079
Netherlands:	$4,063
Austria:	$3,970
Germany:	$3,737
France:	$3,696
Belgium:	$3,677
Sweden:	$3,470

More importantly, what are we getting for this gross overpayment for health care services? Sadly, in terms of health outcomes, the United States does much worse than these other countries in many important areas, as you shall see.

U.S. HEALTH CARE QUALITY: THE SCORES

Infant Deaths

Even if you don't mind spending more of our country's resources on health care than any other country, perhaps the fact that in 2006 we were ranked thirty-ninth in keeping infants alive[8] might raise a red flag. For example, Cuba does a better job than we do, with an infant death rate of 5.82 per 1,000 babies, compared to our 6.22 (CIA World FactBook, 2009) or 6.7 (World Health Organization 2008 report). And that infant mortality rate is the national average; several southern states have infant death rates as high as some African nations. More information on the phenomena is found in the chapter on children's health.

Childhood Vaccination Rate

The national vaccination rate for all recommended childhood immunizations is 83.34 percent, based on 2010 data from the Centers for Disease Control.[9]

The difference in vaccination rates was over 15 percent between the most compliant state, New Hampshire, boasting a vaccination rate of 89.55 percent, and the least, Missouri, with 76.66 percent of their children obtaining early childhood immunizations. Even states with normally good health surveillance systems such as Oregon scored below the national average for childhood immunizations. This degree of variation is not a plus, because the risk of disease outbreak increases as the proportion of unvaccinated residents increases.

And finally, how does our rate of vaccinations compare to other countries? The United States ranks high for its vaccination rate for the big three—diphtheria, Hip B, and hepatitis B—but not as well for other recommended immunizations, such as varicella or chicken pox, which is why the national immunization rate is lower overall.

Adult Life Expectancy

Life expectancy for U.S. residents has actually decreased, though we were not in first place in this measure of healthiness either. The World Health Organization published an update on adult life expectancy in 2000 using the Disability Adjusted Life Expectancy method, or the DALE.[10] This weighs the years of living in full health against total life expectancy, which is felt to be a truer measure of health. In this study, the United States came in twenty-fourth, with a disability-adjusted life expectancy of just seventy years. Japan was in first place at 74.5 years, Australia was second with 73.2, and France in third with 73.1 healthy years. All the rest of the top ten were other European countries. And again, they all have national health care systems. Briefly, here are the highlights of the three top-scoring countries' health care programs.

The United States Compared to Other Countries

Japan.   Health services are provided through either public or private hospitals and clinics in Japan. Patients have universal access to any facility. Public health insurance covers most residents, and the government pays 70 percent or more of the cost of care. The monthly insurance premium is based on individuals' income, somewhat like an income or payroll tax. Supplementary private health insurance is available to cover copayments and other non-covered costs. In 2005, Japan spent 8.2 percent of GDP on health care, and 80 percent of that was paid by the government. This is much different from the United States, which spent twice what the Japanese did on health care, as a percent of GDP. But the U.S. government's investment in health care is less than half of what the Japanese government spends, because the balance comes from the private sector. Using the 2009 figures from the global comparison, the per-person cost of Japanese health care was only $2,249, compared to the United States $5,711.[11] The United States spent 250 percent more than Japan for health care, and the Japanese live longer and are in better health.

Australia.   The Australian health care system is also known as Medicare, and it coexists with a private health system. All legal permanent residents are entitled to free public hospital care. Treatment by private doctors is also free when the doctor directly bills the health department. Medicare is funded by a 1.5-percent income-tax levy (with exceptions for low-income earners) and general revenues. An additional levy of 1 percent is imposed on high-income earners without private health insurance. There is also an uncapped 30-percent government-purchasing subsidy for private health insurance. Australia has a separate pharmaceutical drug program.

In 2005, Australia spent 8.8 percent of GDP on health care, or U.S. $3,181 per capita. Of that, approximately 67 percent was government expenditure. Again, the United States spent nearly double that amount on health care, and 30 percent came from the federal budget. Using the 2009 global comparison, Australia spent $2,886 per person, and the United States spent $5,711 per person for health care. In other words, we spent almost double what the Aussies did.

France.   In its 2000 assessment of world health care systems, the World Health Organization found that France provided the "best overall health care" in the world.[12] In the same report the United States was ranked thirty-seventh.[13] In 2005, France spent 11.2 percent of GDP on health care, or, in terms of U.S. currency, $3,926 per capita. In France, approximately 80 percent of health care spending is a government expenditure, but most French doctors remain in private practice.

French social security consists of several public organizations, distinct from the state government, that finance patient care in private and public facilities. This is somewhat similar to what we have in the United States, with our government-funded health care programs including Medicare, Medicaid, the Veterans Health Administration, and the Bureau of Indian Affairs. Supplemental coverage may be purchased from private insurers, and most of them are nonprofit insurers in France. Until recently, social security coverage in France was restricted to those who contributed to the fund, which is similar to the requirement for Social Security and Medicare eligibility in the United States. Now, universal health coverage allows the entire French population to obtain health care. In the 2009 global health-cost comparison, France spent $3,048 per person compared to the United States' $5,711. Again, the United States spent nearly twice as much as France yet with poorer results overall, and France covered all citizens for health care.

Health Care That Is There When You Need It.   And finally, the French program pays 70 percent of most health care costs and 100 percent for costly or long-term ailments. This is very different from the United States, where health-insurance plans often have strict dollar limits for medical benefits. In fact, as a former insurance broker, I know it was not uncommon to see a group health-insurance program designed so frugally that someone with a serious illness would literally "run out of benefits." Under those circumstances, the medical insurance contracts with private employers were designed to run out of money, regardless of the person's health needs.

I can remember seeing $250,000 caps on lifetime benefits for organ transplants. I also saw a lot of contracts that had overall lifetime limits of $1,000,000. Careful thought was given to employees who were in a high-risk health situation before any plan changes were made, as the new carrier would be liable for future claims. This problem will be addressed if the 2010 U.S. health care reforms are kept intact and implemented in 2014 as scheduled, at which time medical insurance companies will be obligated to offer unlimited lifetime benefit levels for most services.

MEASURES OF CLINICAL EFFECTIVENESS

The *Journal of Health Affairs* published an article in 2004 comparing twenty-one different health care measures in these five countries: Australia, Canada, England, New Zealand, and the United States.[14] These countries were chosen because they all had similar methods for measuring the criteria, which included: five-year survival rates for breast, cervical, and colorectal cancers, childhood leukemia, and non-Hodgkin's lymphoma; kidney and liver organ transplant survival rates; and survival rates for acute myocardial infarction (heart attack) and stroke. In addition, the incidence of these avoidable events was also reviewed: suicide, asthma mortality, pertussis, measles, hepatitis B, and smoking.

In the *Health Affairs* analysis, there was only a single measure for which the United States was first: breast cancer survival, besting the others with 114 lives saved for the five-year cancer survival rates, versus the next best country, Australia, at 107 lives. The United States was last for kidney-transplant survival rates, with a rate of 100 versus 113 for Canada, which scored the highest.[15] These rankings may be an indication that the primary health care system in the United States does not identify these patients early enough in their disease progression. For example, patients with hypertension and obesity are at high risk for renal failure. Also, U.S. health care providers are guaranteed reimbursement for patients with end-stage renal disease, because at that point they qualify for Medicare. Many indigent patients do not receive treatment until their disease is in the chronic stage (i.e., late-stage kidney failure). This postponement of medical intervention costs the health care system more money for intensive care rather than management of the disease. The Canadians have the same national health care system for everyone, so their primary-care surveillance for hypertension and kidney disease is probably better.

THE UNINSURED POPULATION
AND WHY WE NEED TO CARE

It is a fair assessment to say that the United States has been ambivalent about covering all of its residents' health care needs, by virtue of the huge percentage of the national population that lacks health insurance and receives no consistent primary health care. The proportion of the country without medical insurance has increased from 15 percent in 2007 to 17 percent in 2012. According to T. R. Reid's research in *The Healing of America*,[16] at least 20,000 people die each year from nonterminal diseases like lupus or hypertension. They die because they cannot obtain the medication to treat their diseases or are unable to maintain clinical follow-up. This statistic does not include thousands of other people whose lives are diminished by blindness from untreated glaucoma and other preventable diseases.

The number of people who were killed in automobile accidents in the United States in 2009 was 33,808, according to the National Transportation Highway Safety Administration.[17] By comparison, our current health care policy says it is okay to let half that many people die simply because they do not have access to health care.

That there are nearly 50 million uninsured people in the United States[18] may not motivate enough people to change the system, so let's look at the cost of delayed treatment. Yes, that is right, at some point, the nation demands that sick people receive treatment regardless of their ability to pay, and that is for emergency care. There is a federal law called the Emergency Medical Treatment and Active Labor Act that requires all hospitals to treat patients until they are stable enough for discharge, even if there is no insurance or ability to pay for services. This law requires hospitals throughout the country to devote a significant portion of their resources to uncompensated and undercompensated care. These unpaid services can total as much as 25 percent of a hospital's annual services. According to an American Hospital Association Survey, charity care or unpaid care in American hospitals was 6% of gross hospital revenues at the end of 2009.[19] When I worked for a non-profit hospital group in Texas, a considerable amount of our time was spent figuring out how to provide primary care to indigent patients who showed up in the emergency room. Though it isn't a hospital's job to provide primary care for disease management, this was more costeffective than experiencing the revolving door in the emergency department with the same sick people.

Now, you may ask, why does this matter to me? Well, the unpaid charges the hospital absorbs must be paid by others in order for the hospital to operate, and those costs are reimbursed through a cost transfer to the private sector. The hospital negotiates contracts with all insurance companies for reimbursement for services each year, and those charges include additional fees for the unpaid patients. Those fees are then blended into the insurance companies' charges or a self-insured plan's estimated cost for the year. And finally, it is passed down to the individual insured, who then has a portion of the health plan's cost taken out of his or her paycheck. All private-sector plans include charges for uncompensated care from the hospitals.

It would be vastly cheaper for the United States to expand its public health clinics and treat all uninsured patients for free, compared with the present bifurcated pass-through charges for the uninsured burdening health care professionals and private insurance payers. For example, hypertension is an easily treatable disease, and it prevents heart failure, kidney failure, and a host of other chronic diseases. To effectively treat hypertensive people, the country needs a good disease-surveillance program to identify those at risk for the problem and get them into a prevention program. The United States does prevent chronic disease well as a nation, which is one of the reasons why we rank so low for World Health Organization measures, from the DALE index for years of healthy living to life expectancy, as will be revealed throughout the book. Not only are we spending more than any other country, but we also aren't measuring up to those countries that spend much less than we do because they spend their money more wisely for health care. There are many examples of the variances in health outcomes based on national health policy throughout this book.

THE ABILITY TO SEE YOUR OWN DOCTOR

During the Clinton administration's campaign for national health care, one of the tactics the insurance industry used to defeat the proposal for a Canadian-style health care system was the fear of losing one's doctor. However, as you have read, countries that have national health care programs also allow their patients to choose their own doctors. Though the health care programs are largely financed by government payments, the patient also contributes some copayment for services and may also purchase supplemental private insurance as well. These national health care countries tend to have a combination of public and private hospitals, similar to the United States, although there are far more private hospitals here.

In France all 61 million residents are covered by the same electronic medical record system, and patients use a debit card for all services. By contrast, the United States does not have all of its citizens on an electronic medical record system, as there are many different medical-record and insurance-reimbursement standards, and this makes it more difficult to implement. The French also live longer in good health, and fewer of their babies die in the first year of life. They must be doing quite a few things right across the pond.

As a former insurance broker, I can tell you that the any-provider open-panel health plans went the way of the dinosaur because of costs, so this idea that anyone in America can see any doctor is not true. Most health plans have contracts with physicians and hospitals; if you do not go to those providers, you will pay more. In other words, the insurance contract induces you to see its providers by making it extremely unattractive to go outside the ironclad agreements. Even self-insured health plans choose a preferred provider network or PPO for ease of contracting and convenience of paying for services. In fact, one of the first things employees review when there are health-plan changes is whether or not their clinic or doctors are in the new plan. This is especially true for people with chronic diseases or serious illnesses.

Another issue impacting access to clinicians is location; unless you live close to a major urban area or near a university with a medical school, you will probably have very limited access to specialist care. People in rural areas just don't have the access that people living in cities do. As you will see in the chapters on hospital quality, the patient safety standards and reporting vary greatly throughout the United States, and that is not a good thing.

And finally, the type of insurance (or lack of it) dictates which clinic or doctor a patient will be able to see. This is, of course, due to the patchwork system the United States has for paying for medical services. Both the Medicare and Medicaid programs underpay for primary-care doctors' services. In fact, if a Medicare patient does not have supplemental insurance, it is extremely difficult for that person to obtain a primary-care doctor. Doctors cannot afford to serve patients who cannot pay their costs. Medicare is the national health program for senior citizens age sixty-five and up, as well as for certain disabled persons, such as those on kidney dialysis. Medicaid is the state-run medical program for the poor, and one-fourth of the nation's children are deemed to live in poverty.

For the estimated 50 million patients who lack insurance, your health care options are severely limited, so do read the chapter on obtaining health care without insurance.

Hopefully you have a better understanding of the U.S. health care system now. For more details or specific questions on how your state fares, read on, my friend.

NOTES

1. "Employer Health Benefits 2009 Annual Survey," Kaiser Family Foundation, accessed March 11, 2013, http://ehbs.kff.org/2009.html.

2. John Holahan, A. Bowen Garrett, and the Urban Institute, "Rising Unemployment, Medicaid and the Uninsured," Kaiser Commission on Medicaid and the

Uninsured, available online at www.kff.org/uninsured/upload/7850.pdf (accessed April 17, 2013).

3. "Average Single Premium per Enrolled Employee for Employer-Based Health Insurance, 2011," statehealthfacts.org, Kaiser Family Foundation, accessed March 11, 2013, www.statehealthfacts.org/comparetable.jsp?ind=270&cat=5.

4. "Average Single Premium per Enrolled Employee."

5. "2010 United States Federal Budget," Wikipedia, accessed March 11, 2013, http://en.wikipedia.org/wiki/2010_United_States_federal_budget.

6. "2010 United States Federal Budget," Statistic Brain, accessed April 17, 2013, www.statisticbrain.com/2010-united-states-federal-budget.

7. "Health Care Spending in the United States and Selected OECD Countries: April 2011," Kaiser Family Foundation, accessed March 11, 2013, www.kff.org/insurance/snapshot/oecd042111.cfm.

8. Christopher J. L. Murray and Julio Frenk, "Ranking 37th—Measuring the Performance of the U.S. Health Care System," *New England Journal of Medicine* 362 (January 2010): 98–99, available online at http://healthpolicyandreform.nejm.org/?p=2610 (accessed March 11, 2013).

9. "Statistics and Surveillance: 2010 Table Data," Centers for Disease Control and Prevention, accessed April 17, 2013, www.cdc.gov/vaccines/stats-surv/nis/data/tables_2010.htm.

10. Christopher Murray, "WHO Issues New Healthy Life Expectancy Rankings: Japan Number One in New 'Healthy Life' System," World Health Organization press release, available online at www.who.int/inf-pr-2000/en/pr2000-life.html (accessed March 11, 2013).

11. "Healthcare Costs Around the World," Visual Economics, 2010, accessed March 11, 2013, www.visualeconomics.com/healthcare-costs-around-the-world_2010-03-01.

12. Murray and Frenk, "Ranking 37th."

13. Murray, "WHO Issues New Healthy Life Expectancy Rankings."

14. Peter S. Hussey, Gerard F. Anderson, Robin Osborn, Colin Feek, Vivienne McLaughlin, John Millar, and Arnold Epstein, "How Does the Quality of Care Compare in Five Countries?," *Health Affairs* 23, no. 3 (May 2004): 89–99, available online at http://content.healthaffairs.org/content/23/3/89.full (accessed March 11, 2013).

15. Hussey et al., "How Does the Quality of Care Compare in Five Countries?"

16. T. R. Reid, *The Healing of America* (New York: Penguin Press, 2009), 2.

17. National Highway Transportation Safety Administration, U.S. Department of Transportation, "Highlights of 2009 Motor Vehicle Crashes" (Washington, DC: NHTSA's National Center for Statistics and Analysis, 2010), available online at www-nrd.nhtsa.dot.gov/Pubs/811363.PDF (accessed March 11, 2013).

18. "Health Coverage and Uninsured," statehealthfacts.org, Kaiser Family Foundation, accessed April 17, 2013, www.statehealthfacts.org/comparecat.jsp?cat=3&rgn=6&rgn=1.

19. American Hospital Association, "Uncompensated Hospital Care Cost Fact Sheet: December 2010," available online at www.aha.org/content/00-10/10uncompensatedcare.pdf (accessed April 17, 2013).

· 2 ·

Why U.S. Health
Care Is So Expensive

$\mathcal{A}$mericans spend 20 percent more (as a percent of GNP) than any other industrialized country in the world for a health care system, and that system has failed to provide basic health care outcomes equal to those of other industrialized countries. Many smaller countries, like Cuba, do a better job of primary health care than the United States, as evidenced by its lower infant mortality rates, among other measures (chapter 19: "Children's Health Care"). How can the United States spend so much more on its health care and achieve poorer results than other industrialized nations? The answer is complex, but essentially the country is grossly mismanaging its health care investment, due to excess profit-taking, inefficient administration, and a poorly designed system for patient care. In fact, for much of the population their medical care is not linked to any system to generate optimum patient health.

In order to change our health care system we need to have a working knowledge of the variables that create this health care morass. How can the profits of drug and insurance companies continue to skyrocket yet the health care of Americans is not improving? Read on to understand some of the reasons for the current state of U.S. health care.

This analysis explains the relationship among health-system components that contribute to the astronomical cost of health care in the United States. Here are the primary contributing factors to the high cost of health care in the country (not necessarily listed according to precedence):

1. SERVICE ON DEMAND IS NOT NECESSARILY A PLAN

The U.S. service-on-demand policy for most health care treatments contributes to poor queuing and planning for health care delivery and lacks a rational

15

method for curtailing unnecessary services. Examples of these phenomena include patients who show up at a hospital without any insurance and with advanced disease progression. Because many U.S. residents have no medical insurance, they often lack access to a doctor, and the hospital becomes their only clinical intervention. This is an expensive method of providing disease intervention and is indicative of poor planning.

2. MISALIGNED FINANCIAL INCENTIVES FOR CLINICAL SERVICES

Financial incentives from government and private sector insurance programs encourage non-cost-effective and often unnecessary services by reimbursing on volume, not for health outcomes. Because of insurance reimbursement, medical practitioners are paid on volume based on a usual and customary payment schedule for the diagnostic codes. On the provider's side, the clinic or hospital must make the operating budget work to serve a variety of patients, both those who can pay and those who are not full-pay clients. This requires optimizing the services (meaning tests and treatments) for the most lucrative patients in order to keep the doors open for those who can't pay. Consequently, if imaging pays well, there is an incentive to promote MRIs to help offset the unreimbursed and under-reimbursed services, including those covered by Medicaid and Medicare. Additionally, consumers prefer and demand these high-tech services because there is minimal incentive for them not to order expensive tests. Most U.S. insurance policies have front-end deductibles and copayments, and once the insured has met a certain level of expenses, he or she is *home free* and can incur more charges without much recourse.

3. NONSTANDARDIZED CARE IS EXPENSIVE AND DOESN'T PRODUCE EQUITABLE RESULTS

Lack of standardization in clinical protocols and administration throughout the country creates a vast array of treatment protocols, which often add to the cost of care, and patient clinical results vary greatly by facility. Unnecessary differentiation in treatment protocols, without best-practice analysis to support the process, is another reason U.S. health care is so costly. As revealed in the chapters on male, female, and child health, the lack of national, evidence-based medical standards produces vastly different results in patient care, often to the detriment of the patient. Differences in patient outcomes are reflective of many variables, including: ethnicity, geography, income, levels of insurance coverage, clinical practices, overall patient health, and compliance with clinical recommendations.

4. LACK OF PATIENT-CARE COORDINATION

Because there are multiple systems with different interfaces throughout the country, there is a lack of coordination for patient care, even for specific programs such as Medicare. I am not just talking about different medical-records standards; I am also talking about the fifty insurance commissioners who are elected administrators for state insurance laws. This adds a bureaucratic layer to health-insurance coordination because each state may have different standards for consumer protection and product approval. Though the electronic medical-records process has helped improve access to patient information, there are multiple standards depending on the vendor, which also contributes to the cost of care. The private sector demands that electronic medical record (EMR) companies differentiate their products in order to obtain a competitive advantage, which makes it more complex for the end users.

Simpler is better when it comes to administration; why not have EMR standardization? At the very least, a conversion to such a system is easier with digital files than paper. Profit taking has been more of a priority for electronic medical vendors than finding the least expensive process for the country to develop digital records for patient management. Also, EMR firms represent individual health systems, not entire states or regions. Medicare has mandated an EMR standard that is being deployed across the country, with federal financial assistance for implementation.

5. OVERSUPPLY AND OVERUSE OF TECHNOLOGY

The oversupply of technology, such as full-body scan imaging, drives up the cost of care because often unnecessary services are provided to consumers who demand them, contributing to the high cost of U.S. health care. As well, health care providers make money based on the volume of services, so it is to their advantage to provide more services per paying patient, not less. In the case of capitated plans, which pay a fixed fee per enrollee, the incentive is the reverse—to minimize the procedures. However, for patients who are non-paying or not as profitable (the uninsured and those who are on Medicaid), there is no incentive to provide extra services. Unlike computers, which have become cheaper with the spread of technology, this has not been the case with health care imaging and other technology-driven services. Questions we need to ask include: Is the DaVinci robotic surgical system more effective than other surgical techniques? In other words, is it necessary? And finally, do the hospitals that use the machine charge more for comparable surgery than at other non–DaVinci surgical facilities?

6. LACK OF NATIONAL STANDARDS FOR EFFECTIVE PROTOCOLS IN HIGH COST/BENEFIT DIAGNOSIS

The lack of directed health policy for treatment norms encourages unnecessary procedures; for example, the number of hip transplants for octogenarians varies greatly by region, and one wonders how that contributes to the nation's health care. Protocols for heart conditions also vary, even though there is substantial evidence about the most effective treatments for the patient, as cited in chapter 3 of this book.

7. NO RULES FOR MEDICAL SUPPLIERS

Minimal rules govern medical-supply distribution, which creates an incentive for suppliers to maximize profits by seeking unnecessary and clinically inappropriate justification for the purchase of their products. Though some of the 2010 health care reforms increase scrutiny on medical suppliers, this is primarily for billing oversight and not a prescription for patient-utilization changes. Just because a company can sell a certain product, should we as a society encourage this expensive behavior by blanket reimbursement? For example, Medicare reimburses for three-wheeled motorized carts for patients who are mobility-impaired. These devices run several thousand dollars and are now frequently used by younger, able-bodied people. The distributors for these expensive go-carts advertise that they guarantee they can get Medicare to approve payment for the motorized chairs. Would a walker or cane suffice? What are we as a society obligated to pay for? One has to wonder if suppliers weren't promoting them and if the need were based solely on clinical recommendations, would their prevalence decrease? Remember: the cost of expensive medical supply items are figured into what we all pay for health care.

8. DEMANDING U.S. CONSUMERS

Demanding U.S. consumers also contribute to the high cost of health care, partly because other than plan copayments for cost-sharing, there is little financial incentive not to spend "top dollar" for medical services. This phenomenon is especially true if the patient is paying a high cost to buy insurance in the private health care system. The average cost for an employee was more than $5,000 for a single individual in the private insurance system and more than $12,000 for a family in 2010, which has increased to $5,616 for an single employee and $15,745 for a family in 2012. based on the Kaiser Foundation State Health Facts survey.[1] Why wouldn't you want to get your money's worth? The U.S. health care system encourages patient spending, not conservation of resources.

9. POOR SYSTEM FOR DISEASE DETECTION

An inefficient system for disease detection and provision of primary care and chronic disease management creates adverse patient outcomes that become more expensive to the health care system as the diseases and illnesses progress. For example, the lack of early surveillance on elevated blood pressure, which is a primary contributor to kidney failure, is a national problem.

10. CLINICIANS NEED TO BE PAID FOR PRIMARY AND PREVENTIVE HEALTH CARE

Payment to clinicians for medical services is misaligned and rewards specialist care more than primary (preventive) care, even though better primary care could help to prevent many conditions and illnesses that do require further intervention. Surgery is much less prevalent in other countries for many conditions, and those residents do not report poorer health. Perhaps American impatience and the desire to have everything heal quickly are partially to blame. But an outcome of all of this specialist care is apparently not better health, because according to the World Health Organization, the United States ranks forty-seventh for life expectancy, which is behind most other industrialized countries.[2]

11. EXPENSIVE HEALTH CARE ADMINISTRATION FOR PRIVATE-SECTOR PLANS

Waste in plan administration is another problem that contributes to the high cost of health care in the United States. Private-sector medical insurance plans spend 12 percent to 20 percent of total plan contributions (insurance premiums) for administration costs, and government health plans spend about 6 percent of contributions on administration. The complexity of the multiple systems and fifty different state insurance commissioner standards is not cost effective or efficient and also adds to plan-administration expenses for the insurance providers.

12. AMERICANS LACK AN INCENTIVE TO BE HEALTHY ALIGNED WITH THEIR HEALTH CARE COST

Americans are too often unfit and fat, compared to other cultures, a situation that contributes to increases in the incidence of high blood pressure (hypertension), cardiovascular disease, orthopedic issues, kidney failure, and other obesity-related maladies. Even more alarming than current health metrics is the proportion of obese children in the United States: according to the 2008 Kaiser Foundation report, 30 percent of the country's children are obese.[3]

13. EXORBITANT LEGAL COSTS FOR MALPRACTICE

The U.S. legal system is more tortuous than any other system in the world. This practice increases health-system costs by encouraging individuals to make nuisance lawsuits for their own enrichment. Insurance companies, ever on the lookout to reduce expenses, are loathe to litigate and inclined to settle most claims, as that is perceived as more cost effective. The cost of medical malpractice insurance in the United States can exceed $100,000 per year for a single obstetrician.[4] When you combine this with the high cost of a medical education and running a medical practice, it is easy to see why clinician costs are higher in the United States.

14. THERE AREN'T ENOUGH PRIMARY-CARE DOCTORS AND NURSES

The shortage of various clinicians, from nurses to family care providers, is a systemic problem that also drives up the cost of health care for current practitioners who are still able to accept new patients. Economics dictate that a dearth in essential personnel increases the price for services. Though nurses are earning more, primary-care doctors are not. Nurses in the United States can earn $90,000 a year after a four-year financial investment in school, but physicians must shoulder the enormous education burdens of medical school and may only earn $125,000 a year as primary health care providers. In 2007, the average primary-care physician in San Francisco made $130,000 per year and critical-care nurses in the same region earned $90,000 to $120,000, with half the education of the MD.[5]

The U.S. education system expects the individual to shoulder the enormous cost of training to provide an essential medical service to society. The shortage of family physicians can be alleviated through financial support for medical students and the academic institutions training them. The good news is that additional funding for primary-care providers is included in the 2010 health care reforms. I advocate strong federal support to train and finance clinicians in all areas of shortfall, including family practitioners, mental-health specialists, pediatricians, obstetricians, and nurses.

15. HEALTH CARE FINANCING IN THE UNITED STATES IS A COLLAGE OF TAXES, FEDERAL SUBSIDIES, GOVERNMENT PROGRAMS, AND PRIVATE-SECTOR CONTRIBUTIONS

The U.S. health care financing system is based partially on the Medicare tax equivalent of 1.875 percent of payroll, which is matched by employers and employees. This tax was recently increased to 1.90 percent, for both employers and employees.[6] Medicaid financing comes out of both the federal and state budgets and varies widely by state. Federal tax subsidies for employer-sponsored health plans provide a tax deduction for the premium payment (insured model) or the cost of the health plan (self-insured model) and no taxable event for the employee and his or her family. This public/private dual method of paying for health care has been around since Medicare was created in 1967. Previously, insurance was much less prevalent, although collective bargaining by unions contributed to the growth of health plans as well. The primary problem with the present health care financing is a lack of equity and fair distribution of health care resources. People at one company may have medical insurance paid by their employer, and people in another firm may not have anything. Also, people are eligible for Medicaid medical assistance at different levels in each state. With respect to the private insurance sector, some states have much fewer choices for seniors wishing to buy Medicare supplement plans.

16. EXORBITANT DRUG PRICES

The drug prices Americans pay are the highest in the world for one reason: the pharmaceutical companies have been extremely effective at securing their self-interests by spending more money on lobbyists to influence all health care legislation. For example, the Medicare prescription drug benefit approved under the Bush administration expressly restricts the largest health care purchaser in the United States, which is the federal Medicare program, from negotiating with drug manufacturers for better pricing. What this means is senior citizens, the largest customer base for the pharmaceutical industry, pay the highest prices for their medications. Even under the Obama administration, this has not changed, because the discounts the drug companies offered to Medicare enrollees with the 2010 health care reforms were offset by the drug-price hikes the following year. This is typical of the pharmaceutical industry; they dangle a carrot and then leverage it into increased profits without loss of any bargaining power. The powerful pharmaceutical lobby has even blocked the importation of cheaper drugs from our neighbor to the north by inferring Canadian drugs were not safe. This last practice has not prevented enterprising seniors from making regular trips to Canadian pharmacies to save money (or to Mexico, for that matter).

17. NOT EVERYONE HAS EQUAL ACCESS TO CARE

People who fall out of the health insurance safety net (48,000,000 at last count) do not have access to affordable health care for the most part. If you are lucky and live in a city that has a good public health clinic, you can see a primary-care provider for treatment without insurance. However, if you need imaging or specialty care, you will need to access the private health care system, which is prohibitively expensive.

In the following example, an uninsured person was forced to visit the emergency department of a local hospital circa 2009, after a bicycle accident.

Uninsured Ursula was peeled off the pavement and driven home in a good citizen's van because she couldn't afford an ambulance. Once home, she plumbed her stash of previous postsurgical opiates and waited forty-eight hours for the swelling to decrease in her leg. While Ursula was able to manage the pain, the leg ballooned to a frightening level, so a friend drove her to the nearest emergency room a few days later. The emergency physician said the department couldn't really examine her or do any imaging because it would be too painful. She was given a pair of crutches and a prescription for over-the-counter ibuprofen (luckily she already had more robust pain medication at home from a previous surgery). For this service, she was charged more than $500, of which she eventually paid $344. A typical insurance contract pays 60 percent of actual billed charges to a hospital, so Ursula ended up paying an amount equal to that. The difference is the hospital could claim the rest of the amount as charity care, even though insured patients don't pay that amount either.

The emergency physician charges were billed separately, and they accepted $50 instead of their billed $350. Apparently, they are happy to get any reimbursement for uninsured patients. Uninsured Ursula was also told by the treating physician at the hospital that no orthopedic specialist would see her without insurance or guarantee of payment. When the swelling was still evident after ten days, she did finally see a public health practitioner and obtained an X-ray at a different hospital, which luckily showed no broken bones.

Fortunately, Uninsured Ursula was able to drag herself around enough so the muscles in her left leg did not atrophy too much. Through the use of the public swimming pool (less than $3 per visit with a swim pass), she managed her own physical therapy during the next four months.

This incident demonstrates several things about the health care system in America, including the lack of affordable care for patients without insurance, and it also shows the ability of a resourceful patient to self-treat an injury and still fully recover. It should be noted that in this medical situation, the least expensive intervention was at the public health clinic, where her patient care was better than at the very-expensive emergency department of the hospital. Though Ursula had attempted to seek care at a local community health clinic, she was discouraged from treatment because of the requirement to pay an onerous $250 new-patient fee (this from a nonprofit clinic).

An evidence-based health care protocol would advise the patient to visit the lowest cost/optimal care clinic for assessment, and in this scenario, it was the public health clinic.

If Uninsured Ursula had been a privately insured patient, the scenario would have progressed differently. She would have received an MRI or X-ray at the first point of service, which was the hospital emergency department, and probably a consultation with an orthopedic specialist. The specialist may have recommended some special wrap/cast or even a surgical procedure to hasten the healing of the Anterior Cruciate Ligament (ACL) injury. She would have had follow-up visits with a clinician and a physical therapist. The estimated cost to the health-plan system would have been anywhere from $2,500 to $10,000. The patient's clinical outcome, which is full use of the knee and leg, may have been the same as her low-tech approach, but at a premium price.

An evidence-based treatment protocol for this scenario would look like this:

1. Initial patient assessment at an emergent care clinic (not necessarily the ER of a hospital) and diagnosis of an ACL injury without broken bones.

2. Treatment protocol would include medication for swelling and pain, rest, and moderate physical therapy from home using crutches or other mobility aid (cane).
3. Follow-up visit would assess patient's ability to perform more rigorous physical therapy outside the home.
4. Swim therapy at the local pool (swim pass for $28).
5. Continued follow-up with clinician until patient is cleared for full sports activities, allowing time for healing (four to six months).

When you contrast the protocol Uninsured Ursula followed with those for the typical insured patient, the costs would have been much higher, but not necessarily with an improved outcome. Optimal health care planning using evidence-based medical treatment standards would recognize and treat the patient most effectively fiscally and clinically. The goal is to adhere to a process that heals just as well as the other clinical protocols but also considers system costs and patient considerations. Why wouldn't you want evidence-based planning for the health system? It is foolhardy to spend at least 20 percent more than the rest of the world for health care with outcomes that are in many cases worse, as previously indicated in the global comparisons for health care.

NOTES

1. "Employer Health Benefits 2012 Annual Survey," Kaiser Family Foundation, accessed April 17, 2013, http://ehbs.kff.org/?page=charts&id=1&sn=6&p=1.
2. World Health Organization, *The World Health Report, 2000* (Geneva, Switzerland: World Health Organization, 2000), 200, appendix table 10, available online at www.who.int/whr/2000/en/whr00_en.pdf (accessed March 11, 2013).
3. "Percent of Children (10–17) Who Are Overweight or Obese, 2007," state-healthfacts.org, Kaiser Family Foundation, accessed April 17, 2013, www.state healthfacts.org/comparetable.jsp?ind=51&cat=2&sub=14&yr=62&typ=2.
4. Alexis Writing, "The Average Cost for Medical Malpractice Insurance," EHow.com, accessed April 17, 2013, www.ehow.com/about_5514154_average-cost-medical-malpractice-insurance.html.
5. Jeffrey M. Lobosky, *It's Enough to Make You Sick* (Lanham, MD: Rowman & Littlefield, 2012), chapter 8, page 90.
6. "Social Security and Medicare Tax Rates; Maximum Taxable Earnings," U.S. Social Security Administration, accessed April 17, 2013, http://ssa-custhelp.ssa.gov/app/answers/detail/a_id/240/~/social-security-and-medicare-tax-rates%3 B-maximum-taxable-earnings.

Evidence-Based Planning

What It Means and Why You Should Care[1]

EVIDENCE-BASED PLANNING: WHAT IT IS

Evidence-based planning (EBP) is the catch phrase of the health care reform movement. It entails the practice of critically reviewing scientific literature to obtain the most current information about advances in medical-care protocols, and then developing a method for localized testing and adoption within a health care facility or system. EBP is a process, not a single product-driven task. Applying best practices in the process enhances institutional performance metrics. This means that patients who are the beneficiaries of EBP typically live longer and with fewer complications than those who don't, by a population standard. This also means that every individual may not experience this result, but for the larger population, it is the most effective method for the provision of care.

The Institute of Medicine (the IOM) defines *quality of care* as the degree to which health services for individuals and populations increase the likelihood of desired outcomes and are consistent with current professional knowledge. Evidence-based planning is harnessing the enlightenment gained from sharing scientific findings and medical practice and using it to optimize clinical and operational procedures to improve results. The 2010 health care reform mandates have provisions for increased transparency and optimization of service delivery. These processes can only be achieved by deploying the best-practice protocols by diagnosis, whether it is heart disease or diabetes, through the evidence-based planning process.

Large, integrated health care organizations such as the Mayo Clinic, Kaiser Permanente, and the Veterans Health Administration already have work groups that meet regularly to review data, test protocols, recommend changes, and deploy them throughout the organization. Hospitals also have multidisciplinary committees that meet to figure out how to enhance patient outcomes by reviewing and adopting the best data-driven practices; not all clinicians are happy about changing their clinical practices as a result of this scrutiny.

Reducing the Patient's Chance of Dying

One example of successful EBP can be found when reviewing data on secondary myocardial infarctions (heart attacks) in order to develop a plan to reduce the likelihood of a second heart attack. We reviewed a significant body of information, including several dozen peer-reviewed articles, and found a European study that measured time-to-treatment for long-term prognosis impact on myocardial infarction patients[2]; the process revealed a reduction in patient hospitalization costs and increased patient survival of heart attacks. When patients registered for a post–cardiac attack follow-up program (especially a national database like the Minnesota Heart Institute Registry), saw a cardiologist for medication management, and obtained appropriate medication, their chances of a second heart attack were 6 percent less than patients who did not follow these protocols. In a comprehensive review of 40,684 myocardial-infarction hospital admissions in Pennsylvania in 1993,[3] the study cites an estimated cost savings to the Pennsylvania Medicaid program of $71,970 just by improving compliance for prescribing and administering beta-blockers. According to this research, heart-attack patients who had a three-month follow-up visit were 57 percent less likely to die than patients who did not return for their checkup. The beta-blocker protocol alone could save state Medicaid agencies $3.7 million in a single year. And finally, a retrospective cohort study in Scotland also showed a significant difference in patient outcomes post-discharge if they followed up with a cardiologist.[4] So by mapping out a treatment plan, and sticking to it, overall patient health improves, resulting in cost savings as well as better quality of life for the patient.

Bottom Line

It doesn't take a rocket scientist to figure out that following a select set of protocols for heart-attack patients makes a huge difference in clinical performance, which has a significant impact on the cost of health care. The Agency for Healthcare Research and Quality (AHRQ) estimates that 50 percent of Americans will die from heart disease, which is expected to remain the leading cause of death for the United States until 2020.[5] By improving the outcomes for cardiac patients, we can save literally millions of lives, and this is accomplished through the spread of evidence-based planning.

The Carrot

In 2005, Medicare created incentive reimbursements ($6,000 per patient) for the administration of the miracle drug TPA within three hours of a stroke. Patient recovery and mortality were significantly improved if the drug was administered within that window. Medicaid created the financial incentive as a way to get the attention of hospital administrators and improve surveillance and dispensing of this drug in order to have the biggest clinical impact. You might call this the carrot approach.

WHY WE NEED EVIDENCE-BASED PLANNING

The value gained from health care budget allocations, whether premiums, taxes, or fees from direct services, is directly affected by the clinical effectiveness and cost of the services in any health care system. It is in our best interest in terms of patient mortality (death) and morbidity (other complications) to obtain care from institutions that are openly seeking to adopt the best practices worldwide for the management of medical conditions. The 2010 health care reforms under the Accountable Care Organization criteria will specify and encourage the communication of performance metrics and the adoption of best-practice clinical protocols to encourage the best value for your money. It sounds great, so why isn't everyone excited about this process to save money and improve our clinical outcomes?

Evidence-based planning adheres to a scientific discipline that includes reviewing published studies under the Cochrane Central Registry of Controlled Trials and also the Medline Database to discern clinical performance differences of significant impact on populations. In plain English, that means controlled trials and methodical review of existing scientific studies are plumbed to figure out better medical treatments.

THE INSTITUTE FOR COMPARATIVE EFFECTIVENESS, OTHERWISE KNOWN AS THE PATIENT-CENTERED OUTCOMES RESEARCH INSTITUTE

The Institute for Comparative Effectiveness is a new agency that was created to review science findings and make comparative information available to clinicians, insurance companies, and patients as a tool to enhance communication about patient procedural outcomes and system processes. The real value in the Patient-Centered Outcomes Research Institute (PCORI) is the linking of economic cost/benefit analysis to health care delivery processes in order to reveal the most effective methods. The formation of this research and advisory institute builds on the recommendations of the Institute of Medicine (IOM) 2000 report for major changes in health care delivery to improve patient safety and clinical outcomes. Review panels include clinicians and patient and consumer-group representatives.

The PCORI has published its research priorities, and they include:

1. assessment of preventive, diagnostic, and health care treatment options;
2. improving health care systems;
3. improving health care decision-making communications with patients;
4. addressing health care disparities; and
5. accelerating patient-centered research.

Findings from the review of study designs, clinical trials, and patient data become public within ninety days of the completion of each analysis. The new federal agency works in concert with the AHRQ and the National Institutes of Health (NIH), under the fiscal purview of the Government Accountability Office (GAO). Funding for the agency comes from the Centers for Medicare & Medicaid Services (CMS), through a $1 to $2 fee per enrolled employee on private insurance plans and the PCORI Trust Fund.[6] Funding was stipulated for the agency under the American Recovery and Rehabilitation Act (ARRA) in 2009.

Some of the things that will be reviewed by the Institute for Comparative Effectiveness include: cutting waste, reducing unnecessary procedures, resourcing facilities appropriately (we don't all need the DaVinci surgical robot), and improving surveillance of illness to slow disease progression. It will put the spotlight on health care suppliers, insurance companies, and other providers, but if we really intend to address the grossly high cost of the U.S. health care system, this is necessary. The folks who are using the scare tactics about evidence-based medicine are trying to maintain a toe-hold in the current medical practice method, which is each medical practice doing whatever it wants when dispensing health care. That process is too expensive, and the degree of variations in providing medical treatment in this haphazard fashion does not create the same proportion of patient-health improvements as adopting optimal best practices for key diagnosis and disease management in society. For example, Medicare did the right thing by rewarding hospitals that were administering TPA for stroke victims within the optimal window for efficacy. The science behind the administration of this wonder drug was stroke patients showed a remarkable ability to recover if the medication was administered within a few hours of the stroke. In other words, this creates a better health care outcome for the patient and a fiscal savings for Medicare, a win-win scenario. Hopefully, this new institute will help identify and spread other improvements to American health care as well. All you have to do is check the time-to-treat statistics, between the facilities that deploy best-practice protocols and those that don't, which are slated to be more transparent with the Affordable Care Act reporting requirements. As a consumer, this is valuable information, but if you are in the throes of a stroke, you will probably be taken to the nearest hospital, which makes it all the more important that we insist on certain standards for care at all hospitals.

WHAT YOU CAN DO

Use your fingers and do some research on the internet, go to reputable sites like the AHRQ for patient-safety information or NIH for health information. Educate yourself before your follow-up appointment after your initial diagnosis. When you meet with your clinician, ask about best practices for your specific medical condition, and see what they say. If you are uncomfortable with the response, ask more questions, or consider getting a different clinician. You can have an impact on your health and your wallet if you do a little bit of research and ask the investigative questions. If you are dealing with a major illness like cancer or a significant operation it is a good idea to bring someone else along, like a friend or family member.

Public Agencies Dedicated to Providing Health Care Quality and Patient Safety Information

> Agency for Healthcare Research and Quality: www.ahrq.gov
> National Institutes of Health: www.nih.gov
> Patient-Centered Outcomes Research Institute: www.pcori.org

NOTES

1. The citations in this chapter are pulled from a paper authored in 2004 in an academic search, using Cochrane's and other scientific sources for a meta-analysis of available global studies on myocardial infarction and the prevention of a secondary event. I coauthored the work with Wendy O'Shaughnessy.

2. S. Simek et al., "How Does Time to Treatment Affect the Long-Term Prognosis for Patients with Acute Myocardial Infarction Treated with Primary Coronary Angioplasty?," *European Center for Medical Informatics, Statistics, and Epidemiology* 61, no. 8 (August 2004): 91–100.

3. I. H. Zuckerman, S. R. Weiss, D. McNally, B. Layne, C. D. Mullins, and J. Wang, "Impact on Education Intervention for Secondary Prevention of Myocardial Infarction on Medicaid Drug Use and Cost," *The American Journal of Managed Care* 10, no. 7, part 2 (2004): 493–500.

4. I. Abubakar, D. Kanka, B. Arch, J. Porter, and P. Weissberg, "Outcomes after Acute Myocardial Infarction: A Comparison of Patients Seen by Cardiologists and General Physicians," *British Medical Journal Cardiovascular Disorders* 4 (August 2004): 14.

5. John Birkhead, et al., *Acute Myocardial Infarction: A Core Data Set for Monitoring Standards of Care* (London: Clinical Effectiveness & Evaluation Unit, Royal College of Physicians, 1999).

6. "Overview of the Patient-Centered Outcomes Research Institute," Center for Medical Technology Policy, accessed March 11, 2013, www.cmtpnet.org/comparative-effectiveness/overview-of-the-patient-centered-outcomes-research-institute.

Quality and Cost

How the United States Compares with Other Countries

ASSESSING THE REAL COST OF
HEALTH CARE IN AMERICA

*M*easuring the real cost of any public program should include economic factors, such as opportunity cost, which is the cost of spending resources on health care that could otherwise go to something else, such as reducing the national debt or investing in education. Before we can reform U.S. health care, we need to develop some benchmark criteria for a better health care model, which includes an annual budget per person as it relates to individual income and total country wealth.

No matter how you look at it, the United States is throwing more money at health care than any other country, and the clinical results are not the best in the world for life expectancy, infant mortality, or many other health care measures. Unfortunately, the insurance mandates of the 2010 Obama administration health care reforms do not address cost containment sufficiently, as individuals are not put on a health care spending or account-ability allowance, so no cost reductions are in sight. Additionally, private insurance companies charge three times as much for plan administration as government plans do. The pending federal requirement mandating all residents buy medical insurance will only add to insurance-company cof-fers. This is due in part to the fact that the insurance companies can pass their costs on to the private sector, and they will continue to do so until a breaking point is reached.

COST OF U.S. HEALTH CARE
IMPEDES ECONOMIC GROWTH

Health care costs are frequently measured against Gross Domestic Product (GDP), which is the sum of what a country possesses in savings and income at a given point in time, and is reflective of its purchasing power, but not inclusive of cost-of-living differences. As you shall learn in this chapter, the United States is no longer pre-imminent in GDP, which means it does not have the most money to spend, and yet it spends twice what most countries do for their health care plans, 17.9 percent[1] versus 8 percent for other industrialized countries. America's existing health care system must be examined as an impediment to real economic growth and societal development.

In order to assess the U.S. health care system, let's look at what other industrialized countries spend on health care and how that equates to their income. The most recent comparative statistics on the total cost of health care by country are from 2007 data per person values.[2]

To determine world rankings for income, I used public data from the World Bank, which tracks GDP per person.

FIRST-PLACE RIBBON TO LUCKY LUXEMBOURG

What is really interesting is which country is in first place, according to the World Bank, and it is the tiny European country of Luxembourg, which reported a GDP in 2010 of $80,800. This country boasts an income of $74,430 per capita as well. And if that isn't enough to embarrass you, these citizens live three years longer than the average American.[3] The average fulltime wage is $49,663 and is much lower than the income per capita because it does not include cash reserves in investments accounts, but it still keeps them in first place. Singles ads anyone?

ROUNDING OUT THE REST OF THE
TOP TEN COUNTRIES FOR 2009 GDP

Note that the United States has fallen from its once-vaunted first-place role in GDP to seventh place. Luxembourg, a tiny European country, has been in first place for the second year in a row. Note the prevalence of oil-rich countries, accounting for 60 percent of the top ten, including Equatorial Guinea, the newcomer on the list. Information from this list is taken from the World Bank.

Most Income in 2009

This data was drawn from the World Bank data as reported for 2009.

1.	Luxembourg:	$80,800
2.	Quatar:	$75,900
3.	Norway:	$55,600
4.	Kuwait:	$55,300
5.	United Arab Emirates:	$55,200
6.	Singapore:	$48,900
7.	United States:	$46,000
8.	Ireland:	$45,600
9.	Equatorial Guinea:	$44,100
10.	Switzerland:	$39,800

Money Spent on Health Care per Resident as Reported in 2009

The rankings were determined by the latest information from the World Health Organization's Global Health Observatory Data Repository, which included national health care spending per capita as reported in 2009.[4]

1.	Luxembourg:	$8,183
2.	Norway:	$7,662
3.	United States:	$7,410
4.	Switzerland:	$7,141
5.	Ireland:	$4,952
6.	Quatar:	$1,715
7.	United Arab Emirates:	$1,520
8.	Singapore:	$1,491
9.	Kuwait:	$1,416
10.	Equatorial Guinea:	$ 709

COMPARING HEALTH CARE COSTS

In reviewing how the United States compares to other countries for health care expenditures per person, it is no longer in first place for spending the most money per capita on health care, as Norway and Luxembourg both spend more. However, these countries actually have more total income per resident as well, so when you consider the percentage of GDP (essentially total annual output measured in dollars), this puts the United States back in first place for spending more of our national product (money) on health care than anyone else, totaling nearly 18 percent. In other words, the United States spends more money on health care than any other country, period, when you look at the total spent, as opposed to the average spent per person. So where is all of this money going? Hopefully this book will illuminate some of the variances in health care and other contributing factors that contribute to this predicament in the United States. As previously mentioned, the average expense for health care per capita in the industrialized world is 8 percent. So the United States is spending more than twice what most countries with similar infrastructure spend for health care.

Details on U.S. Health Care Spending

According to the most recent Kaiser Foundation reports for health care spending, here is the cost breakdown for U.S. health care expenditures:

- Medicare (2010 report): $10,464.80.[5] This figure is derived from the amount Medicare spent, divided by the number of enrollees for the 2009 data.
- Medicaid (2010 report): $5,795 per individual.[6] This figure is derived from the amount Medicaid spent, divided by the number of enrollees for the 2009 data.
- Children's Health Insurance Program, Medicaid (2007 data): $2,135 per child[7]
- Employer plans (2010 report): $6,438 per individual and $13,770 for a family[8]
- Individual insurance plans (2010 report): $3,606 per individual and $7,102 for a family[9]

Assessing Program Costs

To reveal the true cost of any program, we have to do a solid cost/benefit analysis, which takes into account hidden costs such as pass-through expenses for inadequate reimbursements to clinicians. An example of a hidden cost is when Medicaid fails to pay hospitals or physicians adequately for services, thereby requiring those providers to recoup higher fees from privately insured patients in order to stay solvent. Other hidden costs include reinsurance for catastrophic claims for private plans, which the government could subsidize through a stop-loss guarantee and save employers about 5 percent in administrative expenses. Other areas of expense include plan administration and claims payment, which could be streamlined by requiring regional health care organizations to offer uniform benefits and standardized claims processing.

This could generate another savings of 3 percent to 6 percent in plan costs. Finally, there is the issue of malpractice insurance, which could also be subsidized by the government in areas of clinical shortages, such as primary care, obstetrics, and some specialties.

Budgeting National Health Care

Calculating U.S. health care investment in 2008, using Medicaid, private insurance, and employer insurance premium factors, we arrive at a value that averages $3,758 per person (excluding Medicare). If we then compared that sum to the average American wage at the time, it is the equivalent of 7.68 percent of the average wage. Using the available 2010 data and performing the same calculation, health care costs now consume 8.5 percent of the average income per person. The trend is pretty alarming, since health care costs have eaten up 1.5 percent more of actual purchasing power for Americans in just two years. The reason for this is that wages have been flat for a few years, and health care inflation continues to outstrip earning power. Yet, amazingly, minimal health care cost-containment features were incorporated into the 2010 health care mandates.

CONCLUSION

Considering the big picture, it is important to note that the largest single expenditure in the current U.S. federal budget is now Social Security at 31.27 percent of the annual budget.[10] In 2010 the defense budget was number one, but there has been scaling back in defense spending since the end of the Iraq War. The second-largest federal budget allocation was military defense spending at 28.77 percent of the entire federal budget for 2012.[11],[12] On a positive note, the defense budget has decreased given that defense spending was higher in 2010, when it took 39 percent of the total budget, inclusive of discretionary defense spending. By comparison, the entire 2012 budget for Medicare was 19.46 percent and other federally funded health programs totaled 14.52 percent, not including the Veterans Health Administration allocation.

NOTES

1. Toni Johnson, "Healthcare Costs and U.S. Competitiveness," Council on Foreign Relations, March 26, 2012, accessed March 11, 2013, www.cfr.org.health-science-and-technology/healthcare-costs-us-competiveness.

2. "Healthcare Costs around the World," Visual Economics, accessed March 11, 2013, www.visualeconomics.com/healthcare-costs-around-the-world_2010-03-01.

3. "Luxembourg," World Bank, accessed March 11, 2013, http://data.worldbank.org/country/Luxembourg.

4. "Global Health Observatory Data Repository," World Health Organization, accessed March 11, 2013, http://apps.who.int/ghodata.

5. "National Health Expenditure Data," Centers for Medicare & Medicaid Services, accessed March 11, 2013, www.cms.gov/NationalHealthExpendData/25_NHE_Fact_Sheet.asp.

6. "Medicaid Enrollment by State," Medicaid, accessed March 11, 2013, www.medicaid.gov/Medicaid-CHIP-Program-Information/By-State/By-State.html.

7. "Medicaid Payments per Enrollee, FY2009," statehealthfacts.org, Kaiser Family Foundation, accessed March 11, 2013, www.statehealthfacts.org/comparemaptable.jsp?ind=183&cat=4.

8. Kaiser Family Foundation and Health Research and Educational Trust, "Employer Health Benefits: 2010 Summary of Findings." Available online at http://ehbs.kff.org/pdf/2010/8086.pdf (accessed March 11, 2013).

9. Kaiser Family Foundation, "Survey of People Who Purchase Their Own Insurance," June 2010, available online at www.kff.org/kaiserpolls/upload/8077-R.pdf (accessed March 11, 2013).

10. "Government Spending Details," usgovernmentspending.com, accessed April 18, 2013, www.usgovernmentspending.com/year_spending_2013USbt_13bs1n_0010#usgs302.

11. "United States 2012 Federal Budget," Wikipedia, accessed March 11, 2013, http://en.wikipedia.org/wiki/2012_United_States_federal_budget#Total_revenues_and_spending

12. "Government Spending Details."

II

HEALTH CARE QUALITY

Know Where to Go

Quality Indicators

Best Hospitals for Patient Safety

$\mathscr{P}$art II of this book addresses patient safety and health care quality and includes strategies for consumers to evaluate hospital quality. In this section, I use data from the Leapfrog Group, a nonprofit employer sponsored organization created to alert consumers to patient-safety issues, provide consumer support, and increase transparency in the reporting of key factors to ensure patient safety in hospitals.[1] The Leapfrog Group was created in 1998 after the hue and cry about the medical error rate in U.S. hospitals became public. The Institute of Medicine's 1999 hospital report found more Americans died from hospital errors each year than car accidents![2]

The Leapfrog Group chose its name as a reminder of their goal to help organizations leap over hurdles in achieving best patient-safety standards. The Leapfrog Group's annual hospital survey incorporates seventeen of the thirty-one criteria identified by the National Quality Forum as critical for saving patient lives in hospital settings.[3] The Leapfrog Group's annual hospital survey focuses on the following criteria as key measures of an effective patient-safety program:

1. prevention of medication errors;
2. appropriate staffing in intensive care or ICU;
3. harm-avoidance planning;
4. reduction in pressure ulcers;
5. reduction in hospital injuries;
6. management to prevent serious errors; and
7. reduction in intensive care infections.

Hospitals voluntarily respond to the Leapfrog Group survey and are scored in four quartiles for willingness to report, steps taken to improve each criteria, and degree of achieving the benchmarks. The fourth quartile means 100 percent of the benchmarks were met by the hospital in that reporting period. This information is shared with the medical facility for validation and then is integrated into the reporting matrix and shared with the public on the Leapfrog website. This provides a built-in peer review and empowers patients with important safety information before they choose a hospital.

HEALTHPOLICYMAVEN™ ANALYSIS ON THE BEST HOSPITALS FOR PATIENT SAFETY

In 2009, 1,206 hospitals completed the Leapfrog Group survey, and of those, 12 percent earned scores of 100 percent on four or more of the seven-point scale. Our hats are off to the staff at these stellar facilities for working together so well for the benefit of their communities! I reviewed the Leapfrog Group website for the 2011 hospital safety rankings and found that about 25 percent of the nation's facilities now report their safety criteria. This increase in reporting is in part due to the changes in Medicare reimbursements from the 2008 and 2010 Medicare reforms, which stipulate that hospitals are no longer reimbursed just based on services, but on a formula that will look at important measures for clinical excellence in patient safety. Medicare will pay for performance, which is a great concept for curbing some health care abuses. By comparing the 2009 through 2011 safety rankings for every hospital in the country that reported to the Leapfrog Group, I found there were indeed changes in performance.

2009: Only One Perfect Hospital—Penobscot Bay Medical Center, Maine

Using the Leapfrog safety criteria, only one hospital in the United States in 2009 met all seven of the safety standards 100 percent of the time, and it was Penobscot Bay Medical Center in Maine, with a perfect score.[4] Yet again, the New England States seem to turn out the commendable health care scores.

Updated for 2011: The Quest for Perfection in Hospital Safety

Several hospitals scored 100 percent in all applicable categories of patient safety. This is most assuring news, as patient safety appears to be improving in terms of both the number of hospitals reporting and their scores for achieving safety measures.[5] Though Penobscot Bay Medical Center in Maine is no longer perfect, in 2011 it scored a perfect five out of the applicable six patient-safety measures, putting it in the next-best category and in the top 5 percent of all hospitals for safety.

Perfection: Top-Scoring Hospitals

Arizona—Western Regional Medical Center in Goodyear, Arizona, scored a perfect five out of the five criteria that applied to their patient safety. Since it is a small hospital and does not have an Intensive Care Unit, the ICU safety measures don't apply. Though in 2009 not a single Arizona facility reported meeting the patient-safety criteria for 100 percent of at least four of the seven sentinel event criteria, it is nice to see a stellar facility in 2011.

California—Kaiser Permanente Woodland Hills Hospital scored a perfect seven of seven for patient safety. Kaiser is a health-maintenance organization with an integrated health care system, which means all of their facilities follow the same standards for patient safety and treatment. In 2009 their hospitals were well ahead of other health systems in terms of safety rankings for the Leapfrog Group measures, but some of the other systems are catching up now. All of the Kaiser hospitals in California scored well in 2009 and again in 2011.

Florida—Baptist Health South Homestead Hospital scored a perfect seven of the seven patient safety metrics. Baptist Health is a network of hospitals, and many of their other facilities also scored well for patient safety in this survey.

Pennsylvania—Eastern Regional Medical Center ranked a six out of the six applicable criteria for its patient safety measures in 2010. This hospital has an intensive care unit and scored 100 percent for appropriate staffing levels, but it listed not applicable for ICU infections. Does this mean they did not have a single ICU infection in 2010? In any case, scoring a six is still awesome.

Hospitals Scoring 100 Percent for Six Out of Seven of the Leapfrog Criteria

Starting at the back of the alphabet, these hospitals scored 100 percent for their compliance with at least six of the seven patient safety benchmarks:

- Texas: Cook Children's Hospital in Fort Worth
- Tennessee: Monroe Carell Jr. Children's Hospital
- Pennsylvania: Children's Hospital of Philadelphia, Children's Hospital of Pittsburgh, Lehigh Valley Hospital, Lehigh Valley Hospital–Muhlenberg
- Ohio: Cincinnati Children's Hospital Medical Center, Nationwide Children's Hospital
- New Jersey: Valley Hospital
- Minnesota: Children's Hospitals and Clinics of Minnesota

- Michigan: Helen DeVos Children's Hospital of Michigan, Children's Hospital of Michigan, Huron Valley–Sinai, St. Joseph Mercy Livingston
- Massachusetts: Mount Auburn Hospital, North Shore Medical Center–Union Hospital, Cooley-Dickinson Hospital
- Maine: Penobscot Bay Medical Center (because one of the seven criteria did not apply)
- District of Columbia: Children's National Medical
- Colorado: Children's Hospital in Aurora
- California: Children's Hospital of Los Angeles, Children's Hospital of Orange County, Lucille S. Packard Children's Hospital in Stanford, Presbyterian Intercommunity Hospital, Kaiser Medical Centers in Irvine and Riverside

Hospitals Scoring Five Out of a Seven-Point Range

Hospitals who achieved 100 percent compliance for five of the seven safety criteria received a score of five. With that in mind, here are the stars in reverse alphabetical order:

- Wisconsin: Bellin Hospital, Children's Hospital, Ministry St. Clare Hospital
- Washington State: Mary Bridge Children's Hospital, Northwest Hospital, Seattle Children's Hospital, Virginia Mason Medical Center
- Virginia: Sentara Leigh Hospital
- Texas: Sierra Providence East, St. Thomas
- Tennessee: Memorial North Park, Mercy at St. Mary's
- Ohio: Cincinnati Children's, Southern Ohio Medical Center, Ohio State University Hospital, University Hospital Medical Center at Conneaut, University Hospital Medical Center at Geneva
- North Carolina: Central Carolina Hospital
- New York: Montefiore–Moses, Montefiore–Wellor, Vassar Brothers
- New Jersey: Englewood Medical Center, University Medical
- Nevada: Spring Valley
- Montana: Des Peres Hospital
- Minnesota: Mayo Clinic–Methodist
- Michigan: Harper Hutzel, University Hospital Health Center
- Massachusetts: Bay State Hospitals including Franklin, Mary Lane, and Bay State Medical Center; Children's Hospital of Boston; Brigham and Women's Hospital; Berkshire Medical Center; Boston Medical Center; Faulkner Hospital; Newton-Wellesley; St. Ann's; Carney Hospital; Lahey Clinic; Sturdy Memorial Hospital

- Maryland: University Maryland Medical Center, Northwest Hospital at Randallstown, Carroll Hospital
- Illinois: Swedish Covenant, Metro South Medical Center–North Shore, University Health–Evansville
- Georgia: Gordon Hospital
- Florida: BHS Doctors Hospital, BHS South Miami, BHS Mariners, Florida Hospital Heartland Medical Center, Florida Hospital Medical Center
- Delaware: The Alfred DuPont Hospital for Children
- Colorado: Rose Medical Center
- California: Kaiser Medical Centers at Downey, Fontana, Harbor City, Panorama City, Roseville, Santa Rosa, San Diego, and West L.A.; San Ramon Regional; Sharp-Grosmount; Sierra Vista Regional; Mills-Peninsula Health Services; University of California Hospital at San Diego; Miller Children's Hospital; Long Beach Memorial Medical Center; Clovis Community Medical Center; John Muir Medical Center; Mercy General Sacramento; Scripps Mercy Hospital of San Diego; Presbyterian Intercommunity Hospital

Scoring 100 Percent on at Least Four of the Seven Criteria for the Year Measured

Other high-scoring hospitals, which scored 100 percent for at least four of the patient-safety criteria in the Leapfrog survey, are listed by state in reverse alphabetical order, just to be fair to the folks at the back:

- Wyoming: Wyoming Medical Center
- Wisconsin: Bay Area Medical Center
- Washington: Kadlec, Swedish Medical Center (all three sites), University of Washington Medical Center
- Virginia: Henrico Doctors at Parham, Henrico Doctors at Richmond, Sentara at Williamsburg, Sentara at Virginia Beach
- Utah: Timpangos Regional, Mountainview Hospital, Ogden Regional Medical Center
- Texas: DelSol, St. David's, Baylor Regional Medical Center at Plano, Huguley Memorial, Lake Point Medical, SW Surgical Hospital, St. David's–Georgetown, UT SW at Zale Lipshy
- Tennessee: Baptist of Nashville, Baptist Memorial for Women, Baptist of Collierville, Baptist of Union City, Delta Medical Center, Erlanger East, North Hendersonville Medical Center, Horizon Medical Center Parkwest Medical Center, Skyline, University of Tennessee Medical Center, St. Francis–Memphis, Williamson Medical Center, Cocke, Decatur County, Memorial-Chattanooga, Mercy North,

Mercy West, Methodist–Fayette, Methodist–Germantown, Middle Tennessee Medical Center, Parkridge East, Southern Hills Medical Center, St. Thomas, Vanderbilt

- South Carolina: St. Francis–Downtown, St. Francis–Eastside, Medical University of SCU Medical Center
- Pennsylvania: Lehigh Valley, Allegheny General
- Oregon: Mid-Columbia Medical Center–Dalles
- Ohio: Ohio State University Hospital East, Fairfield Medical Center, Mercy St. Anne
- North Carolina: University of North Carolina–Chapel Hill, Gaston Memorial
- New York: Queens Hospital Center, New York University Hospitals Center, Roswell Park, St. Francis–Poughkeepsie
- New Jersey: Hackensack University Medical Center, Valley Hospital, Roberta Wood Johnson University Hospital, Hunterdon Medical Center, Liberty Health of Jersey City, Lourdes, Newark Beth Israel Medical Center
- New Hampshire: Parkland Medical Center
- Nevada: Desert Springs Hospital Medical Center
- Mississippi: Baptist Memorial–Golden Triangle
- Minnesota: Regions Hospital, St. Johns, St. Mary's of Rochester, Mayo Clinic Methodist
- Michigan: Allegiance Health, Bronson Methodist, University of Michigan, Beaumont Hospital of Grosse Pointe, Beaumont Hospital of Troy, Beaumont Hospital of Royal Oak, Botsford Hospital, Detroit Receiving, Huron Medical Center, Metro Health Hospital, Mid-Michigan Medical Center, Providence Park, Sinai Grace, Spectrum Health of Blogett, Spectrum Health of Butterworth
- Massachusetts: Emerson Hospital, Brigham and Women's Hospital, Falmouth Hospital, Hallmark Health System Melrose–Wakefield, Holyoke, Holy Family Hospital, Lawrence General, Leonard Morse Hospital, Massachusetts Eye and Ear Infirmary, Massachusetts General, Mercy Medical Center, Metro West Medical Center, Milford Regional Medical Center, Morton Hospital and Medical Center, North Shore Medical Center, South Shore Hospital, Saints Medical Center, Good Samaritan Medical Centers–Steward, Norwood Hospital, St. Elizabeth's, Winchester, Wing Memorial Hospital Medical Centers
- Maryland: Anne Arundel Medical Center
- Maine: Central Maine Medical Center, Mayo Regional Hospital Medical Center, Parkview Adventist Medical Center, Sebasticook Valley, St. Andrews

- Louisiana: Women and Children's, P & S Surgical Hospital, Tulane–Lakeside
- Kansas: Allen County Hospital
- Iowa: Grinnel Regional Medical Center
- Indiana: Indiana University at LaPorte, Monroe Hospital, St. John's at Anderson, Indiana Orthopaedic Hospital
- Illinois: Central DuPage Hospital, Children's Memorial, Glenbrook, North Shore University–Highland Park, Memorial Rush University, St. Alexius, Skokie, St. Joseph, West Suburban
- Idaho: West Valley Medical Center
- Georgia: St. Joseph's, Memorial Health University Medical Center
- Florida: Columbia, Mayo Clinic–Jacksonville, Homestead, BHS Coral Gables
- Colorado: Presbyterian St. Luke's Medical Center, Skyridge Medical Center, St. Anthony Summit Medical Center, St. Mary-Corwin
- California: Cedars Sinai–Los Angeles; El Camino Hospital; Fresno Regional Medical Center; John Muir–Walnut Creek; Kaiser Hospitals at Anaheim, Antioch, Manteca, Modesto, Roseville, San Francisco, Los Angeles, Orange County, Mills Peninsula, Placentia Linda, and Pomona Valley; Long Beach Memorial; Marin General Hospital; Mercy at Folsom; Patients Hospital of Redding; Salinas Valley Memorial; Scripps Hospitals at Green–LaJolla and Memorial LaJolla; St. John's Oxnard; Stanford Hospital; Twin Cities Community Hospital; University of California at Davis, San Diego Hillcrest, and Irvine

No-Shows in the Quality Department

The states that had no hospitals meeting either of the criteria above were: West Virginia, North Dakota, New Mexico, New Hampshire, Nebraska, Missouri, Mississippi, Kentucky, Connecticut, Arkansas, and Alaska. I would like to say there is a pattern here, but I can't find one. Though some of these state hospitals reported safety measures to the Leapfrog Group, they did not meet the safety criteria for 100 percent compliance with at least four of the seven hospital safety standards. It is troubling that some of the wealthier states have failed to measure up, including Connecticut and New Hampshire; I guess they all go to New York for treatment. Mississippi is not a surprise, as it also scores low in other health-quality measures, as reported in the state scorecards. Even the Mayo Clinic in Arizona failed to meet at least four of the safety criteria 100 percent of the time in 2009 and 2011, which was quite surprising.

Hospitals Refusing to Report on the Leapfrog Quality and Patient–Safety Survey

For more information on the many hospitals that did not participate in the annual hospital survey by the Leapfrog Group, go to their site for a list of hospital facilities in each state that refused: www.leapfroggroup.org/decline.

One of the improvements in the 2011 survey was that hospitals that declined to complete the survey are shown in alphabetical order along with those that participated in each state survey, so you don't have to hunt around for the no-shows.

Community Hospitals

Though some of the smaller community hospitals lack intensive care units, they were still scored on the other hospital-safety criteria. There were community hospitals that met the benchmark standards for safety, such as Penobscot Bay Medical Center in Rockport, Maine, which only has 110 beds.[6] Though smaller, rural hospitals may have difficulty affording electronic medical-record systems, the current health care reforms provide funding for the conversion of patient data from paper to digital systems. Also, it is difficult for rural hospitals to fully support an intensive care unit. Theoretically, smaller hospitals that scored 100 percent in all of their safety requirements are as safe as larger hospitals, based on their licensure and operating within those mandates. For smaller hospitals that lacked intensive care units but scored well, I have noted it, as demonstrated with the Western Regional Medical Center in Goodyear, Arizona.

Children's Hospitals

Children's hospitals were scored on the applicable criteria for their patients, which did not include pressure ulcers or reduction in hospital injuries, presumably because children are not wandering around the facility unsupervised or unattended for long periods of time in their beds. So, a children's hospital that received a comparable six out of the seven possible benchmarks for scoring would have scored 100 percent for four of the five applicable criteria. Generally, care at children's hospitals is excellent within the United States because they are well funded. Children's hospitals receive strong funding from insurance-company payments, municipal hospital district allocations, state tax support, and donor contributions. These centers also tend to be regional centers for excellence, providing intensive pediatric care for a large population. Interestingly, not all of the children's hospitals scored in the top criteria for the Leapfrog benchmarks.

Score a Big Ten for Managed Care

Through the years, managed care programs (commonly called HMOs) have been lambasted for their design and managed-care methods, but the Leapfrog survey shows that nearly all of the Kaiser Hospitals scored well in their reporting for the seven patient-safety standards. One of their hospitals, Kaiser Woodland Hills, scored a perfect seven of seven for the 2011 survey. Two other hospitals, Irvine and Riverside, scored a six of seven. This shows that the Kaiser Health system effectively manages their hospitals, which should be quite a confidence builder for their patients.

Additionally, the Leapfrog Group publishes a list of the top hospitals each year, and of the sixty-five selected in 2011, nearly a third were Kaiser Hospitals, which is a nonprofit HMO. University hospitals also scored very well over a five-year period for consistently exhibiting patient safety in their surveys, and 20 percent of the top sixty-five were affiliated with university programs, which are also nonprofit state-run organizations.

For more information on the 2011 top performers for over five years, go to the Leapfrog Group's website and view the list: www.leapfroggroup.org/news/leapfrog_news/4810593.

CONSUMER TIPS

First of all, if a hospital is not reporting patient-safety data to Leapfrog, this is an indication that it does not agree with the reporting criteria, does not have adequate staffing to do the reporting, or considers it unimportant. As a patient, you want your hospital to exhibit a culture of transparency and a messianic zeal for safety. Organizations that choose to voluntarily report their safety results are signaling this value. At the very least, you need to find out why nonparticipating hospitals don't report their benchmark error rates and obtain them from another source, like the National Quality Forum (NQF), a national organization devoted to quality assessment of hospital and physician services.[7] The NQF publishes a report about serious hospital errors, which many states make available to their residents.

States that mandate that hospital medical-error information be shared with the general public are: California, Connecticut, Illinois, Indiana, Massachusetts, New Jersey, Oregon, Vermont, Washington, and Wyoming.

Centers for Medicare & Medicaid Services Impact

The Centers for Medicare & Medicaid Services (CMS) have information on hospital errors. They review patient-safety data measures that are linked to levels of payments for services. The CMS reformed their reimbursement policy in 2008 in order to reduce payment for preventable medical complications in hospital settings. This action increases the attention on patient safety by bringing more money into the patient-care mix through financial rewards for achieving patient-safety standards.

HEALTHPOLICYMAVEN™ TIPS

Finally, if you do not get a clear answer to your health care quality questions, consider having your procedure at another facility. The entire hospital survey process is built around assessment of patient safety. Don't be a dummy; ask questions and go online to review reputable data from third-party organizations, not just the hospital's public-relations group. The Leapfrog Group is an easily understandable source to get a quick measure of a hospital's safety practices. If you are going to have a procedure done in one of the states that mandate full disclosure of medical errors for hospitals, you can usually find that information by contacting the state Department of Health.

There is no situation more vulnerable than being unconscious and on "life support" while someone cuts you open and rearranges your bits and pieces. Take it from the healthpolicymaven™, know the score before you give consent for the procedure. Your life may hang in the balance.

NOTES

1. The Leapfrog Group hospital comparison tool, accessed March 12, 2013, www.leapfroggroup.org/cp.
2. "About Leapfrog," The Leapfrog Group, accessed March 12, 2013, www.leapfroggroup.org/about_us.
3. "Safe Practices for Better Healthcare—2009 Update," National Quality Forum, March 2009, accessed March 12, 2013, www.qualityforum.org/Publications/2009/03/Safe_Practices_for_Better_Healthcare%e2%80%932009_Update.aspx.
4. The Leapfrog Group hospital comparison tool.
5. The Leapfrog Group hospital comparison tool.
6. "Care and Services," Pen Bay Medical Center, accessed March 12, 2013, www.penbayhealthcare.org/penbaymedicalcenter/services/Care_and_Services.
7. "Report Cards," National Committee for Quality Assurance, accessed March 12, 2013, www.ncqa.org/tabid/60/Default.aspx.

· 6 ·

Critical Care

U.S. Hospitals with Level-1 Trauma Centers

*I*f you find yourself injured in a city and are unsure of where to go for urgent care, the ambulance will probably take you to the nearest hospital, which will be ranked anywhere from level 1 to level 5 in terms of its trauma treatment resources. Level-1 trauma centers are where the most intensive critical care is given to accident victims, burn patients, and other trauma wounds. The clinical staff members of these nationally designated centers are highly trained in all manner of life-saving procedures. Usually, these hospitals are publicly funded through a hospital district for the region or through a university medical program, such as Harbor View Medical Center, which is part of the University of Washington, or Los Angeles County Hospital, which is part of the University of Southern California Los Angeles Medical Center.

According to a 2008 survey on trauma centers in the United States, 66 percent are affiliated with universities.[1] Though a trauma center will routinely be in the inner city and extremely busy, often lacking in the warmth of a community hospital, it will have highly qualified physicians on staff. Also, the emergency medical team that responds will take you to the trauma center if it is close enough and if they deem it necessary.

A level-1 trauma center is a hospital facility that is certified to handle the most acute care for traumatic injuries, such as mass accidents, burns, and so forth. Trauma centers are located in urban areas and serve as a training ground for medical schools throughout the United States. The American College of Surgeons delineates 108 requirements for level-1 trauma centers, including a minimum of 1,200 trauma admissions per year, an average of thirty-five major trauma patients per surgeon, residency training programs, and ten peer-reviewed medical (scientific) journal submissions every three years.[2]

Because trauma-center hospitals receive preferential public funding, they have to provide care to anyone who needs it, regardless of that individual's ability to pay. Technically, all hospitals in the United States must provide emergency care to stabilize a patient before discharge,[3] but public hospitals provide more care to the indigent than community hospitals. Patients are often transferred to regional hospital trauma centers from community hospitals that may not have the resources for optimal treatment or sometimes just don't want the uninsured trauma patients. Trauma centers tend to treat a disproportionate share of the poor, so they receive a federal subsidy called Disproportionate Share Funding. Additionally, public hospitals are eligible for lower-cost prescription drugs because of 340B federal subsidies.

In a 2005 nationwide survey, there were 218 trauma centers that self-identified as level-1, but upon verification of all requirements, only 188 qualified for that standard as defined by the American College of Surgeons certification standards for trauma centers and reported to the U.S. Centers for Disease Control (CDC).[4]

LOCATIONS OF LEVEL-1 TRAUMA CENTERS IN THE UNITED STATES

The hospitals that are level-1 trauma centers are listed by name for each state. Military hospitals are not listed, as they are covered under a separate health program through the Veteran's Health Administration.

- Alabama: University of Alabama Medical Center
- Arizona: Maricopa Medical Center, Phoenix Children's Hospital, St. Joseph's Hospital, University Medical Center, and Scottsdale Healthcare Osborn
- Arkansas: The Med and University of Arkansas at Little Rock (designated a state level-1 trauma center for the first time in 2010)[5]
- California: Fresno Regional Medical Center, Cedars-Sinai, Children's Hospital of Los Angeles, USC Medical Center, Ronald Reagan Medical Center at UCLA, UCLA Irvine, UC Davis Medical Center and Children's Hospital, Rady Children's, Scripp's Mercy, UC San Diego Medical Center, San Francisco General Hospital and Trauma Center, Santa Clara Valley Medical Center, Stanford University Medical Center, Los Angeles County/Harbor UCLA Medical Center
- Colorado: Children's Hospital of Aurora, Denver Health Medical Center, St. Anthony Central Hospital, Englewood Swedish Medical Center

- Connecticut: Connecticut Children's Medical Center, Yale New Haven Hospital, including pediatric facility
- Delaware: Newark Christiana Care Health System
- District of Columbia: Children's National Medical Center and Washington Hospital Center
- Florida: Broward General Medical Center, Shands at the University of Florida, Memorial Regional Hospital, Shands Trauma One, Jackson Memorial Ryder Trauma Center, Orlando Regional Medical Center, Tampa General Healthcare[6] (under Florida law all trauma centers must also be pediatric trauma centers)[7]
- Georgia: Medical College of Georgia, including pediatrics; Grady Memorial Hospital, Medical Center of Central Georgia, including pediatrics; Memorial Health University Center, including pediatrics; and most recently, Atlanta Medical Center has been designated a level-1 trauma center[8]
- Hawaii: Queens Medical Center is the Hawaiian Islands' only designated trauma center for nonmilitary personnel, but it is unclear at what level it is certified.[9]
- Illinois: Loyola University Medical Center
- Indiana: Clarian Methodist, Indiana University Wishard Memorial, Riley Hospital for Children
- Iowa: University of Iowa Hospitals and Clinics, including Pediatric Trauma Center
- Kansas: University of Kansas; Via Christi Hospitals, including pediatric facility; Wesley Trauma Center
- Kentucky: University of Kentucky Chandler Hospital and UK Children's Hospital, University of Louisville Hospital
- Louisiana: Spirit of Charity Trauma Center (LSU Interim Hospital), LSU Health Science Center
- Maine: Maine Medical Center
- Maryland: UM R. Adams Cowley Shock Trauma Center,[10] Johns Hopkins Hospital[11]
- Massachusetts: Beth Israel Deaconess, Boston Medical Center, Brigham and Women's Hospital, Children's Hospital of Boston, Massachusetts General Hospital and Children's Hospital, Bay State Medical Center, U Mass Medical Center
- Michigan: CS Mott Children's Hospital, University of Michigan Hospital, Children's Hospital of Michigan, Detroit Receiving Hospital, Henry Ford Hospital, Hurley Medical Center, Spectrum Health Butterworth Campus and Helen Devos Children's Hospital, Borgess Medical Center, Bronson Methodist Hospital, Sparrow Hospital, William Beaumont Hospital

- Minnesota: Hennepin County Medical Center, North Memorial Medical Center, Mayo Clinic, St. Mary's Hospital, Regions Hospital including Pediatric Center
- Mississippi: University of Mississippi Medical Center[12]
- Missouri: University of Missouri Hospital and Clinics, Barnes Jewish Hospital, St. Louis University Hospital
- Nebraska: There are no level-1 trauma centers in Nebraska according to the American College of Surgeons criteria.[13]
- Nevada: University of Southern Nevada, Las Vegas
- New Hampshire: Dartmouth Hitchcock Medical Center and Pediatric Center
- New Jersey: Cooper University Hospital, Morristown Memorial, Robert Wood Johnson Memorial University, New Jersey Trauma Center at University Hospital
- New Mexico: University of New Mexico Hospital, Alberquerque
- New York: The Centers for Disease Control and the Department of Health for the State of New York list seventeen level-1 trauma centers within New York City and the boroughs. Here is that list:
  - Lincoln Medical and Mental Health Center in the Bronx neighborhood of Mott Haven
  - New York Presbyterian Hospital's Weill Cornell Medical Center on 68th Street in Manhattan
  - St. Barnabas Hospital in the Belmont section of the Bronx
  - St. Luke's/Roosevelt Hospital Center in Clinton
  - Richmond University Medical Center in West Brighton, Staten Island
  - Staten Island University Hospital in Midland Beach, Staten Island
  - Bellevue Hospital Center in Gramercy
  - New York Hospital Center of Queens in Flushing
  - Jacobi Medical Center on Pelham Parkway in the Bronx
  - Brookdale Hospital Medical Center in Brownsville, Brooklyn
  - City Hospital Center at Elmhurst, Queens
  - Harlem Hospital Center
  - Jamaica Hospital
  - Lutheran Medical Center in Sunset Park, Brooklyn
  - Kings County Hospital Center in Wingate, Brooklyn
  - Children's Hospital of New York, Columbia Presbyterian
- Outside of New York City:
  - Albany Medical Center
  - Erie County Medical Center
  - Strong Memorial Hospital
  - University Hospital SUNY, Stonybrook
  - University Hospital SUNY, Syracuse
  - Westchester Medical Center, Valhalla[14]

- North Carolina: University of North Carolina Medical Center, Carolinas Medical Center, Duke University Medical Center, Pitt County Memorial Hospital, Wake Forest University Baptist Medical Center
- Ohio: Akron General Medical Center, Summa Health System Akron City Hospital, Cincinnati Children's Hospital, University Hospital, Cleveland, Metro Health Medical Center, Rainbow Babies and Children's Hospital, Nationwide Children's Hospital, Grant Medical Center, Ohio State University Medical Center, Miami Valley Hospital, University of Toledo Medical Center, Mercy St. Vincent's Medical Center, the Toledo Hospital, St. Elizabeth Health Center
- Oklahoma: Oklahoma University Medical Center
- Oregon: Legacy Emmanuel Medical Center and Oregon Health and Science University
- Pennsylvania: Children's Hospital, UPMC Mercy Services, UPMC Presbyterian,[15] Children's Hospital, Hospital of the University of Pennsylvania,[16] Penn State Children's Hospital,[17] Penn State Milton Hershey Medical Center[18]
- Rhode Island: Rhode Island Hospital
- South Carolina: Medical University of South Carolina,[19] USC School of Medicine[20]
- Tennessee: Vanderbilt University Medical Center,[21] UTHSC Regional Medical Center, UTHSC Medical Center[22]
- Texas: Dell Texas Children's; University Medical Center in Austin; the following Dallas/Fort Worth hospitals: Baylor University Medical Center at Dallas, Children's Medical Center, Parkland Hospital and Health System, John Peter Smith Hospital; and the following Houston hospitals: Ben Taub General, Children's Memorial Hermann, Memorial Hermann, Texas Children's Hospital; as well as these other Texas facilities: Lubbock University Medical Center, San Antonio University Health System, Scott and White Hospital (multiple locations), and East Texas Medical Center in Tyler
- Utah: Intermountain Medical Center, Primary Children's Medical Center, and University of Utah Hospital
- Vermont: Fletcher Allen Health Care in Burlington
- Virginia: Inova Fairfax Hospital, Virginia Commonwealth University
- Washington: Harborview Medical Center is part of the University of Washington and is a level-1 trauma center for both pediatrics (Seattle Children's Hospital) and adults in Washington.[23] The facility is also the only level-1 trauma center for a four-state region including Alaska, Idaho, Montana, and Washington.[24]
- West Virginia: Charleston Area Medical Center, West Virginia University Hospitals

- Wisconsin: American Family Children's Hospital at University of Wisconsin, University of Wisconsin Hospital and Clinics, Children's Hospital of Milwaukee, Froedtert Hospital, and the Medical College of Wisconsin

SOURCES AND METHODS

American College of Surgeons Guidelines

The American College of Surgeons relies on the guidelines published in *Resources for the Optimal Care of the Injured Patient*[25] to gauge the qualification of individual trauma centers that voluntarily report on staffing and other resources in their facilities. Several states are not listed on the verified trauma-center list for any facilities, which may be because their voluntary report to the American College of Surgeons (ACS) was incomplete. The states not showing any listing based on the ACS-verified criteria include: Arkansas, Florida, Georgia, Hawaii, Maryland, Mississippi, North Dakota, Pennsylvania, South Carolina, Tennessee, and Washington. The methods I used to locate and verify level-1 trauma hospitals in these states are described below.

University Teaching Hospital Status

In order to ascertain trauma-level status beyond the American College of Surgeons 2009 survey information, I researched state university hospital websites for indications of trauma-service status. The University of North Dakota is listed as a level-2 trauma center on its own website, so it has been left off the level-1 list like other states lacking that certification. Of the 133 accredited medical schools in the United States, I researched teaching hospitals that have trauma-center hospitals. My list of trauma centers includes only the university hospital facilities, where it was possible to ascertain their level-1 status.

State Health Departments

Public health departments also provide information on trauma centers, and I have cross-referenced the state hospitals that were not certified by the American College of Surgeons with those state health departments, which may have more current information than the ACS survey, as in the case of Arkansas. In all cases public information was used.

States that lack level-1 trauma centers are: Alaska, Idaho, Montana, Nebraska, North Dakota, South Dakota, and Wyoming

Alpha Hospitals Nationwide

I also cross-referenced the hospitals that scored high for patient safety with the level-1 trauma centers. Here is the list of what appear to be the best purveyors of medical care:

- California: Fresno Community Medical Center, Stanford University Medical Center, Lucille Packard Children's Hospital
- Colorado: Children's Hospital of Colorado
- District of Columbia: Children's National Medical Center
- Indiana: Clarian Methodist
- Massachusetts: Brigham and Women's Hospital, Children's Hospital of Boston, Massachusetts General Hospital, Bay State Medical Center
- Michigan: University Health Center, Detroit Receiving Hospital, Mott Children's Hospital, Bronson Methodist
- Minnesota: Mayo Clinic, St. Mary's Hospital
- North Carolina: University of North Carolina Hospital–Chapel Hill
- Ohio: Cincinnati Children's Hospital, Ohio State University Medical Center
- Texas: Baylor University Medical Center
- Washington: Harborview Medical Center, Seattle Children's Hospital

CONCLUSIONS

States that may not have a level-1 trauma facility but are showing level-2 criteria facilities according to the ACS standards have not been included in certified level-1 facilities list. It is important to note that a level-2 status is still excellent, but the hospital may not have the optimal level of staffing for some surgical specialties that would garner the highest level of certification. The threshold for certification as a level-1 trauma facility is 1,200 trauma admissions per year. Obviously, in some of the less populated states this is unlikely, since the number of trauma procedures per hospital will be less than in an urban area. It is not economical for rural hospital districts to staff for neurology and other infrequent events requiring specializations. When in doubt, if you are in a city with a university medical center, that is a likely place to locate a high-level trauma center.

NOTES

1. Bruce H. Ziran, Mary-Kate Barrette-Grischow, and Barbara Hileman, "United States Level I Trauma Centers Are Not Created Equal—a Concern for Patient Safety?," *Patient Safety in Surgery* 2 (2008): 18, available online at www.ncbi.nlm.nih.gov/pmc/articles/PMC2515286 (accessed March 12, 2013).

2. Ziran, Barrette-Grischow, and Hileman, "United States Level I Trauma Centers."

3. "Emergency Medical Treatment & Labor Act (EMTALA)," Centers for Medicare & Medicaid Services, accessed March 12, 2013, http://cms.gov/EMTALA.

4. "Trauma Care," Centers for Disease Control, accessed March 12, 2013, www.cdc.gov/traumacare/index.html.

5. "Arkansas Trauma System Designates the Med as Level I Center," *Memphis Business Journal*, September 28, 2010, available online at http://memphis.bizjournals.com/memphis/stories/2010/09/27/daily9.html (accessed March 12, 2013).

6. "Florida Trauma Centers Contact Information," Florida Department of Health, accessed March 12, 2013, www.doh.state.fl.us/demo/trauma/PDFs/FLTraumaCntrContactInfo7-09.pdf.

7. Florida Department of Health, Office of Trauma, Division of Emergency Medical Operations, "Florida's Trauma Care System 2003 Annual Report," July 2004, available online at www.doh.state.fl.us/demo/trauma/pdfs/emstraumarept11_04.pdf (accessed April 18, 2013).

8. Edgar Treiguts, "State Adds Fifth Level-1 Trauma Center," GPB News, June 8, 2011, available online at www.gpb.org/news/2011/06/08/state-adds-fifth-level-1-trauma-center (accessed April 18, 2013).

9. "2009 Marks the 150th Anniversary of the Queen's Medical Center," The Queen's Medical Center, accessed March 12, 2013, www.queensmedicalcenter.net/index.php?option=com_content&view=article&id=290:2009-marks-the-150th-anniversary-of-the-queens-medical-center&catid=37:2009-news-stories&Itemid=144.

10. "R Adams Cowley Shock Trauma Center," University of Maryland, accessed March 12, 2013, www.umm.edu/shocktrauma.

11. "Acute Care Surgery & Adult Trauma," Johns Hopkins Medicine, accessed March 12, 2013, www.hopkinsmedicine.org/surgery/div/Acute_Care_Surgery_and_Adult_Trauma.html.

12. "Overview," The University of Mississippi Medical Center, accessed April 18, 2013, www.umc.edu/Overview.aspx.

13. "Verified Trauma Centers," American College of Surgeons, accessed March 12, 2013, www.facs.org/trauma/verified.html.

14. "New York State Trauma Centers," New York State Department of Health, accessed March 12, 2013, www.health.state.ny.us/nysdoh/ems/trauma2.htm.

15. "Penn Medicine Announces New Advanced Care Hospital Pavilion and Trauma Center at Penn Presbyterian Medical Center," news release, Penn Medicine, November 2, 2012, available online at www.uphs.upenn.edu/news/News_Releases/2012/11/expansion (accessed April 18, 2013).

16. "Division of Traumatology and Surgical Critical Care," Penn Medicine, accessed March 12, 2013, www.pennmedicine.org/surgery/cpup/divisions/trauma.html.

17. "Home," Penn State Hershey Children's Hospital, accessed March 12, 2013, www.pennstatehershey.org/web/childrens/home.

18. "Trauma Services at HUP," Penn Medicine, accessed April 18, 2013, www.uphs.upenn.edu/em/clinserv/hup-trauma.htm.

19. Search results for "trauma center, level 1," Medical University of South Carolina Health, accessed March 12, 2013, www.muschealth.com/GSASearch/?q=trauma+center%2C+level+I&SearchGo=Search.

20. "Department of Neurosurgery," University of South Carolina School of Medicine, accessed March 12, 2013, http://neurosurgery.med.sc.edu.

21. "About Us," Vanderbilt University Medical Center, accessed April 18, 2013, www.mc.vanderbilt.edu/about.

22. "Affiliated Hospitals," the University of Tennessee Health Science Center, accessed March 12, 2013, www.uthsc.edu/hospitals.

23. Washington State Department of Health, "Washington State Trauma Services," Office of Community Health Systems, February 2013, available online at www.doh.wa.gov/Portals/1/Documents/Pubs/530101.pdf (accessed April 18, 2013); "Trauma System," Washington State Department of Health, accessed April 18, 2013, www.doh.wa.gov/PublicHealthandHealthcareProviders/EmergencyMedicalServicesEMSSystems/TraumaSystem.aspx.

24. "Harborview Medical Center UW Diversity Appraisal," the University of Washington, October 2004, accessed March 12, 2013, www.washington.edu/diversity/divpdfs/Harborview_Medical_Center.pdf.

25. "Verified Trauma Centers FAQ," American College of Surgeons, accessed March 12, 2013, www.facs.org/trauma/verifiedfaq.html.

Patient Safety

Who Reports Hospital Errors

HOSPITAL ACCREDITATION STANDARDS

$\mathcal{T}$he primary organizations that review hospital medical errors in the United States are the Joint Commission on Accreditation of Healthcare Organizations (Joint Commission), the National Quality Forum, the Centers for Disease Control (CDC) National Health Safety Network, and the Agency for Healthcare Research and Quality. Nearly half the states use the CDC's Health Safety Network. Now that we have learned how to evaluate hospitals that are doing well in terms of patient safety (LeapFrog Group) and the sophistication of their trauma treatment programs (certification for level-1 trauma centers), it is time to review patient-safety reporting and regulation by state.

The Joint Commission

The Joint Commission for Hospital Accreditation Organization or JCAHO recognizes twenty-two criteria for hospital errors, which are referred to as sentinel events for patient safety. The Joint Commission has been tracking this data for over fifteen years. Though the number of adverse patient-safety events has grown each year, so has the patient population. It is also a positive thing to have hospital errors reported, because the data increases institutional awareness and compliance. We have to know the scope of the problem before we can fix the process. Based on the available 2009 data, there was an increase of both self-reported and nonself-reported events. It is also important to note that this database is for all licensed inpatient facilities, including psychiatric hospitals and extended-care facilities. Some of the criteria reviewed by the Joint Commission are obviously more germane to these entities, such as patient escape or suicide. I reviewed 2009 data for the following sentinel events for patient safety:

1. wrong-site surgery;
2. suicide;
3. operation or postoperation complications;
4. medication errors;
5. delay in treatment;
6. patient fall;
7. unintended retention of foreign body (gauze, scissors, etc., in the body);
8. assault/rape/homicide;
9. death or injury of patient while in restraints;
10. perinatal death/loss of function (death during childbirth);
11. transfusion error;
12. infection-related event;
13. medical equipment–related event;
14. patient elopement (patient escapes or is unaccounted for);
15. anesthesia-related event;
16. fire;
17. maternal death
18. ventilator death or injury;
19. utility systems–related event (electrical failure, etc.);
20. infant discharge to wrong family; and
21. other less frequent events.

National Quality Forum Standards

The National Quality Forum (NQF) was created by thirty-two health care organizations to develop consensus about measures for quality indicators and reporting. The NQF requires hospital reporting for the following patient safety metrics from its members:

1. surgery performed on the wrong body part;
2. surgery performed on the wrong person;
3. incorrect surgical procedure;
4. accidental implantation of a foreign object during surgery;
5. interoperative or postoperative patient death;

6. drug- or biologic-induced patient death;
7. patient death or disability caused by infusion pumps, catheters, drains, or specialized tubes;
8. patient death from embolism;
9. infant discharged to the wrong person;
10. death or injury to a patient who leaves the facility prior to discharge;
11. patient suicide or attempted suicide;
12. medication errors;
13. patient death or disability associated with incompatible blood products;
14. patient death or disability due to hypoglycemia;
15. neonatal death associated with hyperbilirubinemia;
16. incurring stage-3 or stage-4 pressure ulcers after admission;
17. patient death or disability from joint-movement therapy;
18. artificial insemination of the wrong sperm or egg;
19. patient death or disability associated with electric shock;
20. patient incident with oxygen or another patient gas;
21. patient burns during hospitalization;
22. death or disability caused by a fall during patient stay;
23. death or disability caused by patient restraints;
24. medical care provided by an imposter clinician;
25. abduction of a patient;
26. sexual assault of a patient; and
27. physical assault of a patient resulting in death or disability of a patient.

FEDERAL GOVERNMENT RECOGNITION OF PATIENT-SAFETY SYSTEMS

AHRQ: Agency for Healthcare Research and Quality

The Agency for Healthcare Research and Quality (AHRQ) is the federal agency for health care quality and patient safety. The agency was created in 1999 to promote methods for improving health care quality and has reviewed patient safety systems throughout the United States. Hospital systems that were cited as effective in patient safety by the AHRQ are:[1]

- Ascension Health: cited for its Safer System
- Columbia University: cited for its Medical Event Reporting System

- Department of Defense: cited for its PSR or Patient Safety Reporting System
- Georgia State Hospital Association: cited for the Partnership for Health and Accountability PHA Event Reporting
- Indian Health Service: cited for the Webcident Reporting System
- Jackson Memorial Hospital Ryder Trauma Center: cited for the Event Reporting Data Base
- Johns Hopkins University: cited for the Intensive Care Unit Safety Reporting System
- Joint Commission Organization: cited for the Sentinel Event Self-Reporting System
- Trinity Health: cited for its Potential Error Event Reporting System
- University of Texas: cited for the Close Call Patient Reporting System
- Vermont Oxford Network: cited for the Neonatal Intensive Care Quality Collaborative Reporting System
- Veterans Administration: cited for the Patient Safety Monitoring System

What to Watch

As a means of encouraging hospitals to prevent unnecessary medical complications from preventable safety errors, CMS, the Centers for Medicare & Medicaid Services, will no longer reimburse at the same level in cases of hospital-acquired infections. In other words, the government is not going to pay for medical "do-overs," so the buck has proverbially stopped at quality control. If a U.S. hospital continues to make certain kinds of preventable medical errors, it will be paid a lower rate for services.

CDC National Health Safety Network

The Centers for Disease Control created a secure internet-based medical-error reporting program in 2005, called the National Health Safety Network. By 2010, twenty-two states had mandated that their hospitals use this system for reporting hospital errors. Presently, three thousand hospitals throughout the United States report their data in this system, making it the largest database for hospital errors in the country. The data is collected for scientific review, and the latest report on hospital infection rates was published in 2009. However, this report does not disclose specific facilities and their performance to the public. So in terms of transparency to the public, the CDC database doesn't help that much.

HEALTHPOLICYMAVEN™ SCORING FOR PATIENT-SAFETY REPORTING

The following criteria were used to evaluate patient-safety reporting by state:

1. availability of public reporting in layperson's terms of hospital safety errors over the internet;
2. government regulation and a legal mandate; and
3. statewide hospital patient-safety reporting.

Three Points for the Highest Level of Oversight for Hospital Safety Standards

States that meet all three of the criteria—a statewide database of patient-safety errors, an enforceable mandate, and transparent public reporting—receive the highest recognition for patient safety. The only state that meets all three standards and that received the maximum score of three points is Minnesota, a founding father for patient-safety reporting.

States Earning Two Points for Patient-Safety Standards

To score two points, there has to be public reporting and a government mandate, but with less ease of public access. For example, if the state's report is not readily available over its website, the state does not get the third point. The states that scored at least two points are Connecticut and Indiana.

States Earning One Point for Patient-Safety Standards

For the award of one point for mandating patient safety, the state must have a government law to track and reveal hospital safety information but with limited reporting. The following states received one point for patient-safety reporting standards: Colorado, Illinois, Maryland, Massachusetts, Michigan, Missouri, New Jersey, Oklahoma, Oregon, Pennsylvania, Rhode Island, Tennessee, Utah, Vermont, Washington, and Wyoming.

Methods

Information was culled from all fifty state health departments and various legislative sites. Additionally, the nonprofit organization Quality and Patient Safety (QuPS.org) provides a state-by-state analysis of patient-safety initiatives and is an excellent resource. In conjunction with the analysis of hospital errors, each state is reviewed for patient-safety programs in development under legislative initiatives. The actual safety incident rates are derived from the Comparative Summary of States' Adverse Event Reporting and Performing Experiences, published in 2005.[2] Not all states were tracking this information at the time, and, therefore, the incident rate for their hospital errors is not reported. In alphabetical order, here are the results of my nationwide review:

- Alabama does not make hospital error information available to the public.
- Alaska does not make hospital error information available to the public.
- Arizona has legislation under review to scrutinize hospital errors more broadly under the Patient Safety and Quality Improvement Act.
- Arkansas does not publicly report medical errors, but it mandates participation in a statewide patient-safety program. The state does have a pilot program among four hospitals to reduce medical errors through increased transfer of medical information.
- California mandates reporting of hospital medical errors to the general public through its Department of Public Health, but this information is not available on the state Department of Public Health website.
- Colorado began reporting on hospital-acquired infections in 2007, with the Infections Disclosure Initiative. This process reviews hospital central-line infections, surgical-site infections, and kidney-dialysis infections. Colorado hospitals are required to report to the CDC National Health Care Safety Network System. The Rocky Mountain state provides information on request for aggregate patient-safety events in hospitals, but not a comparison by facility.[3] Colorado reported 4.2 patient-safety sentinel events per 100,000 patient discharges during a four-year time frame from 2000–2004.[4] Colorado uses its own patient-safety criteria for reporting.
- Connecticut approved Senate Bill 248 on June 30, 2010, mandating that critical hospital errors be disclosed to the public. The bill authorizes the Department of Public Health to conduct random audits of state hospitals and also has whistleblower protection. This state goes beyond the NQF standards for reporting patient-safety information from medical facilities. Connecticut reported only 2.8 patient sentinel events per 100,000 patient discharges, including the six additional Connecticut state metrics, during a twelve-month reporting period from 2004–2005.[5] If you apply the NQF standards alone, Connecticut reported one patient safety event during the same time frame.

- Delaware participates in the CDC National Health Care Safety Network for the reporting of hospital-acquired infections, but it does not make patient-safety information available to the general public.
- District of Columbia has no requirement to disclose hospital errors to the public.
- Florida does not mandate the disclosure of hospital medical errors to the public. Florida does track hospital patient-safety errors using its own criteria. Florida reported 2.5 sentinel events per 100,000 patient hospital discharges, using its criteria during the period from 2000 to 2004.[6]
- Georgia has two statewide medical-error reporting programs: the Partnership for Health and Accountability through the Georgia State Hospital Association and a grant-funded project through the AHRQ. Georgia hospitals use the CMS (Centers for Medicare & Medicaid Services) criteria for reporting. However, the hospital association program is voluntary, whereas the AHRQ grant project is linked to reimbursement eligibility under the CMS. The grant-funded project means Medicare payments may depend on safety outcomes, which is a good thing. There is no state law mandating patient-safety reporting in this state, though.
- Hawaii does not mandate public disclosure of hospital errors.
- Idaho does not mandate public disclosure of hospital errors.
- Illinois passed legislation in 2005 mandating the reporting of hospital medical errors to the public. Its reporting system is based on the twenty-eight NQF criteria for patient safety.
- Indiana does report hospital medical errors, and their 2009 report is online.[7] Indiana was awarded a grant from the CDC to develop a program for prevention of hospital-related infections, which ran through 2011.[8]
- Iowa does not provide disclosure of hospital medical errors on their public health website. However, an article in the *Indianapolis Star*[9] in August 2010 indicates a reduction in reported medical errors by 12 percent compared to the previous year.
- Kansas does not require public reporting on hospital medical errors. In response to a malpractice insurance crisis in 1986, Kansas started a health care provider reportable incident program, but this is primarily for licensing and lacks public disclosure.
- Kentucky does not mandate public disclosure of hospital medical errors.
- Louisiana does not require public reporting for hospital medical errors.
- Maine has published hospital-error data before, but there is no requirement to make it publicly available.[10] The state bases its voluntary

reporting of sentinel patient safety events on the Joint Commission standards for hospital accreditation and reported 1.1 sentinel patient-safety events per 100,000 admissions for the 2004 period.[11]

- Maryland is one of thirteen states that tracks hospital patient-safety performance data and has published reports according to data available through 2006.[12] Maryland reported 1.2 patient safety sentinel event errors per 100,000 patient discharges from 2004 to 2005.
- Massachusetts has a law requiring public disclosure of hospital medical errors. Massachusetts reported 4.2 sentinel events in patient safety for every 100,000 patient discharges during a three-year period from 2001 to 2004.[13]
- Michigan has been a leader in the reporting of sentinel events for hospital medical errors, through a partnership with the Minnesota Hospital Association called the Minnesota Alliance for Patient Safety (MAPS), which was created in 2000. Public Health Code 333.16222 requires the reporting of patient-safety events occurring in hospitals.
- Minnesota has always been a leader in health care, and it created the MAPS patient safety initiative, which is a national initiative to create a scorecard for the measurement of hospital medical errors. This association has fifty member organizations using the NQF patient-safety criteria to track hospital medical errors. Though information is for members only, the group researches and publishes reports on patient safety. Their website lists patient safety reports for 2005 and 2006, which are available to the public. If you are contemplating treatment at a Minnesota hospital, you can review its performance data ahead of time. Of the forty-nine hospitals reporting patient-safety errors, twenty-four had errors in both 2005 and 2006 reporting periods.[14] The report states that 71 percent of Minnesota hospitals were free of any patient-safety sentinel events in this time frame. Another thing I like about the Minnesota report is it provides a very good population measure, which is 3.2 patient-safety events per 100,000 patient days and 14.6 events per 100,000 patient hospital admissions. This makes it easy to compare this metric to a national benchmark. Minnesota is the only state that allows you to see a comparison of hospital patient-safety data online. This is a wonderful example of providing revealing and understandable patient-safety data. I would almost eat some lutefisk for it. Minnesota reported one patient-safety sentinel event according to NQF standards for the 2004 reporting period.[15]
- Mississippi does not require public disclosure of hospital medical errors.
- Missouri has no mandate to report hospital medical errors, but this state did participate in a demonstration grant project by the AHRQ

that assessed methods to reduce medication errors.[16] Missouri reported on surgical site infections in 2007 as a direct result of the 2004 Nosocomial Infection Reporting Act, which reviews health care–related infections from central lines and surgical sites.[17]

- Montana does not require public disclosure of hospital medical errors and in 2003 passed a law repealing the requirement for a health database. Subsequent to that, the 2005 Montana legislature passed the "I'm Sorry Law" giving health care providers additional protections for adverse patient-safety events.[18]

- Nebraska has an adverse-event-reporting requirement for individual clinicians, but no hospital patient-safety reporting mechanism, according to Quality and Patient Safety.[19] The 2011 state legislature is considering a patient-safety and peer review under LB 431.

- Nevada passed a law in 2002 requiring mandatory nonpublic reporting of patient sentinel events. The data on adverse safety events is aggregated, so facilities are not individually identified, and public disclosure is not required. The law was also intended to address medical malpractice insurance concerns.

- New Hampshire reported state hospital errors in 2009, but there is no legal requirement to disclose medical errors to the public.

- New Jersey does not require public disclosure of hospital medical errors, but it does track adverse patient-safety events under the Patient Safety Net legislation, which became effective in October 2004. The state is, however, hampered by the lack of "whistleblower protection" for the reporting of mandatory adverse patient-safety events.

- New Mexico does not require regular public disclosure of hospital medical errors.

- New York bases its reporting of patient-safety errors on ICD9 or medical coding criteria, and it reported eighty adverse patient safety events per 100,000 patients discharged for 2001 data.[20] This is the worst rate for adverse hospital-safety events in the nonprofit group QuPS.org (which stands for "Quality and Patient Safety") report from 2007.[21] Many states reported only one patient-safety event per 100,000, so that gives you an idea of the range for New York, which has about eight times as many patient-safety events as many other states, such as Minnesota or Texas. New York has the Patient Event Tracking System (called PETS).

- North Carolina does not require public disclosure of hospital patient-safety errors.

- North Dakota does not require public disclosure of hospital patient-safety errors.[22]

- Ohio plans to begin mandatory reporting of adverse patient events in hospitals, using 2009 data, but this will not necessarily be made public.[23]
- Oklahoma has the Oklahoma Health Care Information System, which also tracks hospital discharge and surgical information. The data is shared on a web-based system called Ok2share, and pdf reports are accessible on the website. However, there is no mandate for disclosure of hospital errors to the public, and the data is aggregated, not facility specific. Nevertheless, 73 percent of Oklahoma hospitalizations had normal patient discharges in 2006, which is about the same as Minnesota. There is no sentinel-event information.
- Oregon requires public disclosure of hospital medical errors, but compliance is based on hospitals' voluntarily reporting. In 2007, eighteen people died of hospital medical errors, and twenty-seven hospitals in the state reported hospital medical errors, according to an article in *The Oregonian.*[24]
- Pennsylvania has the Health Care Associated Infection Control Act and the Medical Availability and Reduction of Error Act, as well as the State Patient Safety Authority.[25] Pennsylvania is also one of thirteen states that have published reports on hospital medical errors for their state.[26] The Liberty Bell State used Joint Commission criteria for reporting sentinel events on patient safety. The state reported twenty-eight events per 100,000 patient discharges during a twelve-month period from 2004 to 2005.[27]
- Rhode Island has no requirement to disclose patient-safety errors to the public, but it does track hospital-error data in the aggregate.
- South Carolina in 2006 codified the reporting of patient drug reactions, death, or serious injury while hospitalized, but there is no requirement to disclose patient-safety errors to the public.
- South Dakota has an adverse patient-safety reporting requirement for all hospitals, but no information is shared with the public.[28]
- Tennessee has required public reporting of hospital medical errors since 2000. Tennessee reported twelve sentinel events per 100,000 patient discharges in the 2004 reporting period, using the ICD9 medical coding criteria like New York.[29]
- Texas is one of the thirteen states that have published reports on aggregated hospital patient-safety errors, but there is no comparison by facility, and the hospital discharge reporting is not publicly shared.[30] The Lone Star State bases its patient-safety reporting metrics on the Joint Commission sentinel-event criteria, and the composite data for 2004 revealed 0.50 (less than one) sentinel event per 100,000 patient

discharges.[31] This is much lower than any of the other states that reported in the same time frame.

- Utah has no public mandate to report hospital medical errors, and no
data is shown on the state Department of Health website. Utah has
published a report on hospital patient-safety performance but only aggregate data for the state as a whole, not per facility.[32] Utah bases its
patient-safety-reporting metrics on the Joint Commission's sentinel-
event criteria. During a two-year period from 2002 to 2004, the state
reported 0.90 (less than one) sentinel event per 100,000 patient discharges.[33] Utah is also a demonstration state for the AHRQ Patient
Safety Initiative.[34]

- Vermont is making headway with hospital safety by requiring the
reporting of medical errors. Vermont was acknowledged by the
AHRQ for its public-safety surveillance and improvement system,
which is specifically geared to hospitals.[35] This program uses the
NQF criteria and requires each participating hospital to do the following: identify, track, and analyze sentinel events, as well as near
misses; perform causal analysis; and implement corrective action.
Each participating hospital is also required to report hospital errors
to the Patient Safety Surveillance System in Vermont. This information does not have to be shared with the general public, only with
the impacted patient.

- Virginia does not mandate the public reporting of hospital medical
errors. A bill was introduced to require this disclosure in 2010, but it
was defeated.

- Washington requires public reporting of hospital medical errors for
things like infections and other metrics, but it does not share comparison data by hospital to the general public. This information is
only reported in aggregate data and has been available by request since
2008.[36] Washington bases its patient-safety reporting on the Joint
Commission standards for voluntary reporting of sentinel events. In a
four-year period from 2000 to 2004, the state had only 0.70 (less than
one) patient-safety sentinel event per 100,000 discharges.[37]

- West Virginia does not require public reporting of hospital medical
errors.

- Wisconsin has a substantial electronic medical records initiative, but
only one report on hospital quality (from 2001) exists on the Department of Health website. Presently, there is no public-reporting
requirement for hospital medical errors in this state.

- Wyoming does require medical-error reporting to the public, although
it is only aggregated data, not facility specific.

WHAT THIS MEANS TO THE AVERAGE CONSUMER

Having researched all fifty state public health department websites, as well as the National Quality Forum, the Joint Commission on Hospital Accreditation, and the QuPS.org sites, I found that there are several different standards for assessing which patient-safety events to report. The NQF is an entity to which hospitals report safety data and also the organization that the nonprofit hospital-safety watchdog LeapFrog Group uses for its assessments. Some states have their own standards, but for comparison purposes either the Joint Commission or the NQF standards were applied in this analysis.

Here are some tips for assessing patient hospital safety in your state:

1. Look for public reporting of hospital medical errors, as this demonstrates the highest degree of transparency and commitment to improve patient safety.
2. States that apply a nationally vetted patient-safety standard like the National Quality Forum or Joint Commission are using a rigorously tested model for assessment.
3. Information should be available on the state public-health website and also understandable for the average person (like Minnesota's model).
4. Aggregated information for multiple time frames and several hospitals is not that helpful for the health care consumer because it doesn't reveal what you need to know about your hospital of choice.
5. States, like Connecticut, that enforce their reporting with random hospital site visits exhibit rigorous maintenance of patient safety.
6. If your state does not require the reporting of patient-safety sentinel events, you may be able to learn about this from other sources, including the CMS, which also tracks these performance metrics, as well as the Agency for Health Research and Quality (AHRQ). Remember, all states are reimbursed for health care by the CMS, so it tracks information on hospital performance, including infections, surgical errors, and hospital discharge information.
7. Each state has a hospital association, and that organization may have information on hospital safety initiatives.
8. If your state doesn't make hospital patient-safety data available to the average health care consumer, you may be able to obtain information on your hospital from other sources, including the CMS, as well as

the Agency for Healthcare Research and Quality (AHRQ). Both of these agencies are part of the federal Department of Health and Human Services. All hospitals receive Medicare and Medicaid reimbursements from this agency. Finally, talk to your state legislators about sponsoring a bill to require public disclosure and conformance with patient-safety regulations.

Consumer Tips

The federal government's Department of Health and Human Services has a website to compare hospital safety performance. You can select any three hospitals in a geographic area and compare performance for patient readmission rates and patient deaths compared to the national rate for each diagnosis, such as heart failure. This data provides a quick benchmark comparison of your hospital's clinical performance to national measures. Patient experience information is also available. Here is the link to the site: www.hospitalcompare.hhs.gov/hospital-compare.aspx?.

The charts in figures 7.1 and 7.2 summarize the major patient-safety-ranking organizations in the United States.

Patient Safety Watchdog Organizations in the United States of America				
Criteria	Joint Commission	National Quality Forum	Center for Disease Control	Agency for Health Research & Quality
Program	Sentinel Event Reporting-21 events tracked	Hospital Reporting for Safety Metrics-27 events tracked	National Health Safety Network	Researches & reports on patient safety
Inception	1996	2006	2005	1999
Scope	All inpatient facilities	Hospitals	All inpatient facilities	Varies
Enforcement	Yes, Facility Cerification depends on meeting standards; impacts reimbursement & contracts	Concensus based standards established with a public agency/private review process;members must report safety metrics	Data is collected for hospital errors.	No enforcement, but recognition and organizations don't want to lose grant funding for initiatives
Participation	All certified inpatient facilities in the country	Member organizations only;26 states & District of Columbia participate in a state patient safety reporting effort	All facilities getting Medicare or Medicaid funds must meet standards	Voluntary

Figure 7.1.   Patient Safety A.7

	JCAHO	NQF	CDC	AHRQ
Participat ion	All certified inpatient facilities in the country	Member organizations only;26 states & District of Columbia participate in a state patient safety reporting effort	All facilities getting Medicare or Medicaid funds must meet standards	Voluntary
Reportin g	Part of the certification process for care protocols	This is a voluntary organization; reporting is internal, not public	22 states mandate this system for their hospitals; largest in the nation	Only for awards or grant funded projects
Comment s	Organization uses peer reviewed processes to improve health care but specific hospital performance is not publicly reported; unless certification is pulled.	Health & Human Services has contracted with NQF for reporting the Affordable Care Act criteria	Specific hospital performance is not disclosed	AHRQ is primarily a research agency
Web site	www.jointcommission. org	www.qualityforum.org	www.cdc.gov	www.ahrq.gov
Notes	For more information on specific initiatives for patient safety, go to the agency web sites.			

Figure 7.2.   Patient Safety B.7 (cont.)

ANALYSIS

The public reporting of patient-safety errors has illustrated one of the main problems in achieving more affordable health care in the United States: There is no single standard for tracking and reporting safety. Rather, each state labors to identify which model it wants to use and what the political temperament of the legislature is for populous edicts. Though it is great to see all of the innovation, it would be less expensive for everyone if a single standard were adopted. Almost half of the states already use the CMS model (twenty-two), probably because Medicare and Medicaid are responsible for so much of their cash flow. In any case, as I previously cited, multiple standards for measurement do not necessarily add to patient safety, only to the cost of providing it. And that is some food for thought, dear reader.

NOTES

1. "Patient Safety Event Reporting Systems Reviewed," Agency for Healthcare Research and Quality, accessed March 12, 2013, www.pso.ahrq.gov/formats/psersys.htm.

2. "Comparative Summary of States' Adverse Event Reporting and Performance Experiences," Quality and Patient Safety, accessed March 12, 2013, www.qups.org/med_errors.php?c=state_comparison&t=17.

3. "Comparative Summary of States' Adverse Event Reporting and Performance Experiences."

4. "Comparative Summary of States' Adverse Event Reporting and Performance Experiences."

5. "Comparative Summary of States' Adverse Event Reporting and Performance Experiences."

6. "Comparative Summary of States' Adverse Event Reporting and Performance Experiences."

7. Indiana State Department of Health, *Indiana Medical Error Reporting System: Final Report for 2009* (Indianapolis: Indiana State Department of Health, 2010), available online at www.in.gov/isdh/files/2009_MERS_Report.pdf (accessed March 12, 2013).

8. "Statewide Initiative to Help Identify and Prevent Infections," Indiana State Department of Health, accessed March 12, 2013, www.in.gov/portal/news_events/58592.htm.

9. "Indiana Reports Fewer Preventable Medical Errors; Kansas Struggles to Meet Oral Health Needs," Kaiser Health News, August 31, 2010, accessed March 12, 2013, www.kaiserhealthnews.org/Daily-Reports/2010/August/31/State-Round-Up.aspx.

10. "Comparative Summary of States' Adverse Event Reporting and Performance Experiences."

11. "Comparative Summary of States' Adverse Event Reporting and Performance Experiences."

12. "Comparative Summary of States' Adverse Event Reporting and Performance Experiences."

13. "Comparative Summary of States' Adverse Event Reporting and Performance Experiences."

14. "Comparative Summary of States' Adverse Event Reporting and Performance Experiences."

15. "Comparative Summary of States' Adverse Event Reporting and Performance Experiences."

16. "AHRQ's Patient Safety Initiative: Building Foundations, Reducing Risk," Agency for Healthcare Research and Quality, December 2003, appendix 2, accessed March 12, 2013, www.ahrq.gov/qual/pscongrpt/psiniapp2.htm.

17. "Missouri Nosocomial Infection Reporting Data: Report to the Governor and General Assembly—2011," Missouri Department of Health and Senior Services, accessed March 12, 2013, http://health.mo.gov/data/pdf/2011NosocomialReport.pdf.

18. "Montana: Public and Private Policy Medical Errors and Patient Safety," Quality and Patient Safety, accessed March 12, 2013, http://qups.org/med_errors.php?c=individual_state&s=27&t=1.

19. "Nebraska: Public and Private Policy Medical Errors and Patient Safety," Quality and Patient Safety, accessed March 12, 2013, http://qups.org/med_errors.php?c=individual_state&s=28&t=1.

20. "Comparative Summary of States' Adverse Event Reporting and Performance Experiences."

21. "Comparative Summary of States' Adverse Event Reporting and Performance Experiences."

22. "North Dakota: Public and Private Policy Medical Errors and Patient Safety," Quality and Patient Safety, accessed March 12, 2013, http://qups.org/med_errors.php?c=individual_state&s=35&t=1.

23. "Adverse Event Reporting Tools by State," National Academy for State Health Policy, accessed March 12, 2013, www.nashp.org/pst-state-list.

24. "Frequently Asked Questions, Nursing Homes," Oregon Patient Safety Commission, Summer 2007, accessed March 12, 2013, http://library.state.or.us/repository/2007/200710171149033/index.pdf.

25. Bethany Hammer, "Mandatory Reporting of Hospital-Acquired Infections," Thesis Presentation, Loyola University, 2009, available online at http://healthlawonline.luc.edu/documents/Hammer_ThesisPresentation.pdf (accessed March 12, 2013).

26. "Comparative Summary of States' Adverse Event Reporting and Performance Experiences."

27. "Comparative Summary of States' Adverse Event Reporting and Performance Experiences."

28. "South Dakota: Public and Private Policy Medical Errors and Patient Safety," Quality and Patient Safety, accessed March 12, 2013, http://qups.org/med_errors.php?c=individual_state&s=42&t=1.

29. "Comparative Summary of States' Adverse Event Reporting and Performance Experiences."

30. "Comparative Summary of States' Adverse Event Reporting and Performance Experiences."

31. "Comparative Summary of States' Adverse Event Reporting and Performance Experiences."

32. "Comparative Summary of States' Adverse Event Reporting and Performance Experiences."

33. "Comparative Summary of States' Adverse Event Reporting and Performance Experiences."

34. "AHRQ's Patient Safety Initiative: Building Foundations, Reducing Risk," chapter 1, accessed March 12, 2013, www.ahrq.gov/qual/pscongrpt/psini1.htm.

35. "Patient Safety Event Reporting Systems Reviewed."

36. "Comparative Summary of States' Adverse Event Reporting and Performance Experiences."

37. "Comparative Summary of States' Adverse Event Reporting and Performance Experiences."

III

RESOURCING YOUR HEALTH CARE

Surgical Tips

When You Have to Go Under the Knife

$\mathcal{U}$ndergoing surgery is one of the most traumatic things a person can go through, or worse yet if your child has to have surgery. This chapter offers some practical advice for locating the optimal professionals for your procedure and managing your surgery through the recovery process.

VETTING THE SURGEON

The American College of Surgeons certifies physicians based on their surgical training and expertise, so this is a good way to start the verification of a doctor's qualifications. You can go to their website and look up surgeons by specialty and location at: www.facs.org/patienteducation/patient-resources/surgery/acsmember.html.

To ascertain the best facility for your surgical procedure, there are a number of things to consider, such as the type of procedure, where your physician has admitting privileges (hopefully a hospital with really good quality scores), insurance reimbursement provisions (for a covered facility and participating physician), and, of course, the hospital's safety record. For more information on patient safety, you can review the nonprofit Leapfrog Group's hospital rankings in chapter 5 of this book, or go to their website: www.leapfroggroup.org. The federal Department of Health and Human Services has a "hospital compare" website that is easy to use and applies to the entire country: www.hospitalcompare.hhs.gov.

An example of a for-profit company website that may be helpful for assessing health care quality information is www.healthgrades.com, but the patient comments about clinicians tend to be more anecdotal. Healthgrades's website seems to have the most value for judging what the patient has to say about a clinician.

Some questions that you should ask your surgeon are:

1. How many procedures have you performed that are similar to the one you are recommending?
2. At which hospitals do you perform the procedure?

And if you are in Florida, make sure your surgeon has malpractice insurance, as it is not required in that state. Doctors in Florida may also use letters of credit as evidence of their ability to cover a malpractice claim; however, since you never know where you stand in the creditor's queue, this is hardly comforting.[1]

For more information on state-by-state rules regarding the requirement for malpractice insurance, go to the American Medical Association site: www.ama-assn.org/resources/doc/arc/state-laws-mandating-minimum-insurance.pdf.

Once you know this information, you can check the hospital's quality scores with the Leapfrog Group or the Health and Human Services website mentioned in chapter 5 of this book.

RESEARCHING SURGICAL SPECIALTIES

The healthgrades.com website has a tool to find doctors and hospitals by specialty. It lists eighty-six neurosurgeons in Seattle, which is a pretty healthy number, and it indicates that this area does a lot of brain (neuro) surgeries. By contrast, Boston, Massachusetts, has 202 neurosurgeons, and New York City has 321 neurosurgeons. San Francisco has 259, Los Angeles has 285, and San Diego boasts 193 neurosurgeons. Anyway, you get the idea; the larger urban areas have more medical specialists for brain surgery.

To cross-check that, go to the "Find Hospitals" tab and enter "neurosurgery" and your city or zip code and find the doctors who perform head and neck surgery, which is performed by a neurosurgeon. The facilities are also ranked according to health-care quality data reported by the medical facility, which include medical errors and other factors. You can use the website to check out the potential facility and your surgeon ahead of time.

Another good way to compare quality is to look at multiple scores from different evaluators, which could include the Leapfrog Group and healthgrades.com or maybe a list from a news source, like the annual *U.S. News and World Report on Health Care*. In my review of the healthgrades.com list, I saw several hospitals that were also on the Leapfrog Group list for safety excellence, scoring 100 percent in four or more of the seven criteria. These are not all-inclusive measures but merely different resources to help you make an informed surgical-team decision. In any case, if you are going to have any major surgery, it is important to know the safety facts ahead of time. Also, the absolute best way to get a read on a possible hospital or surgical choice is to ask a doctor or nurse where he or she would go for the procedure.

ALPHA HOSPITALS SCORING WELL ON BOTH LEAPFROG AND HEALTHGRADES.COM REPORTS

In a previous review I compared the hospitals that had four out of the five patient-safety criteria on the Leapfrog Group's annual survey and cross-referenced them with the healthgrades.com scores and found facilities that were on both of the "A" lists. I encourage you to do this same exercise when you are contemplating a hospital procedure. The healthgrades.com score tells you what consumers think, and the Leapfrog score is an indication of what the experts think, in terms of both compliance and systemic reinforcement of patient safety. High-scoring facilities are listed by hospital name and state:

- Centura in Colorado
- Skokie in Illinois
- Hackensack in New Jersey
- Lehigh Valley in Pennsylvania
- Memorial in Tennessee

INFORMATION ON SURGICAL SPECIALTIES

Burns: Wound Care

Advanced wound care for burn victims is typically located in level-1 trauma centers throughout the United States, which are listed in chapter 6 of this book.

Cosmetic Procedures

The same rules apply for cosmetic surgery as for any other surgery including checking the certifications, board licensure, and safety rankings for clinicians and facilities. Yes, you can die from plastic surgery, just like any other medical procedure. Finally, your ability to have surgery is based on your health, so if you are overweight, don't exercise, and have a suppressed immune system, it may not be a good idea for you to have elective surgery at all.

Cardiac Procedures (Heart)

Heart surgery is a big deal and has advanced so much in the last decade that even people in very poor health are able to undergo procedures with fewer problems. When reviewing surgeons for this procedure, you can go to the American College of Surgeons site and look under specialty and location. Hospitals that perform complex heart procedures can be found in level-1 trauma centers as well as organ-transplant centers, so find those facilities for a start. Also, researching medical facilities that are affiliated with universities will yield high-quality medical options.

Stand-alone cardiac treatment facilities are common now, but their certification for cardiac procedures, like the balloon treatment for clearing an artery, does not mean they are approved for heart transplants.

Organ Transplants

Hospitals that are approved for organ transplants are always listed by the specific transplants for which they have approval. More information on transplant centers is included in chapter 11 of this book.

Orthopedics

Orthopedic surgeries have tremendous variation and can even be done on an ambulatory or outpatient basis as well as in a traditional hospital setting. The process of vetting an orthopedic specialist is the same as for any other surgery: First, look for a board-certified doctor specializing in the procedure you seek. Then, have the surgery done at a facility with the best patient-safety rating possible. Of course, insurance reimbursement and costs are also a consideration, but insurance companies should seek to cover facilities with excellent patient-safety records because there are fewer procedural "do-overs," and that saves money and lives in the long run.

MANAGING THE DIAGNOSIS, TREATMENT, AND RECOVERY CYCLE

Step 1: Verifying the Accuracy of the Diagnosis

After your initial diagnosis, you need to decide on your treatment team. To locate surgeons who specialize in the procedure you seek, use your internet search engine to get an idea of eligible practitioners for your area, and you should also request a referral from your physician. The next step is to look at the certifications and training, followed by a health grade or safety score from an independent, third-party entity. These will give you a benchmark of competence and patient satisfaction. It is always a good idea to get a second opinion before a surgical procedure even if you have to pay for the opinion.

A word about bedside manner: I think this is overrated, especially for surgeons, because your doctor is not your social worker and this is not as important as having an experienced practitioner who is a member of the American College of Surgeons and is board certified for the designated procedure. Better to have a clinician who needs to work on his bedside manner but is brilliant in his or her field, because when it comes to medicine, brilliance is worth more than charm. Please be careful to evaluate all the factors in selecting the physicians, including the referral source. It is understood that the oncologist is expected to have an empathetic demeanor, as that relationship tends to be more long term, as opposed to a surgeon's short-term relationship with a patient.

Step 2: Taking Control and Selecting the Treatment Team

Assume you are captain of your treatment team and behave accordingly. Do not abdicate your treatment decisions to the oncologist or surgeon. Your decision-making process may include researching treatments on a global scale (not just practices in the United States), obtaining a second opinion, having the surgery performed at a different facility from the primary one for which your surgeon is affiliated, and choosing an atypical postsurgery protocol. In other words, think for yourself and make decisions accordingly.

Step 3: Paying for the Procedure

If you are planning a nonemergency surgical procedure, you will have time to verify any limitations on your insurance plan. Remember, just because the pre-existing conditions limitations have been removed due to the 2010 health care reform mandates, that does not mean the insurance plan is free from contract benefit limitations. For example, specific benefit limits are allowed for certain services, such as physical therapy.

Obviously, if the surgery is due to a traumatic event, you may not have much choice as to the location of the surgery or the procedure itself. Barring that, there still are some general rules to follow to obtain the best surgical outcome, and they are: verify facility licensing, physician certifications, and insurance company approvals; check patient-safety sites like Leapfroggroup. org for health care outcomes; and get a second opinion before you allow someone to cut you open.

Be sure the facility you choose for your nonemergency procedure (ambulatory) is licensed by the state and also approved by your insurance company. To ascertain this, you can check your state department of public health website or call their office to find out about a facility's licensure. If you are super-paranoid, the facility itself will then be able to tell you if your surgeon has admitting privileges for their hospital. Finally, do contact your insurance company's medical claims service department ahead of time and inform them of your pending surgery, which is especially important if you need pre-authorization before having the procedure (typical with back surgeries). This will also allow you to determine if your facility is covered by the insurer and what you will be expected to pay for the services, after your deductible, copayments, and so on.

Also, the facility needs to be approved for the type of procedure you will be having, as all facilities are not equal. Approval for general surgery does not necessarily mean the facility is approved for all surgeries. As indicated in chapter 6, the criteria to become approved for level-1 trauma-center procedures involves a staff of specialists, especially neurologists, who complete enough surgical procedures per year to qualify for the "gold standard," if you will. Your goal should be to find the facility that does a lot of surgeries similar to the one you will be having, because they will have more experience. For example, if you are going to have knee surgery, going to an orthopedic specialty center is probably a good idea. Conversely, if you are having heart surgery, going to a cardiac care center is also advisable. For those of you obtaining organ transplants, read chapter 11 for a list of organ-transplant facilities. For the hospitals that are designated transplant facilities, there are transplant units with special support teams.

If you lack insurance coverage and need to have a surgical procedure, you will probably be encouraged to go to a public hospital, like the local trauma center, or the university hospital. This isn't necessarily bad, because these facilities receive funding to provide a greater proportion of care to those without insurance who lack funding. Don't expect to have a private room or a hotel-like environment, though. And regardless of all of the talk about "free health care" from hospitals, you will be required to contribute to the cost of your care, based on your income. You can arrange for some payment plan, but hospitals do collect on their receivables, and some can be pretty aggressive. For more information on how to obtain health care without insurance, see chapter 9.

Finally, it is always a good idea to bring an advocate with you to the hospital or clinic where you obtain the surgery to make sure you are properly cared for postsurgery. In the United States health care is a volume business, and the surgeons typically complete a high number of procedures per day, because reimbursement from insurance sources is based on the procedure, not the time they spend, ergo less time spent means more money in their pockets. Postsurgery, the nursing team will be responsible for your recuperative care, starting with the postsurgical unit where you recover from the effects of anesthesia. Depending on the procedure, you are moved to either a hospital unit, such as intensive care, or a "med/surg" floor for recovery. If you have had an ambulatory surgical procedure, someone should take you home after the surgery.

CONCLUSION

One of the good things about the U.S. health care system is we have an excellent cadre of highly qualified surgeons. As a surgical customer, take care to find the right surgeon for your procedure, and ask all the necessary questions about intended and unintended consequences of the procedure. Before your surgery, find out what kind of aftercare you'll need as well, and what kinds of medical personnel will be involved. Line them up beforehand if you can. If you will need in-home care, find out what may be covered by your insurance company, and research the best agencies in your area. Be prepared. In other words, know the facts before you go into the operating room, and get all your ducks in a row.

NOTE

1. "Do All Doctors Have Insurance?," Florida Medical Malpractice, accessed March 12, 2013, www.floridamalpractice.com/med20.htm.

· 9 ·

How to Get Medical Treatment in the United States Without Health Insurance

$\mathscr{F}$or the nearly 50 million people without health insurance in the United States, preimplementation of the 2014 health reforms and the 18 million left without insurance postreforms, this chapter is for you. How do you obtain health care if you have no insurance? There are four basic methods for accessing medical care sans health insurance, and they are: pay with cash or credit per clinical visit, frequent public health centers in urban areas, access federally qualified community health centers, and use the old standby—hospital emergency departments. The average person without medical insurance may feel there are few options to get health care, other than paying out of pocket for treatment or, worse yet, avoiding care. Though the lack of health insurance does limit the number of clinicians who will serve those patients, there are two institutional remedies in America: the public health system and federally qualified community health centers. Both of these systems are designed to provide primary health care on an as-needed basis for underserved populations, including the uninsured.

COMMUNITY HEALTH CENTERS

Community health centers (CHCs) were authorized in 1975 to promote health care for medically underserved populations. There are 3,709 federally qualified health care centers in the United States, and eighty-nine are in Washington State. One of the most famous federally qualified health centers is the Pike Market Clinic in Seattle, and the Delta Health Center in Mississippi may be the oldest one in the country, having been established in 1967.[1]

These clinics must periodically reapply for federal funding to support the health care they provide to rural and poor urban communities. The centers also have to conform to certain governance standards, including community representation on the board and auditing for government-grant compliance. Not all community health centers are federally qualified health centers. The federal agency Health Resources and Services Administration (HRSA) has ranked community health centers number one for outcome-driven results, which means good value for their patients. The Bush administration continued to support CHCs and increased relative funding for them, as has the Obama administration.

Patients should have a primary-care provider (regular doctor or nurse practitioner) in a community health clinic in order to have continuity of care, but if you are an occasional patient, you can still get treatment. Patients will be expected to contribute to the cost of their care based on their household income. Community health clinics also accept insurance for reimbursement. The community clinic typically has an on-site pharmacy, so the patient can get his or her prescription filled there as well. All federally qualified community health clinics with pharmacies offer discounted pharmaceutical pricing because of a federal provision called 340B drug pricing. Community health centers will be a major contributor to the medical home and continuity of care provisions under the Medicare and Medicaid reforms, because they are geared for primary health care.

PUBLIC HEALTH DEPARTMENTS

Public health departments are more robust in larger cities, but smaller communities have public health programs as well. In smaller communities, the health department may be more involved in disease surveillance and the health inspection of restaurants. However, even in smaller cities, the health department participates in emergency planning, executing public health directives like childhood immunizations, and disease investigation (e.g., E. coli). In urban areas, residents can go to the public health clinic for primary care, just as they would go to their family doctor, but payment for services is based on a sliding-fee scale according to the patient's income. Lab work is often done right on the premises to save money for the health department. Often the public health departments have the most up-to-date information on international travel vaccinations. For example, if a patient has immunization records at the health department, it may be easier to continue to maintain those in one location. Yes, Virginia, public health is not just for poor folks.

DISPROPORTIONATE SHARE HOSPITALS

America's poor frequent the emergency departments of urban hospitals in droves, which is costly for the community and the hospital system. Consequently, the federal government created the Disproportionate Share Funding program for hospitals that are identified as serving this population. Disproportionate Share Hospital (DSH) money is a federal subsidy for hospitals, so they can continue to provide care for patients who can't pay and have nowhere else to go. There are 1,291 DSHs in the United States, according to the Health and Human Services administrative agency HRSA, but about three times as many hospitals receive some federal subsidy for serving indigent populations. The DSH facility in Seattle is Harborview Medical Center, but there are twelve critical access facilities in Washington. In Austin, Texas, Brackenridge Medical Center has this designation. Even though Texas has designated only a handful of hospitals to serve as critical access facilities, 169 hospitals qualified for federal DSH money in 2002.[2] This phenomenon is due to the formula the federal government uses to calculate the subsidy, which includes the proportion of Medicaid patients served, and thus makes many other nondesignated DSHs eligible. This example is illustrative of the bifurcated means the United States employs to pay for health care, via federal subsidies to support populations that are underserved throughout the country. Generally, hospitals with level-1 trauma-center status will have disproportionate share payment status, as that is where low-income people often go for health care.

DISCOUNTED PRESCRIPTION DRUG PROGRAM (340B)

Qualifying health care facilities are eligible for 340B drug discounts based on the 1992 Veterans Health Care Act. To obtain discounted prescription drugs, go to a community health clinic with its own pharmacy or to a DSH in your city. You do not have to be admitted to the hospital to have your script filled in the hospital pharmacy. Your script should be 25 percent to 40 percent less expensive at these facilities than at your local pharmacy.

NEGOTIATING A HOSPITAL PAYMENT

For anyone in the United States who experiences a hospital admission, here are some crucial things you need to know before you make a payment arrangement. Number one, virtually no one pays retail rates at a hospital, because the patient's bill that lists the hospital charges does not reflect any of the payment arrangements the hospital has with private insurance companies, Medicare, or Medicaid. Number two, cash customers (the uninsured) are charged full retail prices, unless they qualify for discounts in the form of charitable care. If you do not have insurance and are a cash customer, you may pay more for the same services than an insured customer. Number three, hospital charges are not actual costs, but are numbers generated to produce enough money, mostly from Medicare (the largest customer base), to meet budget requirements. The reason hospitals "mark up" their charges is because Medicare reimbursements pay a reduced portion of the gross hospital charges, creating an incentive for hospitals to increase their retail prices in order to net more money from Medicare. The same is true for Medicaid, although the reimbursements are much smaller than from Medicare, so the hospitals are more at risk there. All hospitals do this form of accounting, whether they are a nonprofit or for-profit operation. The dark side of this equation is uninsured patients may be charged the undiscounted rates for services, which are the prices the hospital never expects to get.

To avoid overpaying for hospital services, try to get the hospital to offer a discount. If the discount brings the bill down to 60 percent of their gross charges for your services, this is pretty close to what some insurance-company contracts will pay. If you have ever reviewed an insurance company's state-ment of benefit payment, it shows the total hospital charges and the reduced amount the insurer actually paid, and the insurance company claims the difference as your "savings" for those services. An exception to this rule is children's hospitals, which are reimbursed at about 80 percent to 90 percent of total charges by most insurance companies.

However, for the uninsured patient, the hospital can also deduct the dif-ference between what you actually pay and their gross charges as "charity care." By way of comparison, the hospital is not allowed to take a charitable deduc-tion for the portion of the bill that is not paid by insurance-company contracts. To the extent uninsured patients actually pay their hospital bills, the hospital could come out fine financially. Of course we know many uninsured patients can't pay 60 percent of their hospital charges, and the hospital really does have to throw in money for the difference, which is truly charity care.

If the hospital offers you a discount of 20 percent off their gross charges (retail), this is not much of a discount. Hospitals have charitable-care guide-lines based on the patient's income, levels of poverty in the community they serve, and their corporate mandates. These guidelines are somewhat inflex-ible, but if you are a cash or near-cash payer and can pay your bill quicker than an insurance company (ninety days or longer is not unusual), you may be able to get some additional discount.

TAKE CHARGE OF YOUR HEALTH

The next time you need health care and are without insurance, consider the community clinic and public health alternatives to the emergency department of a hospital. The hospital emergency department is expensive, will require a lengthy wait (several hours), and misplaces resources for primary care, which are geared to urgent care. In a true emergency situation, go to the DSH (also known as the trauma center) for treatment if you don't have insurance. Remember that there are health care alternatives to the emergency department that are accessible to all and for which payment for services is based on your income. Be smart about your health; it's better for everybody.

NOTES

1. "Delta Health Center Receives Major Grant," Bolivar Medical Center, December 2, 2012, accessed March 12, 2013, www.bolivarcom.com/view/full_story/18464032/article-Delta-Health-Center-receives-major-grant-.

2. Carey Eskridge, "Disproportionate Share Hospital (DSH) Program: Your Questions Answered," TLC Research Division, p. 4, accessed March 12, 2013, www.tlc.state.tx.us/pubspol/dshprogram.pdf.

· 10 ·

Medical Tourism

Getting Health Care Outside the United States

*M*edical tourism is exploding in growth for the United States because residents are choosing to obtain health care outside the country. A 2007 study published in MedScape General Medicine found that 750,000 people left the United States to obtain health care elsewhere.[1] Medical tourism was expected to grow to 6 million visits worldwide by 2010.[2] The demand in medical services outside the United States is driven by the high cost of medical services in America, a growing trend of private employers willing to pay for foreign medical services in their health plans, insurance-company reimbursement, and an increasingly sophisticated consumer population. Large employers like Walmart and Boeing have added medical tourism contracting into their medical programs, with the primary motivation of reducing the cost of their health plans.[3] Consumer-driven health care in the United States has encouraged health care purchasers to participate actively in choosing health-plan options. Also, purchasing health services through the use of medical savings accounts has increased the cost/benefit analysis for those consumers. Medical savings accounts allow the participant to sock away money for health care expenses, on a tax-preferred basis, and make withdrawals as needed. Unlike the former cafeteria-plan accounts, there is no requirement to use the funds in the year deposited. Money can be accumulated for health care expenses indefinitely. Savvy consumers now research and seek best values in health care globally, and increasingly, this population is middle class. This demand for health services value will only increase as more globetrotting baby boomers hit the Medicare rolls.

This chapter explains the process of obtaining medical services outside your home country, including identification of global centers of health care excellence, choosing a facility for medical services, and assessment of quality

91

measures. The primary reasons Americans leave their country to obtain medical services elsewhere are:

1. to obtain treatments that are not available in the United States;
2. to save money;
3. to combine health care treatments with travel/vacation
4. for more personalized care than in typical U.S. hospitals.

TOP GLOBAL DESTINATIONS FOR MEDICAL TOURISM

Here are the top accredited destinations for medical tourism based on the existing infrastructure and patient traffic, which was based in part on the Deloitte Medical Tourism Survey of 2008.[4] Also, existing arrangements with U.S. health care providers, insurance companies, university medical centers, and others are noted. The sources for this information come from each one of those entities. The hospital quality measure is based on the Joint Commission International standards for hospital certification.[5] Many other countries are building facilities and programs to promote medical tourism but do not have the volumes or resources of these locations, especially for American consumer-driven contracts.

- Central and South America
  - Brazil: Hospital Alemao Oswald Cruz and Hospital Israelita Albert Einstein, Sao Paulo
  - Costa Rica: Hospital CIMA
- Asia
  - India: Apollo Hospitals Group (Harvard Medical School contracts with them), Fortis Hospital Group (Johns Hopkins contracts with them)
  - Singapore: Johns Hopkins Singapore International Medical Centers, Moh Holdings, Gleneagles Hospital, Raffles Hospital, and Parkway Health Hospitals
  - Thailand: Bangkok Hospital Medical Center and Bumrungrad International
  - Turkey: Acibadem Health Care Group (Harvard Medical School has a contract with them), Anadolu Medical Center, Kent Hospital (affiliated with the Mayo Clinic)
- Europe
  - Ireland: Blackrock Clinic
  - Germany: DRK Kliniken, Kliniken Chemnitz, Kliniken Goerlitz
  - Spain: Centrico Medico

- North America
  - Mexico: CIMA Hospital Group
  - United States: Baptist Health International in Florida, Cleveland Clinic, Harvard Medical School and affiliates, all hospitals at the Houston Medical Center, Johns Hopkins Medical Center, Mayo Clinic facilities, Memorial Sloan-Kettering Cancer Center, UCLA Medical Center, UCSF Medical Center, the University of Pittsburgh Medical Center, as well as various organ-transplantation centers throughout the United States. Refer to chapter 11 for more information on medical centers of excellence within the United States.

According to a study by the American College of Surgeons, the most common services sought by medical tourists are[6]:

1. dentistry: dental implants, teeth restoration;
2. cosmetic surgery: facial reconstruction, figure-enhancement procedures;
3. cardiac surgery: stents, valve replacements;
4. orthopedic surgery: ACL repair, knee replacements, hip replacements;
5. cancer treatment: alternative therapies
6. other specialty care: drug rehabilitation and use of medications not available in the United States.

PRICES FOR MEDICAL PROCEDURES

For a U.S. resident who is insured and travels to a global medical-tourism center, the individual could expect to spend anywhere from one-third to one-half of the cost for the same surgical procedure completed within the United States. It is important to note that patient mortality and other surgical outcomes for the best hospitals globally are similar and in many cases better than the average U.S. hospital.

QUALITY STANDARDS OUTSIDE THE UNITED STATES

The international health care accreditation organization known as the Joint Commission International (JCI) reviews hospital facilities just as the U.S. Joint Commission does. In 2002, there were 220 JCI-accredited facilities promoting care to medical tourists.[7] As a medical tourist, you should look for a hospital that has JCI certification. If a doctor is admitted to perform surgery at a JCI facility, the JCI will have already vetted the physician's qualifications for board certification and other certifications. However, it is always a good idea to verify your surgeon's board certification, to make sure the procedure you are having is one for which he or she is still certified and trained to perform. This process can be done in a variety of ways: by asking your medical-tourism coordinator, contacting the hospital directly, or viewing physician registry information. Hospitals and clinicians who deal with foreign patients are used to answering these types of questions and often have departments specifically supporting medical-tourist needs. Facilities that serve large populations of medical tourists will provide this information on request. For a quick reference, Global Companion Health, the largest medical-tourism provider in the United States, has a website that lists accredited facilities worldwide, for which they have contracts: www.companionglobalhealthcare.com/groupleaders/providernetwork/findbylocation.aspx.

INSURANCE COMPANIES THAT PAY FOR MEDICAL CARE OUTSIDE THE UNITED STATES

Several insurance companies have been covering medical services provided outside the United States through various medical-tourism contracts. A leader in promoting this type of medical outsourcing has been Blue Cross Blue Shield of Georgia, which uses Companion Healthcare to contract with overseas medical facilities. Companion Healthcare has contracts with Parkway Group Healthcare, which owns hospitals in Singapore, Turkey, Ireland, and Costa Rica.[8] Blue Cross Blue Shield of South Carolina created Companion Global Healthcare to do its overseas contracting and has agreements with seven international hospitals. Blue Cross Blue Shield of Wisconsin, a WellPoint subsidiary, has piloted a medical tourism program through Anthem Blue Cross Blue Shield.[9] California Blue Cross Blue Shield incorporated a medical-tourism provision in their contracts in 1999, because their customer base includes a large Spanish-speaking population. United Group in Florida is also providing medical-tourism reimbursement.

TIPS FOR RESOURCING HEALTH CARE
OUTSIDE YOUR HOME COUNTRY

Visas

The North American Free Trade Agreement (NAFTA) dictates that U.S. travelers may go to Canada or Mexico without a visa. There is a significant amount of medical tourism between Mexico and the United States.

Other countries that do not require a travel visa for U.S. residents are: members of the European Union, Costa Rica, Singapore, and Thailand.

A visa may be obtained upon entry to the country for Turkey and does not have to be obtained in advance.

Countries that require the purchase of a visa prior to entering the country are Brazil and India.

Travel Planning

Get your Shots. As a visitor to another country, you may need immunizations, especially if you are traveling to a tropical country (malaria, dengue fever, etc.). In addition, you will need to make other advanced preparations such as obtaining decent first-aid kits and water-purification materials if you are traveling in a developing country. Recently, I updated my immunizations for a business trip to India, which included a cholera series in addition to tetanus and polio updates. Of course, all my other immunizations were current, including the full hepatitis series A and B. Cholera is contracted from unclean water, which is a big problem outside of major cities in India and other parts of Asia. The tetanus shot is essential, as India does not control its dog population, so the country has a higher incidence of dog bites. While I was planning my trip to India, two of my sponsors in India were stricken with the tropical diseases dengue fever and malaria. If the locals contract the disease, you have a pretty good chance of acquiring some nasty bug as well.

Find a good travel clinic—often one may be associated with your city's public health agency—and get the most current updates on disease outbreaks before you leave home.

Safety and Global Terrorism. It is always a good idea to check with the U.S. State Department before going to a foreign country, as it will have the most current information on terrorism and other travel risks by location. For example, Northern India, including Mumbai, has more adverse activity of this kind, including bombings of tourist hotels, than southern India. As an aside, a number of years ago, while traveling in Turkey, I noticed there were very few garbage cans, and I was told they were removed because of previous bombing incidents. Europe also has safety threats, typically at major rail terminals, so it is a good idea not to linger at Heathrow Airport or other major transit hubs.

If you are up for a walk on the wild side, check out Robert Pelton's *Most Dangerous Places* guides. He tells you things no one else does, based on his personal experience. The *Lonely Planet* guides are not as gritty *as Most Dangerous Places* but have solid traveler safety tips, especially for Asia. One I particularly enjoy is *Lonely Planet's* tip for female train travelers in India: "Get a top berth in the sleeping compartment to avoid unwanted groping from male passengers!" Oh well, I guess when you are traveling, you can expect a few surprises.

Medical-Tourism Travel Arrangements.   Travel arrangements as well as the actual hospital contracting are usually coordinated by a medical-tourism travel agent. Unfortunately, there is currently no certification required for this specialized vocation, and people working in this field usually lack medical expertise. It is best to use well-established firms with a track record of resourcing medical needs for international visitors. One of the ways to ascertain if a medical-tourism vendor is qualified is to check with the hospital you intend to use. Also check on the medical-tourism agency's track record by asking for customer references. At a very minimum, review the licensure for your medical-tourism agent, which can be found by checking with the business-licensing agency in the state where the firm is located. A word of warning here: Most medical-tourism providers work on a commission basis, which is then paid by the facility that treats the patient. In India, this may be a portion of the total service charges and is not usually revealed to the customer. Beware when an agent encourages you to use a facility that is unfamiliar and lacks international JCI certification. Also, what kind of "backup" resources does the agent have? Can that person get you in touch with a doctor twenty-four hours a day? Are you able to speak to your clinician before you decide on the procedure? With the economy of Skype and other computerized communications, it is easy to have international teleconferences with digital imaging, prior to complex surgeries. It goes without saying that any reputable doctor is going to want to review your medical records, including labs and images, preferably sent electronically, in advance of the procedure.

Finally, a word to the wise: Doctors in other countries are just as busy as those in the United States, so don't expect them to be your counselor; just expect them to be competent. Any complex procedure requires a care coordinator for postsurgical follow-up and presurgical preparation. Note that most doctors in the United States will not perform postsurgical follow-up care for a procedure performed outside the country unless it has specifically been prearranged. If you have complications, you could end up having to redo the surgery in the United States and saving nothing.

NOTES

1. Michael D. Horowitz, Jeffrey A. Rosensweig, and Christopher A. Jones, "Medical Tourism: Globalization of the Healthcare Marketplace," *MedGenMed* 9, no. 4 (2007): 33, available online at www.ncbi.nlm.nih.gov/pmc/articles/PMC2234298 (accessed April 18, 2013).

2. Deloitte Center for Health Solutions, "Medical Tourism: Emerging Phenomenon in Health Care Industry—2008 Report," available online at www.deloitte.com/us/2008medicaltourism (accessed April 18, 2013).

3. Maria Lenhart and Marilee Crocker, "Walmart Offers Medical Travel Coverage to Employees," Travel Market Report, November 15, 2013, accessed April 18, 2013, www.travelmarketreport.com/articles/Walmart-Offers-Medical-Travel-Coverage-to-Employees.

4. Deloitte Center for Health Solutions, "Medical Tourism."

5. "JCI Accredited Organizations," Joint Commission International, accessed April 18, 2013, www.jointcommissioninternational.org/JCI-Accredited-Organizations.

6. James A. Unti, "Medical and Surgical Tourism: The New World of Health Care Globalization and What It Means for the Practicing Surgeon," American College of Surgeons, June 8, 2009, accessed April 18, 2013, www.surgicalpatientsafety.facs.org/news/medicaltourism0609.html.

7. Zoe Galland, "Medical Tourism: The Insurance Debate," *Businessweek*, November 9, 2008, available online at www.businessweek.com/stories/2008-11-09/medical-tourism-the-insurance-debatebusinessweek-business-news-stock-market-and-financial-advice (accessed March 12, 2013).

8. Bruce Einhorn, "Outsourcing the Patients," *Businessweek*, March 12, 2008, available online at www.businessweek.com/stories/2008-03-12/outsourcing-the-patients (accessed March 12, 2013).

9. Galland, "Medical Tourism."

· *11* ·

Health Care for Visitors
to the United States

$\mathcal{A}$pproximately 6 million people visit the United States each year on temporary visas[1] and another 500,000 obtain immigration visas.[2] In a 2008 report, the consulting firm Deloitte and Touche predicted that by 2011 medical tourists into the United States would reach 800,000.[3] Of these visitors, nearly a third are from Canada, and 26 percent are from Mexico and of the remainder 15 percent are Japanese, and 17 percent are Europeans.[4] According to U.S. Citizenship and Immigration Services (USCIS), the largest group of visitors are Class B visa holders, who are typically short stay tourists and business persons. According to the American Medical Association, approximately 400,000 visitors come to the United States to obtain health care and are referred to as medical tourists.[5] This chapter is organized around your visitor-visa status, so go to your visa-status category to get a quick guide for obtaining health care. For example, if you are a medical tourist, you already have arranged for medical treatment at a U.S. location, which is part of your visa process. This chapter also provides information on centers of excellence for health care in the United States. Information on how to obtain urgent or unscheduled medical care while visiting America is also addressed.

GETTING INTO THE UNITED STATES

I researched immigration requirements with the travel.state.gov website[6] to determine visa requirements for entrance to the United States. Thanks to NAFTA (North American Free Trade Agreement), if you are Canadian or Mexican, a passport is all you need, so welcome to America.

Other countries that are in the visa waiver program for the United States are Andorra, Hungary, New Zealand, Australia, Iceland, Norway, Austria, Ireland, Portugal, Belgium, Italy, San Marino, Brunei, Japan, Singapore, Czech Republic, Latvia, Slovakia, Denmark, Liechtenstein, Slovenia, Estonia, Lithuania, South Korea, Finland, Luxembourg, Spain, France, Malta, Sweden, Germany, Monaco, Switzerland, Greece, the Netherlands, and the United Kingdom.[7]

Individual Eligibility for the Visa Waiver Program

One of the criteria for the visa waiver is to have a passport with an electronic chip in it, which is basically a tracking device. This is not a requirement for all individuals on the waiver list, but it is for anyone from the following countries: Czech Republic, Estonia, Greece, Hungary, Latvia, Lithuania, Malta, the Republic of Korea, and the Slovak Republic. As a medical tourist, you may be eligible for the visa waiver program, if your stay is no longer than ninety days and you are not in one of the excluded categories. Excluded visa categories include foreign media representatives or students. It is to your advantage to obtain the visa waiver if possible, as it gives you more flexibility in travel arrangements for medical care. This is especially critical for something that is health dependent such as an organ transplant, where even an elevated body temperature may postpone the surgery and delay your travel plans.

Medical Tourists to the United States

Medical tourists to the United States who apply for a temporary visa will pay $140 for a Class B visa, which includes all medical tourism and is good for ninety days.[8]

Other Visas

If you are in the United States on a fellowship or as a student, you will be required to have some type of supplemental accident insurance, which will primarily provide health-insurance reimbursement for accidents while in the United States. These contracts do not provide preventive care, and there are minimal primary-care provisions. These short-term medical contracts may be impacted by the 2010 U.S. health care reforms, but the final regulations are not available yet. If you are a student in the United States, every campus has information on how to get health care, often through a campus health clinic. There are also public health clinics in most cities in the United States.

Students

If you are fortunate enough to obtain a student visa into the United States, you will have been informed of the need to purchase student accident insurance, which is a temporary medical-insurance contract, good for a fixed period of time. Typically, this insurance excludes treatment for conditions that existed prior to the date of the contract, so it applies only to accidents and illnesses that occur while visiting the United States. I checked out the americanvisitorinsurance.com website and queried the cost for a twenty-two-year-old student wanting a twelve-month temporary insurance policy in 2010. The cost for the least expensive contract with a $75,000 insurance cap and $100 deductible was $384 for the year. The same insurance quote is listed at $412.45 in 2012.[9] Here are some organizations that sell student accident insurance contracts:

> www.americanvisitorinsurance.com
> www.ehealthinsurance.com

Business Persons

Business travelers are presumed to have money and insurance, and you will be expected to show proof of either should you require health care in the United States. If you need urgent care, go to an urgent-care center or a hospital. If you need a referral for primary care, major hotels can often refer you to medical assistance. Also, please read the chapter on hospital quality in the United States if you are contemplating surgery. A quick note on pharmacies here: They are everywhere, including in the grocery store, but the pharmacist cannot directly prescribe medications, unlike in Italy and other European countries. You will need a prescription from a doctor or nurse practitioner to obtain those medications.

Asylum Seekers

First of all, if you are seeking asylum, you must have a background of persecution in your home country and convince USCIS of this (generally through political support). Second, if you are lucky enough to be granted asylum, there is no visa fee, and you will automatically be granted a longer-stay visa. Third, you will be eligible for social support and assistance, including Medicaid insurance for low-income residents, Aid to Families with Children, and even assistance with housing and finding work. Of course, you will have already had a sponsor and a case worker to help you achieve all of these things.

Tourists

If you are in the United States as a tourist, I hope you purchased medical travel insurance, so you can pay for any medical care you may need while stateside. If not, get ready to cough up your credit card and guarantee some form of payment for medical care. There is no national health system in the United States (except for Medicare), so the cost of care varies by facility and region of the country. Even in 2014, when the health care mandates for insurance are slated to be implemented, this will minimally impact visitor provisions for medical insurance. Visitors to the United States could be required to show proof of insurance upon entry to the country after that date.

Illegal or Undocumented Residents

The United States has made it more difficult for residents to work or obtain services in the States if they lack a formal "green card" or permission to live in the United States. Residents of the United States who do not have legal status are not allowed to receive Medicaid or Medicare insurance benefits (even though they may have lived here for many years and paid these taxes). Thus, the options for illegal poor immigrants are limited. Community health centers in rural areas and urban areas are often geared to these populations. Information can be gleaned from local community centers frequented by these residents. Since these immigrants are most often Hispanic, the community health centers may have a Spanish listing and will certainly have Spanish-speaking personnel. As a last recourse, these patients can go to any hospital emergency department for treatment. In urban areas the community health centers will have interpreter services in several languages, including Mandarin, Korean, Vietnamese, and Japanese.

HEALTH CARE NEEDS AND CENTERS OF EXCELLENCE

Traumatic Injury

Obviously, traumatic injuries are due to accidents and unforeseen situations, so if you are visiting the United States and are involved in an auto accident, you might need to know something about trauma care. It may be comforting to know that virtually all of U.S. urban and suburban areas have a 911 response system for emergencies. All you have to do is dial 911, and help is coordinated by a dispatcher and on the way as soon as possible. Care is generally triaged by emergency medical technicians and the fire department for the district. Once on the scene, they assess the problem, provide on-site treatment, and take the patient to the closest hospital. It is only at the hospital that you will have to show proof of payment. However, if you don't have insurance or enough money to pay for the treatment, the Emergency Medical Treatment Active Labor Act (EMTALA) requires the hospital to treat you until you are stable enough before discharging. Moreover, you will not be deported for owing the hospital money.

Information on critical-care hospitals throughout the United States was previously discussed in chapter 6, which revealed the most sophisticated trauma centers listed by state and city. If you have a traumatic injury, U.S. trauma centers are excellent choices. Assuming you are conscious with an injury that is not catastrophic, you may wish to designate which facility you prefer for treatment. As a visitor to the United States, you don't have to worry about a provider network, as you are not enrolled for primary care here.

Primary Care

As a visitor to the United States who needs nonurgent care, you have a few options: either going to the local public health clinic (mostly in cities) or visiting an urgent-care center (primarily in more suburban areas) for treatment. And finally, most hospital groups also operate nonurgent-care clinics for lesser maladies.

Prearranged Medical Tourist Procedures

For specialized procedures like an organ transplant or complex surgery, the United States is a great place, with lots of quality hospitals and highly qualified surgeons. Presumably your decision to travel to America for this procedure has been well researched, and you have insurance or funds to cover the cost because it will be expensive. The United States has the most expensive health care system in the world—period. Included in this review are centers of excellence based on medical specializations, by city and state, as well as information from hospital-quality and patient-safety reports.

Specialty Care. It is no secret that the United States is well known for specialty care, rather than primary health care. There is a higher propensity for the "surgical solution" in the United States than in most countries in the world. The American College of Surgeons has a very good website for finding qualified surgeons: www.facs.org/public_info/yourhealth/findadoc. html.

For information on board certification for surgeons and surgical centers, go to www.abms.org.

Here is a list of surgical certifications that are granted by this organization:

- cardiovascular;
- colon and rectal;
- critical care surgery;
- general surgery;
- hand surgery;
- head and neck;
- neurological;
- obstetrical and gynecological;
- ophthalmologic (eye);
- oral and maxillofacial;
- orthopedic;
- pediatric vascular surgery;
- plastic surgery, general;
- plastic surgery, head and neck;
- plastic surgery, pediatric head and neck;
- thoracic; and
- urology.

Cardiac Procedures.   The premier cardiac-care facilities in the United States are the Cleveland Clinic and the Mayo Clinic, based on their clinical outcomes over time.[10] Other excellent facilities are: Johns Hopkins Medical Center, Duke Medical Center, Harvard Medical School Affiliates, and many of the university hospitals, including the University of California at Davis and UCLA Medical Center. Houston Medical Center has the DeBakey Heart Center (affiliated with Methodist Hospital), which was where the world's first heart transplant was done.

Orthopedic Procedures.   Orthopedic procedures include knee repair or replacement and joint repairs, including the often-cited hip replacement. Generally, spinal or neck procedures are treated under neurological specialties. Orthopedic surgery may be performed at outpatient surgical centers or as an ambulatory procedure at a hospital, which means you do not stay overnight. Obviously, if you have the surgery performed at a hospital, you can check its quality score by going to the hospital rankings in chapter 5. There are other methods, but these are the simplest. If you are not having your surgery performed in a hospital, then the key criteria to review are the certifications for the physician/surgeon and the facility. Each state grants a license for all medical facilities, so this should be available by checking the Department of Public Health website for the state in which you will have your surgery. You will also want to make sure the facility is approved for the procedure and not just for the appointment or accreditation of the doctor. For information on your orthopedic surgeon, go to the www.healthgrades.com website for ratings and patient feedback. The American College of Surgeons will have a nationwide listing of surgeons and their certifications as well.

Reconstructive and Cosmetic Procedures. For information on certified reconstructive or plastic surgeons, the following website is useful: www.plasticsurgery.org.

Fertility Treatment, In Vitro Fertilization. The U.S. Centers for Disease Control (CDC) provides a website about assisted reproductive technology. The law codifying medical service was passed in 1992. The site has information on fertilization success rates and surveillance information on national results.[11]

Organ Transplantation. The following medical centers each perform at least 150 organ transplants annually in the United States and are members of the Coalition of Major Transplant Centers. These medical centers perform 40 percent of all the transplants in the United States. There are 270 organizations that are certified to perform organ transplants in the United States, but only fifteen of those facilities complete most of the procedures.

Founding members of the Coalition of Major Transplant Centers are: University of Alabama at Birmingham; University of Wisconsin at Madison; University of Minnesota Medical Center, Fairview; University of Michigan; Ohio State University; Washington University Transplant Surgery, St. Louis; St. Barnabas Health Care System, New Jersey; The Health Alliance of Greater Cincinnati and Children's Hospital; Medical University of South Carolina; University of Colorado; Clarian Transplant Center, Indianapolis; University of Tennessee, Memphis; Froedtert Memorial Lutheran Hospital, Milwaukee; Vanderbilt University; and University of Texas at Houston.

Facilities that perform a large number of organ transplants include all of the above and these organizations as well: Cleveland Clinic, Duke University, Johns Hopkins, Massachusetts General (Harvard Affiliate), University of California (several sites), University of Pittsburgh, and University of Washington. For more information on which medical centers are approved for organ transplantation in the United States, go to the Centers for Medicare & Medicaid Services transplant site list[12]: www.cms.gov/CertificationandComplianc/Downloads/ApprovedTransplantPrograms.pdf.

Oral Surgery. Oral or maxillofacial surgeons can be found on the American College of Surgeons website (www.facs.org). This is a highly competitive business of dental reconstruction, the most complex cases typically occurring as a result of a traumatic injury.

Neurosurgery. Neurosurgeons can be found on the American College of Surgeons website (www.facs.org) and are always affiliated with major urban medical centers and level-1 trauma centers. A quick reference tool is to check the trauma-center list in this book (chapter 6) and then find neurosurgeons who are affiliated. Also go to the American College of Surgeons website to locate a specific neurosurgeon.

Alternative Medicine.   Alternative treatments for cancer are becoming more common in the United States as a complement to traditional therapies. Some of the alternative therapies that are used in the United States are oxygen therapy, ozone therapy, proton therapy, and hyperbaric treatment, to name a few. Each cancer care center will list the alternative therapies that are available to patients.

Cost of Care

What you can expect to pay depends on the procedure, location, and duration of care, plus the medications. Some of the wonder drugs cost thousands of dollars. As an example, the arthritis medication Embrel costs about $6,000 a year per patient in the United States. Any medical tourist will be advised on procedure costs and expected to provide a guarantee of payment via credit card or deposit in advance of hospital admission.

U.S. CENTERS FOR TOURISM

This chapter reviews specific health care resources in major international tourist destinations throughout the United States. For those cities that were not mentioned, the list is based purely on the name recognition and drawing cards for international tourists. Although more tourists visit France per year than the United States, the United States brings in more money from tourists than any other country ($86 billion to France's $43 billion in 2006).[13] The following destination cities were chosen for their proximity to iconic U.S. tourist destinations (*indicates that a center for medical tourism is located here):

1. New York City: the Big Apple*
2. Los Angeles: Hollywood offers both adult Disneyland and proximity to the simulated good cheer of family Disneyland*
3. Miami: more affordable beachfront than the Caribbean*
4. Washington, DC: historical center and nation's capital
5. Phoenix: largest urban area close to the Grand Canyon
6. Las Vegas: gambling, adult entertainment
7. San Francisco: cultural center of the West Coast, close to Napa and Sonoma wineries*

8. Seattle: exit point to Alaska, Olympic National Park, and Mount Rainier National Park
9. New Orleans: music, food
10. Honolulu: tropical climate year round, plus U.S. resources

Destinations for Medical Tourists in the United States

Before we get to the prime American tourist destinations, it is important to note that many clinics in the United States already have robust medical services for international clientele. This section reviews specific facilities for visitors who come to the States for prearranged health care services. According to *Medical Tourism Magazine*, top destinations for medical treatment for international visitors to the United States are: Florida, Maryland, Massachusetts, Minnesota, Ohio, New York, North Carolina, Pennsylvania, and Texas.[14] Based on my research, I am also including California as a location for medical in-country tourism. I reviewed the websites for each of the medical sites in this chapter, verifying resources for medical tourists.

California. Los Angeles: The University of Southern California in Los Angeles has an international medical program that offers translation services in six languages and other services. It gets high marks for its care-coordination services, which are key for international visiting patients. According to *U.S. News and World Report*, the UCLA hospital was ranked the fifth best hospital in the United States for 2010, behind Johns Hopkins, the Mayo Clinic, Massachusetts General (Harvard Medical School), and the Cleveland Clinic facilities.[15] Specialties include cancer treatment at UCLA's Jonsson Comprehensive Cancer Center. UCLA's Jules Stein Eye Institute offers ophthalmology services. Another specialty is psychiatry at the Resnick Neuropsychiatric Hospital at UCLA.[16]

San Diego: UCLA San Diego is a top ranked medical facility with a robust international patient-services program including care coordination, assistance with transportation, and translation services. Patient services include treatments for bone marrow transplantation, cancer (oncology), cosmetic surgery, diabetes, eye care (ophthalmology), and hepatitis. Organ transplantation is approved for kidney, liver, pancreas, and lung procedures. Other specialty services include otolaryngology (cochlear implants), neurosurgery, and pulmonary thromboendarterectomy (PTE).[17]

San Francisco: The University of California at San Francisco has an international medical care department, which offers translation services in Cantonese, Mandarin, Spanish, and Russian. American Sign Language is also offered, as it is at most medical facilities. UCSF also offers medical transportation, visa support, home care, and assistance with care coordination.[18]

Patient services include a variety of executive services, including a house-calls program, as well as mindfulness-based patient services including Tai Chi and yoga.[19]

Florida.   Gainesville: The University of Florida medical center is a level-1 trauma center.

Jacksonville: Shand's Trauma One is located in Jacksonville and is rated level 1. The Shand's Proton Therapy Institute brings international medical patients. There is also a Mayo Clinic in Jacksonville, which draws medical tourists as well.

Miami: Jackson Memorial Ryder Trauma Center is rated level 1. Baptist Health International Center in Miami had twelve thousand international patients representing more than one hundred countries in 2008.[20]

Homestead: Homestead Hospital is located in south Florida and is also part of the Baptist Hospital group, and it scored 100 percent on four of the seven criteria in the Leapfrog 2009 patient-safety report. This hospital has a separate international services division, which offers twenty-four hour emergency on-call service and travel arrangements including airport transportation. Baptist Hospital specifies cancer services, gamma knife surgery, and urgent care as specialties.[21]

Naples: The Cleveland Clinic has a location here with 170 physicians and 35 medical specialties including cardiology, neurology, orthopedics, and an international patient center at a separate location called the Weston Campus.[22]

Orlando: Orlando Regional Medical Center is rated a level-1 trauma center. The University of Central Florida in Orlando is involved in medical care for international patients through Orlando Health. The facility treats 4,500 medical tourist patients each year. Practice specialties include: stroke, neurology, orthopedics, memory disorder, epilepsy, brain surgery, radiation-oncology, and gynecologic-oncology.[23]

Maryland.   Johns Hopkins Hospital is located here and also has locations in India, Japan, Singapore, the United Arab Emirates (Dubai), and other countries. Affiliated hospitals include Punta Pacifica in Panama and Fortis Hospitals in India. Johns Hopkins Medicine International coordinates medical care for thousands of international patients a year, representing one hundred countries.[24] For a complete list of their specialties, refer to their website (www.hopkinsmedicine.org).

Massachusetts.   Boston: Harvard Medical School has an international medical tourism program called Harvard Medical International and has affiliations at international hospitals in several countries,[25] including Acibadem Healthcare Group in Turkey, Wockhardt Hospitals in India, and the Apollo Group.

In addition to Harvard Medical School resources, Massachusetts has excellent health care throughout the state including the following two Boston hospitals, which scored 100 percent on six of the seven patient-safety criteria in the Leapfrog 2009 report: Massachusetts General Hospital (Harvard affiliate) and Mercy Medical Center.

Level-1 trauma centers in Boston are Beth Israel Deaconess (Harvard affiliate), Boston Medical Center, Brigham and Women's (Harvard affiliate) Hospital, and Children's Hospital of Boston (Harvard affiliate).

Minnesota. Rochester: The Mayo Clinic (also located in Florida and Arizona) is headquartered here. The Mayo Clinic was ranked number two out of all U.S. hospitals. The Mayo Clinic has affiliates in Canada, Dubai, Guatemala, and Mexico. Their international health care newsletter is available in English, Arabic, Spanish, and Portuguese.[26] The Mayo Clinic is different from many of the international medical tourist centers as it is a nonprofit group and is a completely integrated practice. This has produced treatments in: Wolff-Parkinson White Syndrome (cardiology), Guillane-Barr Syndrome (neurology), immune deficiencies (internal medicine), leukemia (cancer), Huntington's Disease (genetic testing), and Lou Gehrig's Disease, which was diagnosed here in 1939.

In terms of quality, the Mayo Clinic in Minnesota scored a perfect rating on five of the seven Leapfrog patient-safety measures. Rochester Methodist Hospital is also one of the hospitals used by the clinic. St. Mary's is another hospital the clinic uses, and it is also a level-1 trauma center. All of this in little old Rochester, which is eighty miles south of Minneapolis and 370 miles north of Chicago.[27]

New York. Hospitals that scored 100 percent in five out of the seven Leapfrog Group patient-safety criteria were Montefiore Moses Division and Vassar Brothers. Hospitals that scored 100 percent on four out of seven of the safety measures were Montefiore Weller, New York University Hospitals Center, Roswell Park, and St. Francis-Poughkeepsie.

There are sixty hospitals in New York City and the surrounding metropolitan area.[28] Level-1 trauma centers in the metropolitan area of New York as listed by the State Department of Health are also listed in chapter 6 of this book.

New York City Hospitals for Medical Tourists. The hospitals known for serving an international clientele are Memorial Sloan-Kettering Cancer Center, Mount Sinai Hospital, and Cornell Medical School affiliates.

Memorial Sloan-Kettering Cancer Center: This is a world-renowned cancer research center. It offers translations in nine different languages, from Chinese Mandarin to Turkish Cyrillic. Memorial Sloan-Kettering has established relationships with centers in Switzerland, Brazil, Greece, Spain, Turkey, Hong Kong, Singapore, and the Philippines.[29]

Mount Sinai Hospital: This facility has been awarded the Joint Commission gold seal award, which recognizes hospital quality. One of its specialties is robotic prostate surgery (hopefully for the adult population). This hospital does not list a separate international patient program on its website.[30]

Cornell Medical School: The university is affiliated with New York Presbyterian Hospital in New York City. It is also affiliated with Methodist Hospital in Houston, Texas. The Global Health Center through Weil Cornell Medical School is committed to treating chronic disease in programs in Sub-Saharan Africa, the Middle East, the Americas, Europe, India, and elsewhere.

University of New York Medical Centers.   Rochester: Strong Hospital is a level-1 trauma facility, which also has a burn center and specializes in liver transplants (two hundred liver transplants are performed each year).[31]

Stonybrook: University Hospital SUNY is a regional trauma center, which specializes in kidney transplants and has performed more than one thousand.[32]

North Carolina.   Raleigh/Durham: Duke University Medical Center is involved in researching infectious diseases, and its global health program has established medical-research programs in the following countries: China, Haiti, Kenya, Singapore, Tanzania, and Uganda.[33] It should be noted that these are research programs and are not medical-tourism facilities. Duke is an approved organ-transplant center for liver, lung, kidney, and heart transplants.

Ohio.   Cleveland: The Cleveland Clinic is world-renowned for its cardiac services and has had an international patient's program since 1976, which offers translation services in nine languages.[34] Its medical-tourism program serves national and international patients. Its website has an extensive directory of conditions and treatments, with specializations in the following: eye, head and neck, heart and vascular, endocrinology, digestive diseases (Crohn's Disease), cancer, orthopedics, neurology, and executive health. The Cleveland Clinic also performs liver transplants.

Pennsylvania.   Pittsburgh: The University of Pittsburgh has an affiliation with the Royal Berkshire in the United Kingdom for cancer care. The University of Pittsburgh medical program has affiliated programs in Cyprus, Ireland, Italy, Qatar, and the United Kingdom. Its international medical program offers a convenient single-bill, single-price service for patient services[35] and offers translation in Arabic, Italian, Russian, Spanish, and Turkish. Specialties include minimally invasive surgical techniques, clinical trials, rehabilitation services, including specialized fields such as sports medicine. Other services are spinal injury, hand therapy, balance disorders, facial nerve disorders, pain treatment, and industrial rehabilitation.

Texas. Medical tourism is centered in the Houston Medical Center complex, which has many hospitals and health care resources. The medical center offers airport reception and a lounge specifically for medical tourists, located at the George Bush International Airport (formerly the Intercontinental Airport).

Houston Medical Center Facilities. Methodist Hospital[36]: This hospital has other facilities in the United States, including New York City, and an international patient-services program, with twenty-four-hour-a-day reception services.[37] This is home to the world-famous DeBakey Heart Center, which performed the first heart transplant. It is also approved for the following transplantations: heart, heart and lung, left ventricular assist, lung, kidney, liver, pancreas, and Islet cell transplants (can treat diabetes). Memorial Hermann Hospital: This is a level-1 trauma-center facility, as is the Children's Memorial Hermann facility. Some of the services the hospital provides for an international clientele include interventional cardiology, laryngology, genetics, oncology, and maternal fetal health, among others. It offers translation services in Spanish and Arabic and a hospital suite or hotel environment for those patients.[38]

MD Anderson Cancer Center: This medical center has an international patient center with translation services in nine languages, airport transportation, care coordination, and family support.[39] The MD Anderson Cancer Center serves 1,100 international patients yearly, and its primary specialization is cancer care. Translations are available in Spanish, Arabic, and Turkish.[40] Research on cancer is a key component of the center, including research for a vaccine to cure cancer. Baylor Medical Center: Scored 100 percent in five out of seven criteria in the Leapfrog survey previously mentioned in chapter 5, based on the National Quality Forum standards for patient-safety measures. This facility is also a level-1 trauma center. Baylor staffs Methodist Hospital, listed above, and also works with Texas Children's, St. Luke's, and Ben Taub. Both Ben Taub General and Baylor Medical Center are level-1 trauma centers.[41]

Other Facilities Near the Top–Ten International Tourist Destinations for the United States

These facilities are listed by state, according to the top-ten international tourist destinations in the United States. The criteria for inclusion was that the hospitals had to be ranked in either my personal quality analysis, a patient-safety analysis, or a trauma-center analysis, or mentioned as catering to international patients in other media sources.

Arizona—The Grand Canyon. Phoenix: There are four level-1 trauma centers in Arizona, and they are all in the capital city as follows: Maricopa

Medical Center, Phoenix Children's Hospital, St. Joseph's Hospital, and Scottsdale Healthcare Osborn (suburb of Phoenix). In 2009, there were no Arizona hospitals that scored a perfect score on at least four of the seven Leapfrog Group's patient-safety measures, as noted in the hospital-quality review in chapter 5. However, in 2011 Western Regional Medical Center in Goodyear, Arizona, scored a perfect five out of the five applicable criteria for a regional hospital in the annual Leapfrog Group survey from chapter five.

There is a Mayo Clinic in Scottsdale, Arizona, and the Mayo Clinic Hospital has a significant organ-transplant program. It offers international patient-care coordination through the Mayo International Services Program.

If you are injured at the Grand Canyon, you will probably be taken to Flagstaff, a university town that is eighty miles away and has a 270-bed hospital. The hospital is not rated level-1 by the national guidelines, but it is designated as a regional trauma center by the Arizona Department of Health Services. Flagstaff Medical Center features fifty medical specialties.[42]

District of Columbia—U.S. Capital. Washington, DC: The hospitals in Washington, DC, are not end destinations for medical tourism. The main trauma centers are Children's National Medical Center and Washington Hospital Center. If you want to arrange for really great international health care, Johns Hopkins is a short commute away in Baltimore.

Hawaii—Beautiful Beaches and Midway to Asia. Oahu-Honolulu, capital, metropolitan hub: The only designated trauma center in all of the Hawaiian Islands is Queens Medical Center in Honolulu, as previously cited in chapter 6. If you need a major medical procedure in the islands, you will probably end up there. Other hospitals on this island are Leahi (190 beds), Castle Medical Center (160 beds), and Wahaiwa General (162 beds).[43]

Hawaii, also known as the Big Island: Kona has a community hospital that is a seventy-five-bed acute-care facility. Waimea has the North Hawaii Community Hospital, a thirty-five-bed facility, which opened in 1996. Hilo has Hilo Medical Center, which is the main hospital on the east side of the island.[44]

Kuai, the Garden Island: Lihue has Wilcox Memorial Hospital, which is the facility for the north islanders. Kapaa-Samuel Mahelona Memorial Hospital is the south side facility. Both facilities are small.[45]

Lanai, a former plantation: There is a small, thirty-bed facility on this island.[46]

Maui, also known as Big Volcano: Wailuku has Maui Memorial Medical Center, which is operated by the State of Hawaii. The facility has 231 beds with a critical-care unit and was updated in 2006.[47]

Molokai, extremely rural: There is a thirty-bed rural hospital in the only town on the island, which is Kaunakakai.[48]

Louisiana—New Orleans, Known for Its Music and Cuisine. New Orleans: Women's and Children's Hospital scored a perfect score on four of the seven Leapfrog patient-safety criteria from chapter 5 and is a level-1 trauma center designation previously cited in chapter 6. The other designated level-1 trauma center is Spirit of Charity Trauma Center.

Nevada—Gambling and Entertainment. Las Vegas: The level-1 trauma center in Sin City is the University of Nevada Hospital. Other quality hospitals in Nevada are Spring Valley, which scored a perfect rating for five of the seven Leapfrog patient-safety criteria,[49] and Sumerlin, which scored 100 percent on four of the seven rating factors for safety as cited in chapter 5.

Washington—Home to Two National Parks and Gateway to Alaska and British Columbia. Seattle: The hospitals that scored a perfect rating on five of the seven patient-safety Leapfrog criteria in 2009 were Northwest Hospital, Seattle Children's Hospital, and Virginia Mason Medical Center. Facilities that scored 100 percent on four of the metrics in 2009 were Harborview Medical Center, Swedish Medical Center (all sites), and the University of Washington Medical Center. Harborview is the regional level-1 trauma facility for all of Alaska, Idaho, Montana, and Washington and was previously cited in chapter 6 as a level-1 trauma center.

NOTES

1. "Table XVI(B): Nonimmigrant Visas Issued by Classification, Fiscal Years 2008–2012," Travel.state.gov, accessed April 18, 2013, www.travel.state.gov/pdf/FY12AnnualReport-TableXVIB.pdf.

2. "Table XV: Immigrant Visas Issued by Issuing Office, Fiscal Years 2003–2012," Travel.state.gov, accessed April 18, 2013, www.travel.state.gov/pdf/FY12AnnualReport-TableXV.pdf.

3. "Medical Tourism: Emerging Phenomenon in Health Care Industry—2008 Report," Deloitte, May 14, 2012, accessed March 14, 2013, www.deloitte.com/us/2008medicaltourism.

4. "Visa Waiver Program (VWP)," Travel.state.gov, accessed April 18, 2013, http://travel.state.gov/visa/temp/without/without_1990.html#citizen.

5. Christine G. Leyden, "Coming to America—What Medical Tourists Need to Know," Medvoy, August 4, 2009, accessed March 14, 2013, www.medvoy.com/resource.php?industrynews_id=4.

6. "Visa Waiver Program," Travel.State.Gov, accessed March 15, 2013, http://travel.state.gov/visa/temp/without/without_1990.html.

7. "Visa Waiver Program (VWP)."

8. "Fees for Visa Services," Travel.State.Gov, accessed March 14, 2013, http://travel.state.gov/visa/temp/types/types_1263.html#special.

9. "Compare Visitors Medical Insurance," American Visitor Insurance, accessed April 18, 2013, www.americanvisitorinsurance.com/insurance/visitors-medical-summary.asp.

10. "The Top 50 Heart Care US Hospitals," Cardiac Health, accessed April 18, 2013, www.cardiachealth.org/heart-disease-treatment/top-us-heart-care-hospitals.

11. "What Is Assisted Reproductive Technology?," Centers for Disease Control and Prevention, February 12, 2013, accessed March 14, 2013, www.cdc.gov/art.

12. "Medicare-Approved Transplant Programs," Centers for Medicare & Medicaid Services, January 31, 2013, accessed March 14, 2013, www.cms.gov/CertificationandComplianc/Downloads/ApprovedTransplantPrograms.pdf.

13. "World's Top Ten Tourism Earners, 2006," Infoplease, 2007, accessed March 14, 2013, www.infoplease.com/ipa/A0922054.html.

14. David G. Vequist IV and Erika Valdez, "Economic Report: Inbound Medical Tourism in the United States," *Medical Tourism Magazine*, August 4, 2009, available online at www.medicaltourismmag.com/article/economic-report-inbound.html (accessed March 14, 2013).

15. "Best Hospitals," *U.S. News and World Report*, accessed March 14, 2013, www.usnews.com/besthospitals/rankings.

16. "Personalized Services," UCLA Health System, accessed March 14, 2013, www.uclahealth.org/site.cfm?id=169.

17. "Visiting UC San Diego Health System," UC San Diego Health System, accessed April 18, 2013, http://health.ucsd.edu/specialties/international/visiting/Pages/default.aspx.

18. "International Services," UCSF Medical Center, accessed March 14, 2013, www.ucsfhealth.org/services/international_services/index.html.

19. "Patient Services," UCSF Medical Center, accessed March 14, 2013, www.ucsfhealth.org/services/index.html.

20. Vequist and Valdez, "Economic Report: Inbound Medical Tourism in the United States."

21. "International Services," Baptist Health, South Florida, accessed April 18, 2013, http://baptisthealth.net/en/international/Pages/default.aspx.

22. Home page, Cleveland Clinic, Florida, accessed March 15, 2013, http://my.clevelandclinic.org/florida/default.aspx.

23. "International Services," UCSF Medical Center, accessed April 18, 2013, www.ucsfhealth.org/services/international_services.

24. "Medical Tourism Facility: Johns Hopkins Medicine International," Online Medical Tourism, accessed March 15, 2013, www.onlinemedicaltourism.com/Johns-Hopkins-Medicine-International.html.

25. Home page, Partners Harvard Medical International, www.phmi.partners.org.

26. "International Services," Mayo Clinic, accessed March 15, 2013, www.mayoclinic.org/international.

27. "Mayo Clinic in Rochester, Minnesota," Mayo Clinic, accessed March 15, 2013, www.mayoclinic.org/Rochester.

28. Jarrett Murphy, "Trauma Treatment: New York's Level 1 Centers," City Limits, October 7, 2010, accessed March 15, 2013, www.citylimits.org/news/articles/4202/trauma-treatment-new-york-s-level-1-centers.

29. "For International Patients," Memorial Sloan-Kettering Cancer Center, accessed March 15, 2013, www.mskcc.org/mskcc/html/3226.cfm.

30. "About Mount Sinai," Mount Sinai Hospital, accessed March 15, 2013, www.mountsinaihospital.org/about-us.

31. "Burn and Trauma Services Renamed to Honor Devoted Benefactors," University of Rochester Medical Center, accessed March 15, 2013, www.urmc.rochester.edu/news/story/index.cfm?id=3007.

32. "Kidney Transplantation Services," Stony Brook Medicine, accessed March 15, 2013, www.stonybrookmedicalcenter.org/transplant.

33. "Global Health Sites," Duke Global Health Institute, accessed March 15, 2013, http://globalhealth.duke.edu/whos-involved/field-sites.

34. "Language Assistance," Cleveland Clinic, accessed March 15, 2013, http://my.clevelandclinic.org/global_patient_services/patients/international/languages.aspx.

35. "UPMC Global Care," UPMC, accessed March 15, 2013, www.upmc.com/aboutupmc/icsd/Pages/global-care.aspx.

36. "Methodist J.C. Walter Jr. Transplant Center—Houston, TX," The Methodist Hospital System, accessed March 15, 2013, www.methodisthealth.com/mtc.cfm?id=35448.

37. "Professional Services for Patients," The Methodist Hospital System, accessed March 15, 2013, www.methodisthealth.com/basic.cfm?id=37113.

38. "International Services," Memorial Hermann, accessed March 15, 2013, www.memorialhermann.org/international.

39. "Financial Information," MD Anderson Cancer Center, accessed March 15, 2013, www.mdanderson.org/patient-and-cancer-information/guide-to-md-anderson/international-center/financial-information/index.html.

40. William Fitzgerald, "Paving Way for International Patients," *Conquest* (fall 2010), available online at www.mdanderson.org/publications/conquest/issues/2010-fall/international-patients.html (accessed March 15, 2013).

41. "Patient Care at Its Best," Baylor College of Medicine, accessed March 15, 2013, www.bcm.edu/patientcare.

42. "About Flagstaff Medical Center," Flagstaff Medical Center, accessed March 15, 2013, www.flagstaffmedicalcenter.com/AboutFMC/default.

43. "Hospitals," State of Hawaii Department of Health, Office of Health Care Assurance, Medicare Section, accessed April 18, 2013, http://hawaii.gov/health/elder-care/health-assurance/medicare-facilities/directory-hospital.html.

44. "Hospitals."

45. "Hospitals."

46. "Hospitals."

47. "Hospitals."

48. "Hospitals."

49. "Hospitals."

Naturopathic and Alternative Health Care in America

Who Regulates It[1]

NATURAL MEDICINE DEFINED

*N*atural medicine is a practice of health care that seeks to heal the body through its own resources, with stimulation from natural medicines that are derived from plant and animal sources.

The U.S. Census Bureau says the March 2012 national population was 313,125,465.[2] Concurrently there are nearly 7 billion people in the world, and half of those are in Asia.

The National Center for Complementary and Alternative Medicine estimated nearly 5 million Americans used alternative or complementary health care services in 2007.[3] This figure does not include the people who self-treat or use unregistered practitioners. The National Institutes of Health states that the *Pharmacopeia* or universal list of medicines for naturopathic medicine became part of the U.S. Food and Drug Act in 1938. So the concept of "natural medicine" has been recognized for seventy-five years in the United States. Homeopathy, or the practice of treating the whole body system, has been practiced in Germany for over two hundred years, and there are also ancient Asian practices of medicine, which integrate balance and whole-body stimulation for fuller-functioning health systems.

TYPES OF ALTERNATIVE HEALTH CARE

Here is a list of alternative health care treatments in the United States, which does not include any mental-health therapies like biofeedback or hypnotherapy.

For a thorough list of alternative therapies, go to www.healingchoicesonline
.com/modalities.htm.

Acupuncture

Acupuncture is an ancient Chinese treatment that uses long needles to
penetrate and relieve pressure points throughout the body. Acupuncture is
useful for pain management, toxin relief, and to improve circulation. For information on each state's treatment of acupuncture, a good website is www.
acupuncture.com/statelaws/statelaw.htm.

Acupressure

Acupressure is the process of manipulating pressure points in the body to
provide pain relief, release toxins, and stimulate circulatory responses. There
is no standard certification for acupressure service providers, but some states
require these healers to be licensed. Schools that offer a one-year program
for training include the American Organization of Bodywork Therapies of
Asia and the National Certification Commission for Acupuncture and Oriental Medicine. Thirty-eight states use the National Certification Board for
Therapeutic Massage and Bodywork exam for licensing purposes for acupressure providers. For a complete list, go to their website at www.ncbtmb.org/
about_required_states.php.

Birthing Doula

A birthing doula is a birthing coach and labor assistant who is not required to
be licensed. Doulas also serve as advocates when their client is going through
labor and childbirth. There are also postpartum doulas that assist the new
mother after the baby is born, and this process can last for several months.
Doulas can be helpful with breastfeeding facilitation and other mother and
child wellness services. Doulas are not regulated in the United States, but
some states, like Minnesota, have a doula registry.

Chiropractic

In the United States, a professional who practices chiropractic care is licensed
as a Doctor of Chiropractic (DC). Many DC's also practice naturopathic care
and dispense herbal agents and other nonpharmacological remedies. Chiropractic care involves musculoskeletal issues and body spinal alignment as the
focus of good health. Chiropractic care is a holistic health care practice. The
licensing of a DC is provided by a state board.

Oriental Medicine

The title Doctor of Oriental Medicine may refer to one that's applying acupuncture or acupressure or dispensing Asian medicinal herbs. There is no national certification, and licensure varies by state, with Nevada and New Mexico recognizing it. The only school to offer this certification is the National Oriental Medicine Accreditation Agency.

Homeopathy

A nationwide analysis of the licensure and accreditation for homeopathy or naturopathic medicine follows this overview. Thirty of the fifty states have adopted legislation concerning the licensure, education, and scope of homeopathic clinicians.

Massage Therapy

There is no national standard for the licensing of massage therapists, but thirty-seven states have set standards for massage therapists.[4] The agency that certifies massage therapists is called the National Certification Board for Therapeutic Massage and Bodywork. Generally massage therapists attend a massage school and have to undergo a minimum number of treatment hours to obtain a license.

Midwifery

Though midwifery is perhaps the oldest health care field, a midwife can still be considered an alternative health care provider in the United States. Some insurance companies will cover a midwife birth, which is typically done in the home environment. A midwife is a woman who assists another woman in the birthing process. Some states permit midwives to practice independently, and these include[5]: Arizona, Arkansas, California, Florida, Idaho, Louisiana, Minnesota, Montana, New Jersey, New Mexico, South Carolina, Texas, Utah, Vermont, Virginia, Washington, Wisconsin, and Wyoming. The following states also require certification for midwifery: New Hampshire, New York, Rhode Island, and Tennessee. Delaware just requires a midwifery permit. Certification for midwives is provided by the American College of Nurse Midwives or the Certified Professional Midwives through the North American Registry of Midwives.

Reflexology

Reflexology is the manipulation of pressure points in the hands and feet to relieve sinus congestion, promote lymphatic drainage, ease pain, and alleviate a host of other circulatory conditions. Currently, all certification for reflexology is voluntary, but the primary certification organization is a twenty-year-old entity called the American Reflexology Certification Board. Certification involves completion of thirty hours of training for hands and 110 hours for reflexology on the feet. The American Reflexology Certification Board is not affiliated with any school and is an independent organization.

Reiki

Reiki is an ancient health practice involving energy balance through the use of guiding hands. It is not recognized in many states, and there is no certification process. Reiki deals with a person's Chi energy or Chakrah. The practice comes from Asia and strives to balance the energies within an individual to reach full health.

REGULATION OF ALTERNATIVE HEALTH CARE

Naturopaths are primary health care providers, and more Americans are using them as the front line in their health care. Because there are no national standards of certification for naturopaths in the United States, I reviewed all fifty states and the District of Columbia to see what state governments require for licensure and qualifications. Here is a summary of the state laws (as of the end of 2012) regarding the practice of naturopathic medicine.

- Alabama: It is illegal to practice naturopathy in this state.[6]
- Alaska: Requires Naturopaths to pass a state licensing exam.[7]
- Arizona: Naturopaths must be an MD, DO, or DC; naturopathic assistants must also be licensed. Arizona can revoke the license of a practitioner who is six months or more behind on child-support payments.[8]
- Arkansas: According to the Association of Accredited Naturopathic Medical Colleges, there are no licensing requirements for naturopaths in this state.[9]
- California: Requires naturopaths to have a degree from an approved college and also has requirements for naturopathic assistants. A licensing exam is required, but practitioners in practice prior to 1986 are grandfathered in. Sixty hours of continuing education is mandated each year.[10]
- Colorado: There are currently no requirements for licensure or continuing education to practice as a naturopath in the Rocky Mountain State.[11]

- Connecticut: Naturopaths must be an MD, DO, or DC; naturopathic assistants must also be licensed. A naturopath must have completed at least two years of college education prior to professional naturopathic training from an approved school. A state licensing exam is also required but has some grandfathering provisions.[12]
- Delaware: Has a no licensing exam or regulations for naturopaths, but it does have standards for acupuncturists.[13]
- District of Columbia: Requires naturopaths to have a college degree in naturopathy and to pass a state licensing exam. The licensing application also requires financial disclosure and proof the applicant is able to obtain a bond. Thirty hours of continuing education are stipulated every two years.[14]
- Florida: The Florida Department of Health outlawed the practice of naturopathic medicine and only naturopaths in practice since 1959 or earlier have been allowed to continue. Essentially this means there is no naturopathic care there.[15]
- Georgia: Does not currently license naturopaths, so anyone can practice natural medicine.[16]
- Hawaii: Has state licensing and degree requirements for naturopaths.[17]
- Idaho: Requires licensing for naturopaths, requires proof of completing a program from an approved school, and has a state licensing exam. Exceptions to the degree in naturopathy include practicing for twenty years in naturopathy or completing a doctoral-level course with eight hundred hours of accredited study. There are two types of licenses depending on training.[18]
- Illinois: There is no licensing requirement for naturopaths at this time.[19]
- Indiana: There are currently no licensing requirements for naturopaths.[20]
- Iowa: There is no license for naturopaths in Iowa, and a practitioner must be an MD, DO, or DC.[21]
- Kansas: Licensure is required for naturopaths, as well as an examination and continuing education.[22]
- Kentucky: The state has considered legislation to license naturopaths and other alternative health care providers, including acupuncturists, but it has failed to pass any of the bills.[23]
- Louisiana: There are no licensing or continuing-education requirements for naturopaths.[24]
- Maine: Requires thirty-seven hours of continuing education yearly, of which seven must be in pharmacology, as well as a degree from an approved naturopathic college to be licensed.[25]
- Maryland: SB 180, which specifies licensing requirements for naturopaths, made it out of committee and is pending with a legislative hearing set for March 2013.[26]

- Massachusetts: This state does not currently require licensing for naturopaths.[27]
- Michigan: Currently there are no licensing requirements for naturopaths.[28]
- Minnesota: Requires naturopaths to have a degree from an approved school, pass a state exam, and register in the state directory.[29]
- Mississippi: There are no licensing requirements for naturopaths in this state.[30]
- Missouri: Though Missouri has considered naturopathic licensing, as of 2013 there is no such law.[31]
- Montana: Naturopathic practitioners are required to maintain at least fifteen credits of continuing education, five in pharmacology per year.[32]
- Nebraska: There are no licensing requirements for naturopaths in Nebraska.[33]
- Nevada: Naturopaths must be an MD, DO, or DC to practice naturopathy.[34]
- New Hampshire: Licensing and 150 hours of continuing education required every three years. Licensing requires completion of a naturopathic degree from an approved college. Midwives also have licensing and continuing-education requirements.[35]
- New Jersey: There are no licensing requirements for naturopaths.[36]
- New Mexico: There are no licensing requirements for naturopaths.[37]
- New York: There are no licensing requirements for naturopaths.[38]
- North Carolina: Naturopath licensing requires a passing score on a state-administered exam. License renewal mandates forty hours of continuing education.[39]
- North Dakota: Naturopaths must have a degree from an approved school to be licensed in naturopathy.[40]
- Ohio: There are no licensing requirements for naturopaths.[41]
- Oklahoma: There are no licensing requirements for naturopaths.[42]
- Oregon: Naturopaths must have graduated from an approved school for naturopathy and pass a state licensing exam.[43]
- Pennsylvania: There are no licensing requirements for naturopaths in this state.[44]
- Rhode Island: There are no licensing requirements for naturopaths in this state.[45]
- South Carolina: It is illegal to practice naturopathy in this state.[46]
- South Dakota: There are no licensing requirements for naturopaths in this state.[47]
- Tennessee: There are no licensing requirements for naturopaths in this state.[48]
- Texas: There are no licensing requirements for naturopaths in this state.[49]

- Utah: A naturopath license requires a degree from an approved school and a twelve-month residency in naturopathy.[50]
- Vermont: To be licensed as a naturopath in Vermont, a degree from an approved school is required.[51]
- Virginia: There are no licensing requirements for naturopaths in this state.[52]
- Washington: To practice naturopathy in Washington, the practitioner must have graduated from an approved school and pass a state licensing exam. Washington State has been a leader in the integration of alternative medical treatments, requiring insurance companies to include alternative health care treatment provisions in their contracts for twenty years.[53]
- West Virginia: In order to be licensed as a naturopath in West Virginia, the applicant must be an MD and have a naturopath certification from an approved school.[54]
- Wisconsin: There is no licensing requirement for naturopaths, nor are there naturopathy schools in this state, although legislative efforts are ongoing to create state standards.[55]
- Wyoming: There are no licensing requirements for naturopaths in this state.[56]

WHO CERTIFIES NATUROPATHS

These organizations certify education programs for licensure of individuals practicing homeopathic medicine, including naturopaths. Through certification and licensing standards, the health care consumer is at least able to gauge the experience of the practitioner.

Council for Homeopathic Certification

The Council for Homeopathic Certification was formed in 1991 and is the main agency for certification of homeopathy programs. It administers national exams in March and October of each year.

For a complete list of certifications provided by the Council for Homeopathic Certification, refer to their website: www.homeopathicdirectory.com/index.php.

American Board of Homeotherapeutics

The oldest certifying organization for homeopathy in the United States is the American Board of Homeotherapeutics, which has been around since 1844.

In order to obtain ABH certification, a candidate must be an MD, DO, or DC with a valid license, have three years of homeopathic practice, have 350 hours of education in the field, meet ethical and caseload requirements, and pass a national exam. The designation it awards is called the Diplomat in Homeopathy.

Homeopathic Academy of Naturopathic Physicians

The Homeopathic Academy of Naturopathic Physicians was founded in Ashland, Oregon, and is a relatively new entity. Certification for Homeopathy is in three stages: an application to take an oral exam, a fellowship period with five hundred hours of education, and a case-study analysis in the final part of the exam.

The U.S. Department of Education

Though the U.S. Food and Drug Administration does require homeopathic medications to meet certain legal standards for product authenticity and packaging, it does not police the licensing of homeopathic practitioners. Further, there is wide variation throughout the United States on homeopathic licensing: some states don't recognize it at all, and others have laws stipulating naturopathic practices. There are few randomized control studies on homeopathic treatments, and most studies review data on a patient cohort, so the treatment protocol is going to depend greatly on the provider the patient seeks.

HEALTHPOLICYMAVEN'S™ NOTES

As a person seeking optimal health, I have utilized nearly all of these alternative health care purveyors, including both birthing and postpartum doula services, massage therapy, and reflexology. Reflexology was extremely beneficial, because the feet have so many nerve endings, and by manipulating the various pressure points I have noticed some health improvements.

NOTES

1. Most of the regulations for alternative health care providers address naturopathic clinicians as they are providing primary care. The investigation looked at licensing requirements and continuing education mandates for alternative health care providers, primarily naturopathic practitioners.

2. "U.S. and World Population Clock," U.S. Census Bureau, accessed April 18, 2013, www.census.gov/population/www/popclockus.html.

3. "Homeopathy: An Introduction," National Center for Complementary and Alternative Medicine, accessed March 15, 2013, http://nccam.nih.gov/health/homeopathy#keys.

4. "Massage Therapy Certification," Natural Healers, accessed March 15, 2013, www.naturalhealers.com/qa/massage.html.

5. "Direct-Entry Midwifery State-by-State Legal Status," Midwives Alliance of North America, May 11, 2011, accessed March 15, 2013, http://mana.org/statechart .html.

6. "Naturopathic Licensing Jurisdictions in the United States/Canada," Oregon. gov, accessed April 18, 2013, www.oregon.gov/obnm/popdocs/naturopathicboardso-famerica.pdf.

7. "Statutes and Regulations: Naturopaths," Alaska Department of Commerce, Community, and Economic Development, March 2008, available online at www .dced.state.ak.us/occ/pub/NaturopathyStatutes.pdf (accessed April 18, 2013).

8. Homepage, State of Arizona Naturopathic Physicians Medical Board, accessed April 18, 2013, www.aznd.gov/agency/pages/home.asp.

9. Licensure map, Association of Accredited Naturopathic Medical Colleges, accessed April 18, 2013, www.aanmc.org/images/licensuremap-shaded_October2012.gif.

10. "Business and Professions Code, Section 3630-3637," Legislative Council, State of California, accessed April 18, 2013, www.leginfo.ca.gov/cgi-bin/displaycode ?section=bpc&group=03001-04000&file=3630-3637.

11. "Naturopathic Doctor Licensure," Association of Accredited Naturopathic Colleges, accessed March 15, 2013, www.aanmc.org/careers/naturopathic-doctor-licensure.php.

12. "Naturopathic Physician Licensing Requirements," Connecticut Department of Public Health, accessed April 18, 2013, www.ct.gov/dph/cwp/view.asp? a=3121&q=389384.

13. "Board of Medical Licensure and Discipline," State of Delaware, accessed April 18, 2013, http://dpr.delaware.gov/boards/medicalpractice/index.shtml.

14. "District of Columbia Municipal Regulations for Naturopathic Medicine," District of Columbia Department of Health, May 1, 2012, accessed April 18, 2013, http://doh.dc.gov/sites/default/files/dc/sites/doh/publication/attachments/naturo-pathic_regulations.pdf.

15. "Naturopaths," Florida Department of Health, August 31, 2012, accessed March 15, 2013, http://doh.state.fl.us/mqa/naturopath/index.html.

16. Martha Allen, "What Is Naturopathic Medicine?," Athens Natural Medicine, accessed March 15, 2013, www.drmarthaallen.com/naturopathicmedicine.html.

17. "Licensing Area: Naturopathic Medicine," Hawaii Department of Commerce and Consumer Affairs, accessed March 15, 2013, http://hawaii.gov/dcca/pvl/boards/naturopathy.

18. Legislature of the State of Idaho, House Bill no. 220, 61st legislature, 1st regular session, 2011. Available online at http://legislature.idaho.gov/legislation/2011/H0220.pdf (accessed April 18, 2013).

19. Licensure map, Association of Accredited Naturopathic Medical Colleges.

20. "Licensing," Indiana Association of Naturopathic Physicians, accessed March 15, 2013, www.inanp.com/?page_id=25.

21. "A Policy Statement on Naturopathy," Iowa Board of Medicine, accessed March 15, 2013, http://medicalboard.iowa.gov/policies/naturopathy.html#.

22. Home page, Kansas State Board of Healing Arts, accessed March 15, 2013, www.ksbha.org.

23. Licensure map, Association of Accredited Naturopathic Medical Colleges.

24. "Naturopathic Physician Continuing Education Requirements," OnlineCE, accessed March 15, 2013, www.onlinece.com/pages/naturopathic_requirements.php.

25. "Naturopathic Doctor," Maine Office of Professional and Occupational Regulation, accessed March 15, 2013, http://maine.gov/pfr/professionallicensing/professions/complementary/naturopathic_doctor.htm.

26. Home page, Maryland Association of Naturopathic Physicians, accessed March 15, 2013, www.mdanp.org; "Support Licensure of Naturopathic Doctors in Maryland," Maryland Association of Naturopathic Physicians, accessed April 18, 2013, www.ndaccess.com/MDANP/Page.asp?PageID=5.

27. Home page, Massachusetts Society of Naturopathic Doctors, accessed March 15, 2013, http://msnd.org.

28. Licensure map, Association of Accredited Naturopathic Medical Colleges.

29. "Naturopathic Doctor Registry," License Minnesota, accessed April 18, 2013, http://mn.gov/elicense/licenses/licensedetail.jsp?URI=tcm:29-3569&CT_URI=tcm:27-117-32.

30. "Licensed States & Licensing Authorities," American Association of Naturopathic Physicians, accessed April 18, 2013, www.naturopathic.org/content.asp?contentid=57.

31. "Licensed States & Licensing Authorities."

32. "Montana Licensing Information," Montana Association of Naturopathic Physicians, accessed March 15, 2013, www.mtnd.org/licensing.htm.

33. "Naturopathic Licensing Jurisdictions in the United States/Canada," Oregon Board of Naturopathic Medicine, accessed March 15, 2013, www.oregon.gov/OBNM/PopDocs/NaturopathicBoardsOfAmerica.pdf?ga=t.

34. "Overview of Naturopathic Regulation," NaturoWatch, accessed April 18, 2013, www.naturowatch.org/licensure/laws.shtml.

35. "Naturopathic Examiner," New Hampshire Department of Health and Human Services, accessed March 15, 2013, www.dhhs.nh.gov/oos/blc/naturopath.

36. "Naturopathic Licensing Jurisdictions in the United States/Canada."

37. "Naturopathic Licensing Jurisdictions in the United States/Canada."

38. "Naturopathic Licensing Jurisdictions in the United States/Canada."

39. "General Assembly of North Carolina: Session 2011," North Carolina General Assembly, accessed March 15, 2013, www.ncleg.net/Sessions/2011/Bills/Senate/PDF/S467v1.pdf.

40. "Licensing States and Licensing Authorities," American Association of Naturopathic Physicians, accessed March 15, 2013, www.naturopathic.org/content.asp?contentid=57.

41. Licensure map, Association of Accredited Naturopathic Medical Colleges.

42. Licensure map, Association of Accredited Naturopathic Medical Colleges.

43. "Oregon Formulary & Jurisprudence Exams—Applications, Requirements, Dates," Oregon Board of Naturopathic Medicine, accessed March 15, 2013, www.oregon.gov/OBNM/Exams.shtml.

44. Home page, Pennsylvania Association of Naturopathic Physicians, accessed April 18, 2013, www.panp.org.

45. "Naturopathic Licensing Jurisdictions in the United States/Canada."

46. "Traditional Naturopathy Licensing," The License Commission of the Americas, accessed March 15, 2013, www.tlcta.com/naturopathy.

47. Licensure map, Association of Accredited Naturopathic Medical Colleges.

48. Licensure map, Association of Accredited Naturopathic Medical Colleges.

49. "Naturopathic Physician Practice Act," Utah Division of Occupational and Professional Licensing, accessed March 15, 2013, www.dopl.utah.gov/laws/58-71.pdf.

50. "Naturopathic Physician Practice Act."

51. "Links and Resources," Vermont Association of Naturopathic Physicians, accessed March 15, 2013, www.vanp.org/links.php.

52. Licensure map, Association of Accredited Naturopathic Medical Colleges.

53. "Washington State Credentialing Requirements," Washington State Department of Health, accessed March 15, 2013, www.doh.wa.gov/Portals/1/Documents/2600/630112Naturopath.pdf.

54. "H. B. 3089," West Virginia Legislature, accessed March 15, 2013, www.legis.state.wv.us/Bill_Status/bills_text.cfm?billdoc=hb3089%20intr.htm&yr=2001&sesstype=RS&i=3089.

55. Licensure map, Association of Accredited Naturopathic Medical Colleges.

56. Licensure map, Association of Accredited Naturopathic Medical Colleges.

Health Care Reforms

A Consumer Perspective[1]

$\mathcal{U}$nless you have been in a coma since 2010, you are probably aware that the U.S. Congress passed a landmark health care reform bill that impacts most people living in the United States. Here are the key provisions of the consumer reforms, followed by some examples of how the changes will impact individual health care purchasers of various incomes.

The Patient Protection and Affordable Care Act[2] (PPACA) and the Health Care Education and Reconciliation Act of 2010 attempt to address nearly all segments of U.S. private-sector health care. Under the Accountable Care Organization provisions, hospitals and clinicians will be paid based on clinical performance and not just on the volume of procedures. Insurance companies will be required to disclose how they use the premium dollars you contribute. Medicare Advantage plans (where there has been abuse in administrative costs) will have to spend 85 percent of the money collected to actually pay medical claims. Medical records and medical claim forms are also in the process of being standardized across the country because of Medicare mandates.[3] Medical suppliers will now be subject to greater scrutiny before the Centers for Medicare & Medicaid Services will pay their invoices for the equipment. All of these changes are part of an overarching process to eliminate or reduce unnecessary health system expenses, as a means to lowering health care costs and improving clinical results.

Additionally, since there has been a great deal of rancor over the government health care mandates, like the insurance exchanges and the statewide implementation by 2015, I have included a progress list, showing each state and its position relative to the mandates in this chapter, but it appears that only a handful of states will be ready with their SHOP or Small (Business) Health (Insurance) Options Programs by the 2015 enrollment deadline.

INSURANCE CHANGES FROM THE PATIENT PROTECTION AND AFFORDABLE CARE ACT

Here is a summary of the changes to health care and health insurance from the Patient Protection and Affordable Care Act mandates[4]: This information has previously been published in the monthly health care column, Straight Talk on Health Care, under the trademark Healthpolicymaven™. All regulatory citations are from the Patient Protection and Affordable Care Act[5] and the Public Health Service Act,[6] both from 2010 unless otherwise indicated.

1. The creation of the Federal Supplementary Medical Insurance Trust Fund in 2010 is an attempt to provide subsidies and expansion of health-insurance coverage for individuals and small businesses. This will be funded through a variety of new taxes on medical suppliers, insurance companies, and drug companies by 2014.

2. In 2014 medical insurance will be required for most U.S. residents, and proof of insurance will be required upon the filing of the annual income tax return, or a tax penalty will be due. The penalty will start at $95 per insured per year and increase to as much as $695 by 2016. Tax penalties for children (persons under age eighteen) will be capped at 50 percent of the adult penalty for the family.

3. As of 2010 new group health-insurance plans are mandated to cover eligible employees without excessive waiting periods for preexisting conditions. Existing group health insurance plans had until their plan's renewal in 2011 to conform to this mandate.

4. As of 2011, newly issued group insurance contracts are prohibited from limiting essential benefits under medical insurance contracts. There is a phase-in schedule for existing group medical contracts under the grandfathered provisions. By 2014 all group medical insurance contracts must comply with this mandate.

5. By 2014, insurance companies are required to post a minimum loss ratio for health-insurance claims if participating in federal health plans like Medicare Advantage plans. This means they have to spend a targeted percent of the insurance premiums collected to actually pay for medical services for the insured.

6. As of 2010 children up to the age of twenty-six are eligible to remain covered on their parents' health insurance plans (previously children were eliminated from the parents' medical coverage by age twenty-three, except in the case of developmental disability or incapacitation). Given the dearth of jobs, many offspring in this age group have returned home with their college degree in hand and remain unemployed, but at least they have medical insurance.

7. As of 2012, the prescription drug "donut hole" exclusion for Medicare Part D recipients is closed, which helps more low-income seniors be able to afford their medications by eliminating the stop-gap problem.[7] Though this change helps seniors, the CMS, through Medicare's Part D Prescription Drug Plan, are currently prohibited from negotiating for lower drug prices directly with the pharmaceutical suppliers.[8] So government health plans actually overpay for prescription medications while private-sector plans are able to negotiate for better drug pricing through pharmaceutical benefit-management programs. Both the Bush and Obama administrations have failed to make this "market correction."

8. Drug rebates are effective in 2013 for oral medicines that are reformulations (generic brand) for existing drugs (name brand) in an attempt to lower the cost of certain prescription medications. This is a drug company end-run around the loss of patent revenues when drugs become generic. A reformulation of a drug is just a minor change by a pharmaceutical company to extend its patent and generate higher revenues at the expense of the consumer. The rebate or discount is completely offset by higher drug prices. This is probably the biggest rip-off in the health care bill.

9. By 2014, establishment of regional health insurance exchanges and drug purchasing cooperatives will make standardized group medical plans available to individuals and small businesses that lack access to affordable health care. The degree of affordability will depend on the price of the insurance and the largesse of federal subsidies.

State-by-State Status for Insurance Exchange Adoption

Using the Kaiser Family Foundation Health Reform Source website,[9] read on for a quick update on statewide progress for adoption of the health insurance exchange mandate (as of 2013).[10] Also please note that the federal grant award information for implementation of the insurance exchanges was taken from the Health & Human Services website, called the Center for Consumer Information and Insurance Oversight, an agency under the Centers for Medicare and Medicaid Services.[11]

- Alabama: Has adopted insurance exchange implementation legislation and been awarded a level-1 planning grant for $8,592,139.
- Alaska: Has not passed legislation to implement a health insurance exchange and did not apply for the $1 million planning grant. On July 17, 2012, Alaska announced it will allow the federal government to operate its insurance exchange.

- Arizona: Has adopted legislation to implement a health insurance exchange and been awarded a level-1 planning grant of $29,877,247.
- Arkansas: Passed legislation for implementation of a health insurance exchange in 2011 and has received two level-1 grants totaling $26,260,555.
- California: Has passed legislation to implement the health insurance exchange law and has been awarded a level-2 planning grant for $673,705,358, which stipulates the program. California is the largest state, and it will integrate the MediCal Medicaid program, the SHOP program for the insurance exchange, and other partners.
- Colorado: Has passed legislation to implement the health insurance exchange law and has been awarded a Level I planning grant totaling $61,437,747.
- Connecticut: Has passed legislation to implement the health insurance exchange law and was awarded a level-2 grant for $107,358,276.
- Delaware: In 2011, Delaware passed legislation to adopt a health insurance exchange and has been awarded level-1 grants worth $11,936,639.
- District of Columbia: Passed a bill to implement a health insurance exchange and has been awarded a level-2 grant for $72,985,333.
- Florida: Has not passed health insurance exchange legislation, but did pass a law prohibiting the coverage of abortion in insurance exchanges except for the federal Hyde criteria. Though a recipient of the $1 million planning grant, they plan to return the federal money. Since Florida has not passed state legislation approving a state-run insurance exchange, they will default to a federally run model.[12]
- Georgia: The legislature was not in favor of a health insurance exchange, but the governor has signed an executive order to implement one, and they have received the $1 million planning grant.
- Hawaii: Has passed legislation to implement a health insurance exchange and has received level-1 grants totaling $76,255,636.
- Idaho: Has declared the intent to operate a state insurance exchange.[13] The state has also enacted a law to prohibit abortion in exchanges except for the federal Hyde criteria. Idaho has been awarded a level-1 planning grant for $20,376,550.
- Illinois: Passed legislation authorizing health insurance exchange implementation and has received level-1 grants totaling $37,917,831.
- Indiana: Has not approved health insurance exchange legislation and will default to a federally run exchange.[14] The state has passed a bill to prevent an insurance exchange from covering abortions except for the federal Hyde criteria. Indiana has received $6,895,126 in level-1 grants.

- Iowa: Has approved legislation for a state-run insurance exchange,[15] and it received $34,376,665 for a level-1 planning grant. Governor Branstad prefers a state-run exchange.
- Kansas: Law was signed prohibiting health insurance exchanges and also prohibiting private insurance plans from offering abortion coverage. Kansas did receive the $1 million planning grant. Because Kansas has not passed legislation for a state-run insurance exchange, it will default to a federally run exchange.[16]
- Kentucky: On July 12, 2012, Governor Beshear signed an executive order to establish the Kentucky health benefit exchange. Kentucky has been awarded $182,707,738 in level-2 grant funds.
- Louisiana: Will allow the federal government to operate their health insurance exchange but passed a law prohibiting exchanges from covering abortions, with no exceptions, not even the Hyde criteria (including rape or incest). This state has received $998,416 in level-1 planning grant funds.
- Maine: Has established a commission to study the health insurance exchange process and was awarded $5,877,676 in level-1 grant funds. Since Maine has not established legislation authorizing a state-run insurance exchange, it will default to the federally run model.[17]
- Maryland: Adopted federal health insurance exchange legislation April 12, 2011, and has received the following grants: $1 million for planning, over $6 million for development, and $27 million to conduct data and policy analysis. To date Maryland has been awarded $123,048,693 in grants (I guess it pays to be close to the capitol).
- Massachusetts: In 2006, Massachusetts established its own statewide insurance exchange under Governor Romney, and it is the model for the federal plan. Initially the state invested $25 million to provide near-universal coverage for its residents, under the Health Connector program, which is self-sustaining. This bayside state has been awarded $81,256,970 to transition its statewide Health Connector plan to the federal insurance exchange model.
- Michigan: Has signed a law to create the MI Health Marketplace in support of the health insurance exchange mandate and has received level-1 grant funds totaling $40,517,249.
- Minnesota: Legislation on health insurance exchanges failed in 2012. It has received level-1 grants totaling $112,169,007. Governor Dayton signed an executive order to improve state health care delivery and oversee development of an insurance exchange.
- Mississippi: As of April 1, 2013, Mississippi has decided to default to the federally run insurance exchange model.[18] Mississippi has received

$29,865,716 in level-1 grant funds. State law prohibits abortion from being included in any health insurance exchange.

- Missouri: Legislation to approve a state-based insurance exchange failed twice, but a law was passed that prohibits abortion from being offered in the exchanges, except in the event of a life-threatening situation. The state has accepted level-1 grant funds of $20,865,716. Missouri has opted to default to the federally run insurance exchange.[19]
- Montana: Has not passed a law to adopt or prohibit an exchange and has accepted the $1 million planning grant. Montana will default to a federally run exchange.[20] Governor Schweitzer vetoed a bill that would have prohibited the creation of an insurance exchange in 2011.
- Nebraska: Bills to approve a health insurance exchange failed in 2012, but LB-22 was passed, which prohibits insurance exchanges from offering abortions. As of April 1, 2013, Nebraska has defaulted to a federally run insurance exchange model.[21] Nebraska has accepted a level-1 planning grant award of $5,481,838.
- Nevada: Passed health insurance exchange legislation on June 6, 2011. Nevada has also been awarded a level-2 grant (for early adopters of the exchanges) totaling $50,016,012. The Nevada state insurance exchanged must meet certification requirements by January 2013, be prepared to enroll state residents by January of 2014, and be self-sustaining in 2015.
- New Hampshire: SB 148 was passed, which prohibits a health insurance exchange, but it accepted the $1 million federal planning grant. On June 18, 2012, Governor Lynch signed HB 1297, which allows the state agencies to interact with the federal government for the creation of a federal insurance exchange and the state has received level-1 funds totaling $894,406.
- New Jersey: Governor Christie vetoed a bill to approve a health insurance exchange on May 1, 2012, though the state has received level-1 planning grant funds of $7,674,130. As of April 1, 2013, New Jersey has elected to default to the federally run insurance exchange model.[22]
- New Mexico: Governor Martinez vetoed the insurance exchange act bill, but the state has since declared the intent to establish a state-run insurance exchange.[23] New Mexico has been awarded $34,279,483 in level-1 grant funds.
- New York: A health insurance exchange bill failed in 2011, but the state received $1 million in planning, $27 million for technology infrastructure, and over $10 million for technology systems from the federal government. The governor signed an executive order to establish the New York Health Benefit Exchange in 2012, and the state has received level-2 grant funds totaling $185,822,357.

- North Carolina: All three bills for health insurance exchanges failed in 2011, but the state accepted $86,357,315 in level-1 grant funds. North Carolina has defaulted to the federally run insurance exchange model.[24]
- North Dakota: health insurance exchange legislation was approved in 2011, and it was awarded the $1 million planning grant, but the state has elected to let the federal government run the insurance exchange.[25]
- Ohio: Ohio decided to let the federal government run its insurance exchange, after analyzing the information using the $1 million planning grant.[26]
- Oklahoma: The state has not passed a health insurance exchange law, but on April 4, 2011, it did pass a law outlawing abortions except for cases of rape, incest, or life endangerment. Senate Bill 547 does allow insurance exchange plan enrollees to purchase abortion coverage as necessary. Oklahoma has been awarded the $1 million planning grant, but it has elected to allow the federal government to operate its insurance exchange.[27]
- Oregon: A law authorizing health insurance exchanges was authorized on June 22, 2011. Oregon has received $1 million for planning, $48 million for early innovation, and $48 million for a level-1 establishment grant. Oregon has received level-2 grant funds totaling $226,472,074.
- Pennsylvania: This state has opted to allow the federal government to run its insurance exchange. Governor Corbett supported a state-run exchange.[28] The state has received level-1 funds totaling $33,832,212.
- Rhode Island: Legislation authorizing a health insurance exchange failed in 2011, but the governor signed an executive order on September 19, 2011, to establish an exchange. They have also received $1 million for planning and $58 million for level-2 development of a health insurance exchange. So, again, unless they are returning the money, they are planning on offering a health insurance exchange.
- South Carolina: Failed to authorize a health insurance exchange legislatively, but it did accept the $1 million planning grant. South Carolina has defaulted to the federally run insurance exchange model.[29] Governor Haley signed law S-0102 prohibiting insurance exchanges from offering abortion coverage except in the case of rape, incest, or to avert the death of the pregnant woman.
- South Dakota: Legislation to approve an insurance exchange failed in 2012, and the state has defaulted to the federally run exchange model.[30] The state accepted the $1 million planning grant. In March 2012, the legislature passed a law prohibiting the state from offering

abortion coverage in exchanges except to preserve the life or health of the pregnant woman. South Dakota has received level-1 funds totaling $5,879,569.

- Tennessee: Has no health insurance exchange legislation yet, but it did pass a law restricting abortion coverage under exchanges. Tennessee has received level-1 grant funds totaling $8,109,965. Tennessee has decided to let the federal government run its insurance exchange.[31]
- Texas: All bills for health insurance exchanges failed in 2011, but the insurance commissioner's office and the state Health and Human Services Commision have partnered to run a Texas Insurance Exchange. Texas has accepted the $1 million planning grant. On July 9, 2012, Governor Perry announced that Texas would not establish an exchange. As of April 1, 2013, Texas has defaulted to the federally run insurance exchange.[32]
- Utah: An insurance exchange was authorized in 2008 and has since been amended to include the Affordable Care Act and insurance exchange requirements. Utah has been awarded the $1 million planning grant. On March 2011, Utah passed a law banning abortion in any private insurance plans, with exceptions for the Hyde Amendment criteria and for fetal abnormality.
- Vermont: This state is working toward a single-payer system under Green Mountain Care, and it will be administered by the Vermont Department of Health Access (VDHA), as authorized on July 1, 2012. Vermont has applied for a federal waiver to transition from the Vermont Benefit Exchange to the single-payer Green Mountain Care program. The VDHA will transition the publicly funded health insurance program to meet the federal requirements. To date Vermont has received $104,178,965 in level-2 grant funds.
- Virginia: Health insurance exchange legislation was signed on April 6, 2011. Virginia has indicated a preference for administering its own exchange and has been awarded $4,320,401 in level-1 grant funds, but it elected to accept the federally run insurance exchange.[33]
- Washington: The Washington Health Benefit Exchange was authorized on May 11, 2011, and the state has received $24 million in federal grants. To date, Washington State has received $127,852,056 in level-1 grant funds.
- West Virginia: The state established a health insurance benefits exchange on April 4, 2011, and has been awarded level-1 funds of $9,667,694.
- Wisconsin: On March 30, 2011, health insurance exchanges were authorized; however, Governor Walker reversed his earlier position on insurance exchanges and said they would not be implemented until

after the elections. Further, he also closed a health care agency he had created called the Office of Free Market Health Care. As of April 1, 2013, this state has defaulted to the federally run insurance exchange model.[34] That said, Wisconsin has been awarded early innovator level-2 grant funds totaling 37,756,266, and one wonders if they will have to repay HHS.

- Wyoming: On March 10, 2011, health insurance exchanges were authorized, but Wyoming has accepted $800,000 of level-1 grant funds to implement an exchange. Wyoming has defaulted to the federal insurance exchange model.[35]

Pay or Play: Provisions for Taxing Employers Who Don't Offer Health Insurance

The Patient Protection and Affordable Care Act amended section 4980H of the Internal Revenue Code in order to provide tax penalties for employers with fifty or more employees who do not offer health insurance for their employees. The penalty will be between $2,000 and $3,000 per eligible employee, depending on the size of the employer.[36] For some employers, it will still be worth it to avoid the expense of a medical insurance plan, which could cost more than $4,000 per employee and more than $12,000 per family. According to the Kaiser Foundation's Statehealthfacts.org, the average cost for family medical insurance for private employer plans was $13,027 in 2009.[37] But no matter how you look at this provision, it mandates more people buy medical insurance, which is a *huge* win for the insurance sector, but I am not sure about everyone else. The U.S. Supreme Court affirmed the government's ability to require medical insurance and assess tax penalties for noncompliance in July 2012.[38]

The Affordable Care Act and Implementation of the Insurance Subsidies

The Affordable Care Act of 2010 has several stipulations for medical-insurance contracts including benefit provisions, allocation of premium payments, and enrollment subsidies. The medical-insurance requirement is one of the lynchpins of the act, in order to reduce the uninsured population and stabilize the safety net for hospitals, which bear the brunt of the uninsured patient expenses. Another goal of the mandate is to get patients into the care continuum earlier when they are able to see a clinician for primary health care and increase prevention of chronic conditions, thereby improving the quality of our health care. Of course, whether or not this will save any money is to be determined and will require a long-term view.

Out-of-Pocket Expenditures for the Poor

All of the citations for this section were drawn from the ACA guidelines for health care mandate implementation.[39]

The Affordable Care Act limits the out-of-pocket expenditures for annual health services for families within 250 percent of the federal poverty rates, which is based on a government formula.[40] This means that the insurance companies will not be able to pass-through extra charges that impact insurance-plan costs to these modest-income residents. In 2012, the federal poverty rate is defined as an annual income of $11,170 for a single individual and $23,050 for a family of four.[41] For individuals with an annual income up to $27,935 or a family of four with earnings up to $57,625, both the amount paid for health-insurance premiums and copayments for health services over the year are taken into consideration in determining the total federal health insurance subsidy. In other words, what you are actually expected to pay when you use the medical-insurance contract is considered in the plan design for subsidizing health insurance purchasing under the PPACA formula. Prior to this act, insurance companies would file for insurance plan provisions and rate approval with their state insurance commissioners, but often little thought was given to overall individual cost-sharing. This predicament reflects the market-based insurance system where the insurance companies tend to target corporate clients and design plans that meet their fiscal objectives, which are not necessarily designed to support the individual.

Individual Out-of-Pocket Limits

All citations in this section are drawn from the Patient Protection and Affordable Care Act Mandates.[42]

One of the curiosities of the PPACA is that individual health insurance out-of-pocket spending limits are set by a government-determined actuarial formula. However, the factors contributing to the individual's out-of-pocket health care expenses to create the target are complex. For example, deductibles, copayments, and coinsurance requirements all contribute to the price a patient must bear in U.S. health care. Here are some examples of how this administrative provision will affect various individuals and families.

Insurance plan subsidies for individuals earning 150 percent of the federal poverty level would have a maximum out-of-pocket expense of $1,981, and a family in that income level would be capped at $3,963 in expenses per year.[43] This doesn't sound too bad, but then remember, this does not include the medical-insurance premium payments. However, at that income level, the federal tax credit would equal 98 percent of the insurance premium for qualifying plans.

Health savings account cost-sharing would be limited to a maximum of $5,950 for an individual in 2010 and $11,900 for a family in that year.[44] After 2014 these allowances are indexed, so that people who fall within 400 percent of the federal poverty level would continue to be eligible. It is hard to imagine that someone within the federal poverty level would choose a medical savings account, but I suppose it could save money upfront, making it a more affordable method of meeting the law's requirement.

Table 13.1 (below) shows the reductions in medical cost-sharing for those within 400 percent of the federal poverty level (2010 standard) who are enrolled on medical savings plans.

Insurance Premium Subsidies

Individuals and families who fall within 400 percent of the federal poverty level will be eligible for a tax subsidy to help pay for medical-insurance premiums.[45] According to IRS regulations issued on May 23, 2012,[46] the federal tax credit can be paid in advance to an insurance company, so that low- and moderate-income folks don't have to shell out all of the premiums up front.[47] Insurance companies will also have to provide a ninety-day grace period before a health-insurance policy can be cancelled for nonpayment, but cancellation can be retroactive to the last payment date.[48]

Table 13.2 (below) shows the subsidies that would apply to a medical-insurance plan that has an actuarial benefit level of 70 percent or higher (also known as the Silver Insurance Exchange Benefit Plan).[49]

Measurement of the Medical Plans to Determine the Level of Subsidy Necessary

The PPACA through the U.S. Department of Health and Human Services has derived actuarial values to determine what the benefit caps may be for individuals within 400 percent of the federal poverty rate.[50] An actuarial value is a calculation determined by an enrolled actuary who is someone who has a mathematics degree and certification for actuarial science. The measurement of overall cost-sharing is based on the hypothesis that people who are of modest incomes will not benefit equally with the purchase of health insurance if

Table 13.1.

Federal Poverty Level	Maximum Out-of-Pocket Limit
100 percent to 200 percent	66 percent
200 percent to 300 percent	50 percent
300 percent to 400 percent	33 percent

Table 13.2.

Federal Poverty Income Level	Tax Credit for Buying Health Insurance
133 percent of FPL	98 percent
133–150 percent of FPL	96–97 percent
150–200 percent of FPL	93.7–96 percent

Other Income Levels	Tax Credit for Buying Health Insurance
200–250 percent of FPL	91.95–93.7 percent
250–300 percent of FPL	91.95–90.5 percent
300–400 percent of FPL	90.5 percent

they can't afford to use the coverage because of the ongoing cost-sharing at the time of treatment. So the subsidies are meant to improve access to health care by eliminating some financial barriers for the working class.

Employer Subsidies

Only employer-sponsored health plans with an actuarial value of 60 percent or higher will be eligible to receive the tax-credit subsidies,[51] so this is important information for small businesses who are considering starting or modifying their health-insurance plans. Also, if the employee's share of the premium exceeds 9.5 percent of their income, that makes them eligible for a federal tax-credit subsidy.[52] So there are two ways an individual may qualify for a federal subsidy to buy insurance through their employer, either through the plan design or the income level of the individual.

Medicaid Expansion

Sources for this section are all drawn from the Public Health Services Act of 2010.[53]

Medicaid subsidies will also continue for those within 135 percent of the federal poverty level, but each state will have the option of expanding Medicaid as a means to covering their low-income residents with incomes beyond this level. Some states will choose not to expand Medicaid beyond the federal minimum levels. The federal subsidies, through tax credits for the purchase of medical insurance, will still roll out in 2014, for families with incomes up to 400 percent of the federal poverty rate. This means many working-class Americans will have subsidies to buy medical insurance.

Medicaid Expansion and the Impact on Hospitals

For hospital systems, more patients with insurance means there will be fewer uninsured services, and this is a stabilizing factor for the health care safety net. What remains to be seen is how many of the 48 million uninsured will be able to afford insurance for their families and will actually enroll. The Obama Administration forecasts that an additional 32 million will obtain some form of health insurance,[54] either through government or private-sector means, because of the PPACA. However, since the July Supreme Court ruling, which allows states to decide how much they want to expand their Medicaid plans, the number of new people with insurance may be considerably smaller.

To encourage participation, the PPACA stipulates a tax penalty for those residents who don't enroll in an insurance plan. Medicaid changes are a bright spot for hospitals, as more people will be eligible for Medicaid, versus having no health care coverage now, and this should reduce the stress on hospitals for the uninsured population. Historically, these plans do not reimburse for total cost recovery for clinics or hospitals, so pass-through costs to private-sector insurance participants are still a problem. Hospitals must charge private insurance plans more money for the same health services in order to make up for the Medicaid and uninsured patient underpayments. I believe it is called "robbing Peter to pay Paul." Although Medicaid reimbursement is marginal, it is still better than no reimbursement, so this will increase viability for some hospitals, especially those serving a lot of lowincome folks. To achieve this increased funding level, the health care reform bill increases the allowance for the Federal Medical Assistance Percentage for Medicaid managed-care plans.

Primary-Care Providers Get a Raise

Under traditional fee-for-service reimbursement plans, family medicine, general internal medicine, and pediatric practitioners will have increased reimbursement for primary-care services. This is to serve as an incentive to provide more patient care in a clinic setting by getting doctors to accept Medicaid patients into their practices. Though this increase is paltry, it is at least a start in the direction of aligning clinical reimbursement with desired patient services.

Health Care Purchasing Subsidy for Low-Income Residents

For individuals who are not eligible for Medicaid or Medicare, but who qualify for subsidized insurance purchasing, here is the subsidy range under the PPACA for the forty-eight states (Alaska and Hawaii have different standards) and the District of Columbia[55]:

If your household income is no more than 133 percent of the federal poverty rate or the equivalent of $14,856 in 2012[56] for a single individual, you would be required to pay only 3 percent of the insurance premium from the regional insurance-purchasing exchanges. Government subsidies would pay the balance of the cost. The amount of income a family can have and still get the subsidy is based on the number of children and total family members. For example, if you have a family of two, you can earn $20,123 and still receive the same subsidy for 97 percent of the health-insurance premium. Families with eight members could post incomes of $51,724 and get the same subsidy. Most U.S. families are not that large, but for larger families, for every child above that number you may add $5,267 in income for each child to determine if you qualify for a subsidy (includes the 133 percent above federal poverty level).

This type of federal subsidy continues until the reported income is up to 400 percent of the federal poverty level for that year. In other words, a single individual could have an income of $44,680 and get a subsidy from the government to buy medical insurance. The amount of the subsidy would be 91.5 percent, meaning the individual would have to pay 9.5 percent of the plan cost. Likewise, for a family of two, the income could be as high as $60,520 and still receive government assistance to purchase medical insurance. When you ratchet this up to the family of eight, the income could be as high as $155,560 and still receive the same 91.5 percent of the insurance plan cost subsidy.

These subsidies may seem a bit generous, but when you consider that family medical insurance premiums averaged $12,000 a year for group insurance plans in 2010, when the PPACA was enacted, and grew to $15,980 in 2012,[57] you can see how even middle-class families would have difficulty paying for the insurance. The government's perspective with this subsidy is it is better to have people insured and able to obtain health care because they can pay the doctors and hospitals than to go without care. For illustrative purposes, I have used the most recent medical insurance plan cost data available for family coverage from the Kaiser Foundation's survey of individuals who buy their insurance directly from insurance companies.[58]

Individual Penalties for Residents Who Do Not Obtain Health Insurance

Section 4980H of the Internal Revenue Code also stipulates that individuals who do not elect health insurance will be subject to a tax penalty, which would run between $325 and $695, depending on modified adjusted gross income levels on their annual tax returns. Many people may choose to pay the penalty rather than buy insurance because it is less expensive to pay the tax. The tax will be used to fund the federal health insurance trust, so it is a targeted allocation.

The combination of insurance tax subsidies, coerced employer contributions, and required individual insurance plan participation should help reduce some of the uninsured expenses which health systems experience, although it is difficult to forecast the level at this time. According to Hewitt Associates, an employee-benefit consulting firm, when the Obama administration created the COBRA subsidy for unemployed workers, enrollment increased by 20 percent for those individuals electing to continue their group medical insurance on a self-pay basis.[59] Finally, individual participation in regional purchasing cooperatives is going to depend on how well those plans are communicated and, ultimately, the cost of the plans.

Paying for the Health Insurance Subsidies and Mandates in 2014

All citations in this section are drawn from the federal regulations for the Patient Protection and Affordable Care Act of 2010.[60]

Insurance Company Tax.   Insurers will be assessed a premium tax to help pay for the health care provisions under the Patient Protection and Affordable Care Act. Basically, there is a formula that excludes certain activities from tax, contains an offset, and has special provisions for insurers that derive 80 percent or more of their revenue from low-income clientele (like Molina Healthcare). The tax will also impact companies that work with the Medicare population (Medicare Advantage plans like AARP), and disabled populations.

Health Insurance Luxury Plan Tax.   High cost or "luxury" health plans will have to pay an excise tax up to 40 percent for health insurance premiums which exceed an expected premium, with risk adjustments by geographic regions. If your health insurance premiums exceed that threshold, a tax will be assessed on the residual, so if your annual premium was $15,000 for an individual the $4,800 over the threshold would be assessed a tax of $1,920 using 2010 values. The formula for determining which plans are high cost will be based on a per-employee factor derived from national Blue Cross/Blue Shield industry standards. It will include rates that are age adjusted for risk as well as by sex. This threshold was $10,200 for an individual medical insurance premium and $27,500 for a family medical insurance premium and is indexed for medical inflation when the law was passed in 2010.

Please note that these premiums are more than twice the cost of the average U.S. health insurance premium,[61] so the luxury tax will affect very few people, and union plans are exempt. Union plans are exempt from this tax because their insurance plans are composite-rated, meaning they typically have a single premium or cost factor per union member, regardless of family enrollment. This rate calculation is different than a single individual premium with separate charges for dependents, which is the standard to which the new tax assessment refers.

Other New Taxes

All citations in this section are taken from the Patient Protection and Affordable Care Act Provisions of 2010.[62]

Medical Device Excise Tax.   Medical devices such as cardiac pacemakers are now taxed at 2.9 percent of the purchase price.Orthopedic devices presumably are included in this category. Exceptions to the tax include hearing aids, glasses, contacts, and over-the-counter devices purchased at the drugstore. This tax will simply make these devices more expensive and will be passed directly through to the ratepayers and health care consumers. Also, in a nod to medical tourism, since this is an excise tax, even if you obtain health care outside the United States, if the device is manufactured in this country, you will pay the tax. One would think a sales tax is worth it for a new ticker.

Estate and Trust Tax.   A tax equal to 3.8 percent will be levied on estates and trusts for their undistributed net income.

Medicare Changes

Medicare enrollees benefit by the following changes in reimbursements as defined in the Patient Protection and Affordable Care Act of 2010[63]:

1. *Closure of the prescription drug "donut hole" exclusion under Medicare Part D*: Medicare enrollees who have used all their prescription drug allowance will be reimbursed up to $250 to close this loophole. This reimbursement will be allowed once per year per enrollee for Medicare Part D drugs. For more information on the Medicare drug benefit, review Medicare in chapter 15.
2. *Changes in Medicare Advantage (HMO) payment*: Qualifying counties will receive increased allowances, based on enrollment, which is meant as a subsidy for areas with low-income density.
3. *Quality rankings will impact Medicare payments*: Health care facilities with a health care quality ranking of four or more (although the phase-in requirement is lower to give health care providers an opportunity to conform to the new expectations) will receive increased reimbursement payments from Medicare. Reimbursements will also depend on Medicare Advantage plan enrollment by county, which has specific reporting and patient-management requirements.
4. *Transparency about plan expenses and administration costs*: Under the Public Health Services Act, Medicare Advantage plans are required to have a claims loss ratio of 85 percent of premiums paid, or the plan will have to pay a penalty to the government.
5. *Physician ownership/referral (medical home provision)*: This provision requires provider agreements to be signed for patients, designating a medical home status. This is part of Medicare's efforts to improve primary care for Medicare patients by strengthening the primary-care relationship.

Medicare Payroll Tax Increase

It should come as no surprise that there is an increase in the Medicare payroll tax, from 2.9 percent of total payroll to 3.80 percent, split evenly between the employee and the employer.[64] Given the state of the Medicare fund, a bigger tax increase is warranted and is probably on its way. And for all of the seniors who get frustrated when they hear the word *tax*, unless you are working for a wage, you are not paying this tax.

Efforts to Rein in Health Care Costs

Durable Medical Equipment Oversight. Durable medical equipment suppliers will be subject to an additional ninety-day period of claim review before receiving government reimbursement.[65] This is because of a high degree of suspected fraudulent activity in this supply sector. I guess this means they will be getting paid later. This is a good thing, as it is meant to cut down on abuse in the medical-supply chain.

Fraud Detection. The Commission of Medical Services in the U.S Department of Health and Human Services is now going to compare notes with IRS tax records as an enhanced Medicare fraud-detection procedure. We'll just add this to the list of Big Brother invasiveness post-9/11.

On a closing note, the Public Health Services Act imposes a slew of new taxes on corporations, individuals with investment income, and trusts. I just hope there is transparency in the spending of those funds and that it does actually go toward health care for those who need it.

Medicaid Changes under PPACA and the Agency for Health Care Administration Reforms

The Kaiser Family Foundation has the best summary of health care reform changes for Medicaid, and here are the highlights.[66]

Medicaid Highlights of the 2010 Health Care Reforms

1. Eligible low-income, childless adults will now be eligible for federal Medicaid coverage for those states that choose to accept the federal criteria.
2. The reforms create a state option to provide family planning services for low-income women, and again this will be subject to state-approved Medicaid criteria (as mentioned in this chapter and chapter 17).
3. Eligible low-income *state employees* will now be able to apply for the CHIP or Children's Health Insurance Plan, which is federally subsidized.

4. Free-standing birth centers are now eligible for coverage from Medicaid (including Planned Parenthood).
5. Complex increases in the Medicaid drug formulary rebates will lower the net cost for prescription drugs for some participants.
6. Home- and community-based services are now eligible under Medicaid, even if states have not made the election (could be an administrative challenge if a program is not in place).
7. The reforms create a demonstration project for hospitals targeting a global payments program for safety-net stabilization (to prevent hospitals from closing).
8. The reforms create funding for hospitals that must provide care to mental-health patients to help offset uncompensated care; this is important for Disproportionate Share Hospitals that serve a large proportion of indigent patients.
9. The reforms create the Centers for Medicare & Medicaid Services to develop, deploy, and measure methods for improving cost and efficiency in Medicare and Medicaid programs.
10. The reforms create the Federal Coordinated Health Care Office to align Medicare and Medicaid financing and administration for optimization of program performance.
11. The reforms require the U.S. Department of Health and Human Services to establish a process by which states can apply for 1115 Medicaid waivers to redesign state Medicaid programs.

2011 Medicaid Changes[67]

1. Establishes a voluntary program called CLASS to purchase community assisted-living facilities for the disabled and elderly, which has since been put on hold due to cost.
2. Creates Medical Home Language for Medicaid patients with at least two chronic conditions, since enhanced disease-monitoring will improve clinical outcomes and save money over time. This provides a budget for two years of care management, care coordination, and care promotion for these patients.
3. Improves federal funding for matching state provisions for noninstitutional long-term care under Medicaid.
4. Establishes a Community First Choice option under Medicaid for disabled enrollees in community-care-based programs.

NOTES

1. Much of the health care reform information has previously been published in the monthly health care column Straight Talk on Health Care, under the trademark

Healthpolicymaven™. Sources include the Patient Protection and Affordable Care Act and the Public Health Service Act, both of 2010, as well as other U.S. government agencies tasked with implementation and administration of the regulations.

2. "Insurance Changes from the Patient Protection and Affordable Care Act," Straight Talk on Health Care blog by Healthpolicymaven™, March 26, 2010, accessed March 15, 2013, http://healthpolicymaven.blogspot.com/2010/03/insurance-changes-from-patient.html.

3. "CMS 1500 Claim Form," EMR Consultant, accessed April 18, 2013, www.emrconsultant.com/education/cms-1500-claim-form.

4. "Insurance Changes from the Patient Protection and Affordable Care Act."

5. "The Patient Protection and Affordable Care Act," Public Law 111–148, 111th Congress, March 23, 2010, available online at www.gpo.gov/fdsys/pkg/PLAW-111publ148/pdf/PLAW-111publ148.pdf (accessed April 18, 2013).

6. "Compilation of Title XXVII of the Public Health Service Act (and Related Provisions)," 111th Congress, 2nd session, available online at www.nadp.org/libraries/hcr_documents/phsa027.sflb.ashx (accessed April 18, 2013).

7. U.S. Congress. H. R. 1, 108th Congress, 1st session, January 7, 2003, available online at www.gpo.gov/fdsys/pkg/BILLS-108hr1enr/pdf/BILLS-108hr1enr.pdf (accessed April 18, 2013).

8. "Medicare Prescription Drug, Improvement, and Modernization Act of 2003," Public Law 108–173, 108th Congress, December 8, 2003, www.gpo.gov/fdsys/pkg/PLAW-108publ173/pdf/PLAW-108publ173.pdf (accessed April 28, 2013).

9. "Establishing Health Insurance Exchanges: An Overview of State Efforts," Kaiser Family Foundation, accessed April 18, 2013, www.kff.org/healthreform/8213.cfm.

10. "State Decisions For Creating Health Insurance Exchanges, as of April 1, 2013," Statehealthfacts.org, accessed April 18, 2013, www.statehealthfacts.org/comparetable.jsp?ind=962&cat=17&sub=205&yr=1&typ=5.

11. "Creating a New Competitive Health Insurance Marketplace," The Center for Consumer Information & Insurance Oversight, accessed April 18, 2013, http://cciio.cms.gov/Archive/Grants/exchanges-map.html.

12. "Florida: Health Insurance Exchanges," Statehealthfacts.org, accessed April 18, 2013, www.statehealthfacts.org/profileind.jsp?cat=17&sub=205&rgn=11.

13. "Idaho: Health Insurance Exchanges," Statehealthfacts.org, accessed April 18, 2013, www.statehealthfacts.org/profileind.jsp?cat=17&sub=205&rgn=14.

14. "Indiana: Health Insurance Exchanges," Statehealthfacts.org, accessed April 18, 2013, www.statehealthfacts.org/profileind.jsp?cat=17&sub=205&rgn=16.

15. "Iowa: Health Insurance Exchanges," Statehealthfacts.org, accessed April 18, 2013, www.statehealthfacts.org/profileind.jsp?cat=17&sub=205&rgn=17.

16. "Kansas: Health Insurance Exchanges," Statehealthfacts.org, accessed April 18, 2013, www.statehealthfacts.org/profileind.jsp?cat=17&sub=205&rgn=18.

17. "Maine: Health Insurance Exchanges," Statehealthfacts.org, accessed April 18, 2013, www.statehealthfacts.org/profileind.jsp?cat=17&sub=205&rgn=21.

18. "Mississippi: Health Insurance Exchanges," Statehealthfacts.org, accessed April 18, 2013, www.statehealthfacts.org/profileind.jsp?cat=17&sub=205&rgn=26.

19. "State Decisions for Creating Health Insurance Exchanges, as of April 1, 2013."

20. "State Decisions for Creating Health Insurance Exchanges, as of April 1, 2013."

21. "State Decisions for Creating Health Insurance Exchanges, as of April 1, 2013."

22. "State Decisions for Creating Health Insurance Exchanges, as of April 1, 2013."

23. "State Decisions for Creating Health Insurance Exchanges, as of April 1, 2013."

24. "State Decisions for Creating Health Insurance Exchanges, as of April 1, 2013."

25. "State Decisions for Creating Health Insurance Exchanges, as of April 1, 2013."

26. "State Decisions for Creating Health Insurance Exchanges, as of April 1, 2013."

27. "State Decisions for Creating Health Insurance Exchanges, as of April 1, 2013."

28. "State Decisions for Creating Health Insurance Exchanges, as of April 1, 2013."

29. "State Decisions for Creating Health Insurance Exchanges, as of April 1, 2013."

30. "State Decisions for Creating Health Insurance Exchanges, as of April 1, 2013."

31. "State Decisions for Creating Health Insurance Exchanges, as of April 1, 2013."

32. "State Decisions for Creating Health Insurance Exchanges, as of April 1, 2013."

33. "State Decisions for Creating Health Insurance Exchanges, as of April 1, 2013."

34. "State Decisions for Creating Health Insurance Exchanges, as of April 1, 2013."

35. "State Decisions for Creating Health Insurance Exchanges, as of April 1, 2013."

36. "Affordable Care Act—Pragmatic Implementation," Straight Talk on Health Care blog by Healthpolicymaven™, March 6, 2013, accessed April 18, 2013, http://healthpolicymaven.blogspot.com/2013/03/affordable-care-act-pragmatic.html.

37. "Health Costs and Budgets," Statehealthfacts.org, accessed March 15, 2013, www.statehealthfacts.org/comparecat.jsp?cat=5&rgn=6&rgn=1.

38. "Supreme Court Upholds the Affordable Care Act: What the Experts Are Saying," Rand Health, June 28, 2012, accessed April 18, 2013, www.rand.org/health/feature/aca_ruling.html.

39. "2012 HHS Poverty Guidelines," U.S. Department of Health & Human Services, accessed April 18, 2013, http://aspe.hhs.gov/poverty/12poverty.shtml.

40. "Affordable Care Act—Pragmatic Implementation."

41. "2012 HHS Poverty Guidelines," Office of the Assistant Secretary of Planning and Evaluation, accessed March 15, 2013, http://aspe.hhs.gov/poverty/12poverty.shtml#thresholds.

42. "Affordable Care Act Tax Provisions," Internal Revenue Service, accessed April 18, 2013, www.irs.gov/uac/Affordable-Care-Act-Tax-Provisions.

43. Kaiser Family Foundation, "Explaining Health Care Reform: Questions about Health Insurance Subsidies," Kaiser Family Foundation Focus on Health Reform, July 2012, accessed March 15, 2013, www.kff.org/healthreform/upload/7962-02.pdf.

44. Kaiser Family Foundation, "Explaining Health Care Reform: Questions about Health Insurance Subsidies."

45. "The Patient Protection and Affordable Care Act."

46. "Affordable Care Act Tax Provisions."

47. Internal Revenue Service, "Health Insurance Premium Tax Credit," Federal Register 77, no. 100 (May 2012), available online at www.gpo.gov/fdsys/pkg/FR-2012-05-23/pdf/2012-12421.pdf (accessed March 15, 2013).

48. Federal Register volume 75, no. 123, June 28, 2010, Rules and Regulations, pp. 37187–37241, available online at www.gpo.gov/fdsys/pkg/FR-2010-06-28/html/2010-15278.htm (accessed April 18, 2013).

49. Kaiser Family Foundation, "Explaining Health Care Reform: Questions about Health Insurance Subsidies."

50. "Patient Protection and Affordable Care Act; Standards Related to Essential Health Benefits, Actuarial Value, and Accreditation; Proposed Rule," Federal Register volume 77, no. 227, November 26, 2012, available online at www.gpo.gov/fdsys/pkg/FR-2012-11-26/pdf/2012-28362.pdf (accessed April 18, 2013).

51. "Patient Protection and Affordable Care Act; Standards Related to Essential Health Benefits, Actuarial Value, and Accreditation; Proposed Rule."

52. "Patient Protection and Affordable Care Act; Standards Related to Essential Health Benefits, Actuarial Value, and Accreditation; Proposed Rule."

53. "Compilation of Title XXVII of the Public Health Service Act (and Related Provisions)."

54. "Insurance Changes from the Patient Protection and Affordable Care Act."

55. Kaiser Family Foundation, "Explaining Health Care Reform: Questions about Health Insurance Subsidies."

56. "2012 HHS Poverty Guidelines."

57. Kaiser Family Foundation and Health Research & Educational Trust, "Employer Health Benefits: 2012 Summary of Findings," available online at http://ehbs.kff.org/pdf/2012/8346.pdf (accessed April 18, 2013).

58. Kaiser Family Foundation, "Survey of People Who Purchase Their Own Insurance," June 2010, available online at www.kff.org/kaiserpolls/upload/8077-R.pdf (accessed March 11, 2013).

59. Matt Scroggins, "COBRA Enrollment Rises after Subsidy Enacted: Hewitt," Business Insurance, December 23, 2009, accessed April 18, 2013, www.business insurance.com/article/20091223/NEWS/912239997.

60. "The Patient Protection and Affordable Care Act."

61. Kaiser Family Foundation and Health Research & Educational Trust, "Employer Health Benefits: 2012 Summary of Findings."

62. "Affordable Care Act Tax Provisions."

63. Centers for Medicare and Medicaid Services, "Affordable Care Act Update: Implementing Medicare Cost Savings," available online at www.cms.gov/apps/docs/aca-update-implementing-medicare-costs-savings.pdf (accessed April 18, 2013).

64. "Affordable Care Act Tax Provisions."

65. "Affordable Care Act Tax Provisions."

66. "Medicaid and Children's Health Insurance Program Provisions in the New Health Reform Law," Kaiser Family Foundation, accessed March 15, 2013, www.kff.org/healthreform/7952.cfm.

67. "Affordable Care Act," Medicaid.gov, accessed April 18, 2013, www.medicaid.gov/AffordableCareAct/Affordable-Care-Act.html; "How Hospitals Will Fare under the 2010 Public Health Service Act," Straight Talk on Health Care blog by Healthpolicymaven™, March 23, 2010, accessed April 18, 2013, http://healthpolicymaven.blogspot.com/2010/03/how-hospitals-will-fare-under-2010.html.

When It's Terminal

How to Die Well

WHY YOU NEED TO PLAN FOR A GOOD DEATH

$\mathscr{D}$ue to the collapse of my brother, Russ's, pulmonary function at age forty-one, following complications from a kidney transplant, we made the decision to respect his wishes and take him off the ventilator. When the day came to allow him to pass, we surrounded his hospital bed, the anesthesiologist administered some morphine, and he breathed shallowly until he went from white to gray in the space of a few minutes.

February 2, 2011, was the fourth anniversary of my brother's death, who courageously requested that his breathing tube be removed, so he could die with dignity. He couldn't breathe on his own after a failed final course of treatment for a rare strain of pneumonia. It took approximately three weeks from the time of his initial plea to end his suffering until he was at peace. Though Russell entered the hospital with a Do Not Resuscitate document (DNR) and had instructions on what he would accept for lifesaving treatment, the process of allowing a patient to die on his own terms is not a simple one. My sister, an experienced hospice nurse, also held his medical power of attorney. Once the family had gathered, we discussed his wishes, and everyone was in agreement. A meeting with a member of the ethics committee of the hospital was required, followed by explicit instructions for the transplant unit. With each shift change, we needed to make sure the directive specifying no additional interventions was respected. The failure of a transplant patient is hard on everyone in the hospital unit, as the intensity of the care creates bonds between the patient and the staff. Death was much easier than life had been for him.

Though we were all grateful that he was allowed to have his suffering eased and die with dignity, the complexity of the process confounds those who must navigate the health care system. Even though we had several family members present with significant health care expertise, an entire family in agreement with the protocol, written advanced directives upon admission, and an informed patient, it was still mentally and organizationally difficult taking the final step. There was one family in the transplant unit whose elderly father had been on life support one month prior to my brother's ventilator experience and was still there when we left. The lesson is: though your paperwork may be in order, you will still need to navigate each exchange in the care continuum with people who are trained to cure. Sometimes death is the only way to alleviate the suffering of a loved one. I have never been more proud of my family than during this process where we all came together with dignity and respect and courage for my brother. I truly think it was harder on us than it was for him, as he wanted to be released.

FACTS AND FIGURES

According to the Agency for Health Care Research and Quality, 36 percent of the health care expenditures in the United States were for Medicare patients, who comprised 13 percent of the population in 2002 and are expected to grow to 30 percent by 2030.[1] Increasingly, these patients are left to die in hospitals because there are no family members available to support them and a lack of facilities for patients requiring end-stage-of-life care. We have plenty of conversations about quality of life in health care, but what about a good death? Is being hooked up to machines, wasting away immobile, and suffering from bed sores a life of quality? And who should be able to make those decisions when they need to be made?

Alternatives to hospital deaths for the terminally ill include in-home hospice care, long-term care facilities with hospice programs, private-duty nursing, and, of course, family member care. According to the Kaiser Family Foundation's June 2007 report on Medicare spending, 30 percent of all expenses paid in 2004 were for long-term-care facilities.[2] The average cost per beneficiary was $12,763. Average spending in the last year of life was $22,107 for Medicare recipients. Only 2 percent of Medicare reimbursements went for hospice care, 4 percent for home health care, and 5 percent for skilled nursing facilities in 2006. This means the 19 percent balance was for long-term-care expenditures in the hospital. Given the growth in our Medicare population and the ability of hospitals to keep patients alive longer with increasingly invasive procedures, as a society we need to review the equity of this spending pattern and the optimal patient care.

ALTERNATIVE WAYS TO FADE AWAY

One of the alternatives to inpatient hospital care for the terminally ill is in-home palliative care. Palliative care means symptom management and includes ease of pain and suffering. In July of 2007, the *Journal of American Geriatrics* published the results of a study assessing patient satisfaction for in-home palliative care versus inpatient care.[3] The randomized trial was sited within two different health-maintenance organizations located in two states and reviewed patients who were diagnosed with a year or less to live. The study showed an increase in patient-care satisfaction and a reduction in the use of medical services and corresponding cost of care for end-stage treatments. Perhaps more importantly, the patients who received in-home care were less likely to visit the emergency department or be admitted to the hospital than were the patients treated through typical acute-care modalities.

POLICY IMPLICATIONS

One of the challenges in determining health care policy is to assign values to patient health-intervention outcomes. A Canadian study, published in December of 2006, reviewed valuation methods for assessing human life outcomes.[4] The study suggested setting a common threshold of cost-effectiveness that could be applied to all health care interventions. Since health care resources are limited, based on our ability to pay, either through taxes, insurance premiums, or direct reimbursement, examination of the value achieved for a health care program seems reasonable. Medicare data indicate that more than 16 percent of all health care expenditures are spent in the last month of life. Methods currently used in the United Kingdom study include weighing each year of life gained to the cost of the services. The legal community has become adept at valuing human lives for tort actions, so certainly the health care community can work toward a reasonable method for measuring value versus the cost of the intervention.

Barriers remaining to improve palliative care in hospital settings include quality-of-life considerations and a dignified death. There are hospital-based palliative care programs with specific measures for end-of-life treatments and demonstrated cost savings, as cited in "Evidence Base for Developing a Palliative Care Service," published in the *Medsurg Nursing Journal* in June 2007.[5] Recommendations include the development of a multidisciplinary support team for terminally ill patients, separate hospice wings for acutely ill and terminal patients, alignment of patient care with the patient's wishes, and a hospital-consulting service for the administration of palliative care off-site. The following criteria were listed as success factors of palliative-care programs:

1. early discussions on end-of-life procedures and processes;
2. patient outcomes include less time spent in intensive-care units;
3. elimination of unnecessary tests and procedures;
4. better pain management through measures linked to patient-satisfaction surveys and medical-record integration;
5. reduction in the length of stay;
6. reduction in hospital charges; and
7. reduction in hospital readmission.

PLANNING FOR YOUR DEATH AND LEGAL DOCUMENTS

In order to make sure your last wishes with respect to being unplugged or not resuscitated are followed, you need to have certain legal documents in order, including financial power of attorney, medical power of attorney, medical directive, and, of course, a will. If minor children are involved, you will need a guardianship as well. Here is a brief explanation of these legal documents and what they do for you and your loved ones.

Durable power of attorney is also called the financial power of attorney and stipulates who will have checkwriting ability when you are incapacitated, as well as other financial decisionmaking authority. In my case, I have my accountant appointed for this role. I have another friend who is also an accountant as my backup in this role. Call me prudent.

Guardianship is a legal document that authorizes an individual to take care of your minor children or an incapacitated adult. Each state has rules regarding the appointment of a legal guardian in that event. There are people whose entire law practices are devoted to this.

Health care durable power of attorney stipulates who will make the final health care decision regarding your life when you are incapacitated. I am lucky, as I have a sister with hospice nursing experience, so she would be in charge in my case. It is *not* a good idea to name your mother or father to this role, as it puts undue strain on them emotionally, and they may not be healthy at the time either. It is also a good idea to have a backup representative outside your immediate family in the event you are involved in a natural disaster or car accident as a group; someone else can step into this legal designation.

Medical or health care directive is a document that delineates under what terms you would choose not to be resuscitated (electric shock), tube fed (bypasses normal digestive system), or have oxygen mechanically blown into your lungs (ventilator). This is not the all-inclusive list, but it covers the big three. For example, in my health care directive, I state that I choose not to have artificial nutrition or water, which means if I am a vegetable and I can't eat, *au revoir*. There is, of course, more clarifying language about a terminal incurable and irreversible condition. It does get dicey when a medical decision has to be made about a coma or persistent vegetative state, as there is no specific time frame. This is why you want to be careful about to whom you give the power to unplug your artificial life support, who is your medical power of attorney appointee. Most people do not want to go the route of having an extremely protracted and public process regarding the medical decision to die on their own terms.

Hospital medical directives are legal documents regarding care instructions and are typically required when a patient enters a hospital for any procedure requiring an overnight stay. If you are going to be under general anesthesia, you will want to make sure that your admission papers reflect what your personal medical or health care directive states. This may seem like duplication, but it is necessary also to sign the hospital's legal documents regarding your care instructions in the event that something goes wrong. Do not assume that your doctor or any of the caregivers will agree with your medical-directive instructions, so there could be a process of enforcement. In that case, hospitals have an ethics committee that meets and reviews patient criteria for the last goodbye, so it is not based on one person's opinion. However, as long as the individual who has the medical power of attorney is there to make sure your wishes are respected, you will be able to fade away as you planned. Of course, there are cases where one relative sues to prevent the removal of the artificial device, but ultimately the courts find in favor of the properly drawn health care directives.

Will and testament is, of course, your instruction for disbursement of your property. Each state has laws regarding allocation of property for those who die intestate, which means without a will, so unless you want the state distributing your goodies, plan accordingly. Pretending that you are not going to die by avoiding planning for it will not change your mortality. I am not going to discuss estate planning at all except to say that a trust is a useful tool to preserve assets, and an attorney can advise you on the applicability for your needs. On a final note, please review these documents from time to time—some suggest annually—to make sure no changes are in order. We are, after all, flawed human beings, and relationships do change.

TAKING CONTROL

Reaching the end of the road after a terminal illness or other life-abbreviating event does not mean that you have to die in a hospital or even a nursing home. You can die at home surrounded by comforts, with people who care about you, and the guardians who help you do this are hospice nurses. Hospice services are generally provided for patients who have been identified as having less than six months to live, and insurance companies are required to pay for these services. Hospice care is primarily symptom management, typically dealing with pain relief. However, sometimes people do not want to experience a painful loss of mental or physical faculties predicated by their medical condition, and they decide to take matters in their own hands. This is referred to as assisted suicide, and it is legal in some states.

Assisted Suicide: When You Know It's Time to Go

Booth Gardner, former governor of Washington State, successfully campaigned to have physician-assisted suicide legalized in Washington in 2008, in part because of his own medical condition.[6] Since the *New York Times* published an article[7] on his initiative the same week that I (as the healthpolicymaven™) posted an article about palliative care and medical directives,[8] a closer look at the ramifications of the legislation, which became law in March 2009, follows. Here are the provisions for the Death with Dignity Acts in Washington[9] and Oregon[10,11]:

1. The law permits legally competent patients who are at least eighteen years old, who are state residents, and who suffer from a terminal disease to obtain lethal prescriptions.
2. Each patient applying for assisted suicide must make two requests to end his or her suffering, with at least a fifteen-day separation between the pleas.
3. The patient must obtain two separate opinions from physicians indicating the person has less than six months to live in order to qualify for the medication.
4. Physicians are allowed to prescribe a lethal dose of medications to patients, but not administer the drugs.
5. The state health department tracks and reports the number of assisted suicides, just as it tracks other causes of death.

Prevalence of Death-with-Dignity Laws in the United States

Oregon's Death with Dignity Act was passed with a 51 percent majority in 1994 and enacted in 1997 after overcoming legal challenges. Oregon has reported just 673 assisted suicides since the law began.[12] Though many people in that time-frame obtained prescriptions for lethal medications, only 64 percent acted on the desire to end their life. When you compare the number of Oregonians who died a natural death from similar causes, less than one-tenth of 1 percent of the residents opted for assisted suicide.

In 2009, the first year of data for Washington's Death with Dignity Act, thirty-six people choose assisted suicide, which relies on a lethal dose of medication prescribed by a physician. Most of the patients had cancer. Ninety-five people obtained the life-ending prescription, but only a handful elected to go through with it. All physician-assisted suicides are monitored, and all but three people died within ninety minutes of taking the lethal dose. Two awoke after the lethal dose but died later, and one person did not die until the next day.[13]

States that have acknowledged the rights of the individual to commit medical suicide include Montana, whose supreme court upheld the right of physicians to provide lethal medications to terminally ill patients in December of 2009.[14] Additionally, New York State passed the Palliative Care Patient Information Act on February 9, 2011, which requires clinicians to provide terminally ill patients with end-of-life-options and counseling.[15] Vermont passed a similar law in May 2009, An Act Relating to Palliative Care and Pain Management.[16] Other states have considered Death with Dignity legislation as well. It should be noted that suicide, let alone assisted suicide, is still illegal in some states.

Difference between Terminal Sedation and Euthanasia

It is important to differentiate terminal sedation from euthanasia, and both practices were analyzed in a Netherlands study in 2006.[17] *Terminal sedation* refers to the permanent use of drugs, typically morphine, to alleviate suffering. Euthanasia is the more aggressive approach, which is to eliminate suffering by putting the patient out of his or her misery, also with the use of drugs. In the Netherlands study, clinical practices were reviewed for 410 physicians and their patients who were primarily diagnosed with cancer. The report showed that patients who requested euthanasia were typically more concerned about loss of dignity and were less anxious (15 percent) than patients requesting sedation (37 percent). Physicians reported that terminal sedation had shortened participants' lives by one week in 27 percent of the cases, whereas 73 percent of the euthanasia cases were shortened by a week.

Opponents of suicide frequently express concerns that the uninsured and vulnerable will be taken advantage of with a formalized right to assisted suicide. First, let's hope the United States provides health care for all its residents in the near future. Second, since such a small group of people who are eligible for assisted suicide in Oregon and elsewhere actually make this choice, there isn't a huge financial incentive for a health care system to hasten the death process.

Using the Netherlands example of a life reduced by one week, we could apply the Medicare reimbursement to the number of patients who would make that choice. This scenario would depend on whether or not the patient was in an acute-care or long-term-care setting and the geographic location of the facility. Let us assume all the patients were Medicare eligible and apply the Oregon average of thirty-eight assisted suicides per year to calculate the potential reduction in Medicare charges. According to the Washington State Hospital Association, the average Washington State hospital payment under Medicare was $4,603 in 2005. The average length of stay for all patients was 4.37 days, but slightly higher for Medicare patients at 4.88 days.[18] Based on the Netherlands study, we could assume Washington might save $1,053 per day of avoided hospitalization or $7,373 per patient for a week of inpatient care for end-of-life treatment.

Who Else Does It: A Global View of Assisted Suicide

Other countries have legalized assisted-suicide protocols; the foremost of them is the Netherlands, which reports two thousand assisted suicides per year. The Netherlands is the only country that also permits legal euthanasia. In 2002, the Council of Europe conducted a comprehensive survey on assisted-suicide provisions, which found eight countries that responded that do allow the practice of assisted suicides.[19] However, only four countries had legal and transparent provisions for assistance with suicide, including the Netherlands, Switzerland, Belgium, and, at that time, only Oregon in the United States.

CONCLUSION

Some practitioners in the medical profession have raised concerns about the violation of their Hippocratic Oath by assisting patients with suicide. However, in a 1996 survey sample of 3,102 physicians, *The New England Journal of Medicine* reported that 16 percent of the clinicians indicated they had written prescriptions to hasten death and 4.7 percent said they had administered lethal injections.[20] It would seem the practice of helping patients end their suffering is not new, just lacking in formality for some parts of the United States.

Since we have a huge population ready to become Medicare eligible, and there are proven methods for addressing end-of-life care besides acute hospital settings, isn't it about time the United States develops some standards for delivering appropriate palliative care to terminally ill patients? Focusing on quality end-of-life care means helping the patient remain as comfortable as possible in *this* life, as opposed to focusing on the next life. If grandma is heaven-bound, then why make her suffer unnecessarily? Let her die at home, if possible, not in some institution. As I previously shared, the social inequities of health touch the young as well as the old.

Though I'm sure this will earn some hellfire and damnation coupons, remember, "In God We Trust" was not on the original United States currency and was only added to the coins in 1861 during the Civil War strife. This phrase did not become the official U.S. motto until 1956, when it became emblemic on paper currency. Last time I checked the remnants of the Constitution, we still have separation of church and state in this country under the 14th Amendment.

The 2010 U.S. census reveals that the second largest demographic in the religious response section was for those without any religion, including atheists, representing 21.87 percent of all of census responses, and not including the agnostics, who add another half a percent. Protestants accounted for 57.88 percent of the total responses, and Catholics were 19.36 percent. Additionally, the census identifies forty-three religions in the United States. All religious findings were drawn from table 75—"Self-Described Religious Identification of the Adult Population," from the U.S. 2010 census.[21] Given this disparity of beliefs, it would seem using religion is not a sound method to cast social policy for such a diverse nation's health care delivery. A social policy that reflects science and medical evidence in the allocation of public resources may result in better end-of-life care for the terminally ill, an easier and more peaceful road for patients and their families, and an easing of the burden on health care costs to everyone.

NOTES

1. Mark Stanton, "The High Concentration of U.S. Health Care Expenditures," *AHRQ Research in Action* 19 (June 2006).

2. "Medicare Spending and Financing," Kaiser Family Foundation, June 2007, accessed March 16, 2013, www.kff.org/medicare/upload/7305-02.pdf.

3. Richard Brumley et al., "Increased Satisfaction with Care and Lower Costs: Results of a Randomized Trial of In-Home Palliative Care," *Journal of American Geriatrics Society* 55, no. 7 (July 2007): 993–1000.

4. Michael Drummond and Deborah Marshall, "Putting a Price on Life," *The Globe and Mail*, December 8, 2006, p. A25.

5. Elizabeth Rice and Denise Betcher, "Evidence Base for Developing a Palliative Care Service," *MedSurg Nursing* 16, no. 3 (June 2007): 143–48.

6. "Former Governor's Death with Dignity Initiative Booth Gardner," Straight Talk on Health Care blog by Healthpolicymaven™, January 11, 2008, accessed April 19, 2013, www.healthpolicymaven.com/?p=47 and http://healthpolicymaven .blogspot.com/2008/01/former-governors-death-with-dignity.html.

7. Daniel Bergner, "Death in a Family," *New York Times*, December 2, 2007, p. 1.

8. "The Cost to Die; an Insiders View on Terminally ill Patients and Advanced Directives," Straight Talk on Health Care blog by Healthpolicymaven™, January 3, 2008, accessed April 19, 2013, http://healthpolicymaven.blogspot.com/2008/01/ cost-to-die-insiders-view-on-terminally.html.

9. "Chapter 70.245 RCW: The Washington Death with Dignity Act," Washington State Legislature, accessed April 19, 2008, http://apps.leg.wa.gov/rcw/default. aspx?cite=70.245.

10. "Death with Dignity Act," Oregon Health Authority, accessed April 19, 2013, http://public.health.oregon.gov/ProviderPartnerResources/Evaluationresearch/ deathwithdignityact/Pages/index.aspx.

11. "Death with Dignity Acts," Death with Dignity National Center, accessed April 19, 2013, www.deathwithdignity.org/acts.

12. "2013 Summary of Oregon's Death with Dignity Act," Oregon Health Authority, p. 4, accessed April 4, 2013, http://public.health.oregon.gov/ProviderPartner Resources/EvaluationResearch/DeathwithDignityAct/Documents/year15.pdf.

13. William Yardley, "Report Finds 36 Died under Assisted Suicide Law," *New York Times*, March 4, 2010, p. 1, available online at www.nytimes.com/2010/03/05/ us/05suicide.html (accessed March 16, 2013).

14. Yardley, "Report Finds 36 Died under Assisted Suicide Law," p. 1.

15. "Palliative Care Information Act," New York State Department of Health, accessed April 19, 2013, www.health.ny.gov/professionals/patients/patient_rights/ palliative_care/information_act.htm.

16. "Act 25 & the Palliative Care and Pain Management Task Force," Vermont Ethics Network, accessed April 19, 2013, www.vtethicsnetwork.org/act25_task_ force.html.

17. J. A. Rietjens et al., "Terminal Sedation and Euthanasia: A Comparison of Clinical Practices," *Archives of Internal Medicine* 166, no. 7 (April 2006): 749–53.

18. www.wsha.org/files/61/AHA2005stats.ppt.

19. Derek Humphry, "Tread Carefully When You Help to Die: Assisted Suicide Laws around the World," Euthanasia Research and Guidance Organization, March 1, 2005, accessed March 16, 2013, www.assistedsuicide.org/suicide_laws.html.

20. Diane E. Meier, Carol-Ann Emmons, Sylvan Wallenstein, Timothy Quill, R. Sean Morrison, and Christine K. Cassel, "A National Survey of Physician-Assisted Suicide and Euthanasia in the United States," *N Engl J Med* 338 (1998): 1193–1201, available online at www.nejm.org/doi/full/10.1056/NEJM199804233381706 (accessed April 19, 2013).

21. U.S. Bureau of the Census, "Table 74. Population in Group Quarters by State: 2000 to 2010," in *U.S. Census Bureau, Statistical Abstract of the United States: 2012* (Washington, DC: U.S. Census Bureau, 2012), available online at www.census.gov/ compendia/statab/2012/tables/12s0075.pdf (accessed April 19, 2013).

What You Need to Know
Before Your Medicare Election

$\mathcal{I}$nformation for this chapter was drawn from the U.S. Government Medicare and Social Security publication EN-05-10043.[1]

Medicare was established in 1967, after it became law under President Johnson in 1965. It was created as a hospital plan to assist the aging population with inpatient medical expenses; this coverage is called Medicare Part A today. Part A is financed by a 1.95 percent tax on wages, which is matched by employers. Medicare Part A is offered as an automatic enrollment once an eligible U.S. resident has reached age sixty-five and starts to draw Social Security income.

ELIGIBILITY

The Medicare *initial enrollment period* is a seven-month time frame that encompasses the three months before and after becoming sixty-five, plus your birth month. In order to be eligible, you must have accrued ten years of covered payroll or wages for yourself or your spouse. This means that you must have worked in a job where you paid taxes into the Social Security Administration, called FICA on many payroll statements. There are exceptions to the ten-year requirement if you are blind, in endstage renal disease (on kidney dialysis), or approved for some other disability.

Once an applicant elects to draw Social Security income benefits (which is a single, irrevocable election), he or she will receive notification of eligibility for Medicare and may elect or decline benefits at that time. Those who are not eligible for Social Security income benefits may still be eligible for

Medicare. In this case, you must initiate the enrollment in Medicare during the *initial enrollment period* and can do so online by visiting www.social security.gov and clicking "apply for Medicare" or by visiting your local Social Security office.[2] The effective date for Medicare will be either the first day of the month of your sixty-fifth birthday or the first day of the month after the application is received following your birthday month.

You may continue to work and be covered by employer insurance past age sixty-five and still be eligible for and enrolled in Medicare, especially Part A. Part A benefits are normally offered at no cost to the enrollee. If you choose not to enroll in Medicare Part A or B and are enrolled in an employer group insurance policy, you may be eligible for a Medicare special-enrollment provision. The caveat is that enrollment must occur within eight months of the termination date of the employer medical plan. Please note: COBRA coverage, which is an extension of a previous employer's health plan, is not considered employer coverage, and therefore it is not eligible for this special enrollment provision.

If you do not elect Part B during the initial enrollment period and do not have qualified employer insurance, you may still elect Medicare Part B during the general enrollment period from January 1 through March 31 annually. Delayed enrollment in Medicare Part B results in a July 1 effective date and penalties for Part B premiums.

Open enrollment for Medicare Part C, Medicare Advantage Plans, and Medicare Part D is the annual period when beneficiaries are able to make plan changes. In 2011, this was from October 15 to December 7, for a January 1, 2012, effective date. You may also elect or change your Part D (prescription drug) coverage at this time.

If you do not enroll in Part D when first eligible, you may enroll during the annual open-enrollment period or during special enrollment periods. Part D premiums are subject to late-enrollment penalties if you delay enrollment and do not have creditable group coverage. Check with your group-coverage carrier to determine if your current prescription coverage is "creditable" for Part D purposes.

Employer medical plans (for companies with more than twenty employees) are required to pay medical claims before Medicare contributes. This means the employer plan is the primary payer, and Medicare only contributes to the cost of any eligible health services as a secondary payer.[3] This provision only applies to firms that employ people above age sixty-five who are covered on both employer and Medicare health plans. This stipulation is a transfer tax, making the private sector pay for medical costs previously covered by Medicare, which is an attempt to shore up the financial strain on the Medicare system.

MEDICARE PART A IS THE
HOSPITALIZATION COVERAGE[4]

Medicare enrollees have cost-sharing requirements for services (this information is drawn from the Medicare.gov website[5]). Part A enrollees will incur a $1,184 hospital deductible per admission in 2013. After the deductible, the first sixty days of each hospitalization are paid at 100 percent for eligible charges. Beyond that, there is no copayment (one would hope not). There is a daily cost share for the hospital stay of $296 from the sixty-first to ninetieth day, and $592 per day from the ninetieth day, with up to sixty "lifetime reserve days." It should be noted that this is per hospital stay, so that is one heck of a long time to be hospitalized. The sixty lifetime reserve days can be used for hospitalizations that run beyond the ninety-day cap. All costs beyond 150 days in the hospital are born by the Medicare participant. Part A covers hospital charges and hospital-related charges.

Things excluded from Part A coverage are:

1. physician visits either inside or out of the hospital;
2. long-term care in a nursing home or a facility that addresses the needs of patients who will always need care, including specialized facilities, like Alzheimer's care; and
3. intermediate-care facilities, which are a type of rehabilitation facility, where stroke patients and those requiring long-term recovery are sent upon discharge from a hospital.

MEDICARE PART B OR THE DOCTOR'S COVERAGE[6]

Medicare Part B is optional, and it primarily provides coverage for physicians' services, in and out of the hospital. After a $162 deductible, Part B pays 80 percent of charges, and you pay 20 percent. You may also be billed Part B excess charges by your doctor.

The monthly premium for Medicare Part B was a maximum of $110 in 2011 and is billed every three months or deducted from your Social Security check. In 2012, this was changed to a flat $99.90 per month. In 2013, the cost was $104.90 per month.[7] If you don't sign up when you are initially eligible, the premium for Part B will increase by 10 percent each year you delay.[8] Also, if you have income that is 200 percent of the retirement amount as determined by Medicare, you will pay a higher premium for your Part B coverage. As of 2013, this is income over $85,000 for a single person and over $170,000 for a married couple, based on the modified adjusted gross income declared on one's tax return. In 2010, the maximum surcharge for Medicare Part B premiums only applied to individual incomes over $160,000 and $320,000 for those filing jointly, with a cap on the monthly assessment of $259.70.

The following preventive services are paid at 80 percent without a deductible:

- abdominal aortic aneurysm screening;
- cardiovascular screening;
- colorectal screening;
- diabetes screening;
- mammograms;
- pelvic exams; and
- annual physical exams.

Also, influenza and pneumonia immunizations are offered at no cost for providers who accept Medicare's reimbursement rate. There are a few other preventive-care services that are covered, but they are subject to the deductible.[9]

PREMIUM ASSISTANCE FOR LOW-INCOME SENIORS[10]

Each state has different provisions for assistance for low-income seniors, typically through state Medicaid programs, but generally, if you fall within 125 percent of the federal poverty level and you have less than $6,000 in assets, you will most likely be eligible for some subsidy. Seniors enrolled on both Medicare and Medicaid plans are referred to as dual-eligible beneficiaries. Check with your state Medicaid office to determine if you are eligible for health care assistance.

MEDICARE PART C, OR MEDICARE ADVANTAGE PLANS[11]

Part C was established as a managed-care (HMO) component, which means the insured typically would select a doctor from a provider group that contracted to provide care for Medicare patients for a fixed fee. These plans are now called Medicare Advantage plans and were created under the Medicare Modernization Act of 2003 to provide inpatient and outpatient care as well as prescription drug coverage. Recent changes allow traditional insurance plans, preferred provider organizations, and Medical Savings Accounts to come under the Medicare Advantage umbrella as well. Typically, these plans provide some enhanced coverage for wellness and health assessment, although when the 2010 health care reforms are phased in (by 2014), all Medicare plans will have to offer annual wellness exams. All these plans receive a fixed reimbursement from Medicare for each enrolled participant. Medicare members who choose this option do not purchase MediGap supplemental insurance coverage.

SPECIAL NEEDS PLANS[12]

Medicare has a provision for health care advocates, who are court appointed and represent disabled participants that receive benefits under plans designated as special needs. These plans seek to provide assistance to beneficiaries in institutions, skilled nursing facilities, or those with disabling diseases, and also dual-eligible Medicare enrollees.

MEDICARE PART D, OR THE DRUG COVERAGE[13]

Part D provides an annual reimbursement for prescription drugs and was created under the Bush administration's Medicare Modernization Act of 2003. The annual deductible is no more than $310, and the enrollee then pays either a copay or percentage of the drug charges until all charges paid by the enrollee and insurance carrier add up to $2,840 (initial coverage limit for 2011). At that point, you reach the coverage gap or, as it has been called, the "donut hole," because no drug benefits are payable until the enrollee has incurred expenses of $4,550 out of pocket. After that, you pay the following copayments: $2.50 for generic drugs, $6.30 for brand-name drugs, or 5 percent of drug charges, whichever is greater. Effective in 2011, coverage for prescription charges between the $2,840 level and $4,550 out-of-pocket maximum are covered. Please refer to your Medicare contract for details on which prescription drugs are covered under this provision.

To be eligible to enroll on the drug plan option, you must be enrolled on Part A or B of Medicare. The monthly premium for Part D Medicare drug coverage varies based on many factors. Medicare Part D can be purchased on its own or as part of a Medicare Advantage plan. For individuals earning over $85,000 per year as retirees and $107,000 for joint income-tax filers, there is a surcharge premium that starts at $11.60 and is capped at $66.40 per month.[14]

MEDICARE SUPPLEMENT PLANS

You might be wondering why you need to purchase supplementary insurance if you have Medicare parts A and B. The answer is Medicare does not pay physicians very much, so if you want to have any reliable primary care with a doctor, you need to have secondary insurance. This predicament is not the fault of the physician, who may be paid as little as $10 for an office visit, but rather, it's a program design flaw in Medicare. There has been a recent attempt to remedy this by creating some additional reimbursements for managing a patient's care using quality metrics, but this does not apply across the physician payment system yet. In addition to these Medicare components, there are private Medicare supplements that provide supplementary coverage for copayments, deductibles, and other medical expenses.

Through June 2010, there were twelve Medicare supplement plans, labeled A through N. Here is the summary of how these supplements differ:

- Plan A pays the deductible and copayments for hospitalizations beyond the 150-day limit (365-day lifetime maximum), and it pays for home health care (plus blood).
- Plan B covers everything Plan A provides and the deductible for Plan A.
- Plan C pays for the Part B deductible, the skilled nursing facility coinsurance amount, and emergency care while traveling in another country.
- Plan D pays everything Plan C covers except the Plan B deductible.
- Plan F provides the same benefits as Plan E but also pays providers more because it reimburses for charges beyond the Medicare scale, which are referred to as the "excess charges" provision. Also, there are now two Plan Fs because one is a high-deductible option.
- Plan G covers the same benefits as Plan F, except it is for retirees who may spend a good part of their time as expatriates. The plan provides insurance while undergoing medical treatment in other countries, up to $50,000 each year.
- Plan K has a 50/50 coinsurance and a higher out-of-pocket requirement at $4,640 and does not provide additional compensation for physicians who are underpaid by Medicare.
- Plan L pays 75 percent for Part B benefits, with a maximum out-of-pocket for the insured of $2,320 each year.
- Plan M provides the same coverage as Plan K and foreign emergency travel, but it has no out-of-pocket limit.
- Plan N pays the same as Plan L, with some additional copays (cost sharing) on the coinsurance portion and also covers foreign emergency travel.

Some plans were phased out because of the Medicare changes on June 1, 2010. Plans E, H, I, and J became obsolete in June 2010, and that is why they are not mentioned.

PLAN-SELECTION TIP

A word about excess charges: these are not fees in excess of usual and custom-ary charges but reflect the physician's normal billing for services rendered, which Medicare does not recognize. *For all seniors enrolled on Medicare plans: unless you have a provision to cover these uncompensated charges, you may have difficulty finding a doctor.* Physicians cannot afford to practice medicine at a loss, and the current reimbursement levels for most outpatient services are far below usual and customary rates.

MEDICARE MEDICAL SAVINGS ACCOUNTS

Medicare Medical Savings Accounts, or MSA plans, are high-deductible major medical insurance plans tied to a medical savings account, which can accumulate funds for medical services without taxation. These plans are typi-cally for the wealthier enrollee. Another feature of an MSA is the ability to transfer unused funds from one year into the next without penalty.

CONCLUSION

Medicare was designed when there was nothing available for senior health care, but with the advent of national health care purchasing pools and insur-ance mandates, is it time for the country to reevaluate how it manages health care for elders? Wouldn't it make more sense to include retirees in a national purchasing pool, so the risk could be shared across a larger, healthier popu-lation? It is a basic tenant of risk management to spread the risk of a given population across a bigger continuum to enhance predictability, optimize ad-ministration, and lower costs for individuals. The way the Medicare program is established, there is a disproportionate burden on seniors, who are often low-income residents, which is grossly unfair. Though the working-class population in America is burdened by the high cost of health care, seniors are dedicating far more of their proportional incomes to buy health care. Surely we can find a better way to finance health care, pay physicians fairly, and provide care. Unfortunately, the health care reforms of 2010 did little to address these concerns for this population; one can only hope changes will come in the near future.

If you are not totally confused yet, private insurance companies each have their own marketing and plan design twists that will confound you. I took twelve hours of Medicare continuing education courses just to write this chapter, and I still find it bewildering. For information on which insurance companies provide products for Medicare enrollees, you can go to your state insurance commissioner's website or call its customer service number. Also, the politically active AARP (American Association for Retired Persons) promotes certain MediGap insurance plan(s) for its members, and you can go to its website as well. Now that you have worked for decades and managed to make it to retirement age in the United States, your health care really starts to cost you money. It is important to note that a good number of federal employees and, of course, veterans do not have to participate in the Medicare program and have very good lifetime health care benefits. Unfortunately, this makes them unsympathetic to the plight of the rest of the private-sector Medicare participants.

For more information on Medicare and Medicare Supplement coverage, contact a Medicare specialist or go to the official government website: www. medicare.gov.

NOTES

1. Social Security Administration, "Medicare," available online at www.ssa.gov/pubs/media/pdf/EN-05-10043.pdf (accessed April 19, 2013).

2. "Medicare Eligibility Tool," Medicare.gov, accessed April 19, 2013, www.medicare.gov/MedicareEligibility/home.asp?version=default&browser=Chrome%7C25%7CWindows+7&language=English.

3. Hinda Chaikind, "Medicare Secondary Payer—Coordination of Benefits," Congressional Research Service, July 10, 2008, available online at http://aging.senate.gov/crs/medicare11.pdf (accessed April 19, 2013).

4. "What Does Medicare Part A Cover?," Medicare.gov, accessed April 19, 2013, www.medicare.gov/what-medicare-covers/part-a/what-part-a-covers.html.

5. "Part A Costs," Medicare.gov, accessed April 19, 2013, www.medicare.gov/your-medicare-costs/part-a-costs/part-a-costs.html.

6. "What Does Medicare Part B Cover?," Medicare.gov, accessed April 19, 2013, www.medicare.gov/what-medicare-covers/part-b/what-medicare-part-b-covers.html.

7. "Part B Costs," Medicare.gov, accessed March 17, 2013, www.medicare.gov/your-medicare-costs/part-b-costs/part-b-costs.html.

8. "Medicare Eligibility Tool," Medicare.gov, August 3, 2012, accessed March 17, 2013, www.medicare.gov/MedicareEligibility/Home.asp?dest=NAV|Home|Gen eralEnrollment|PremiumCostInfo#TabTop.

9. "Preventive and Screening Services," Medicare.gov, accessed April 19, 2013, www.medicare.gov/coverage/preventive-and-screening-services.html.

10. "Get Help Paying Costs," Medicare.gov, accessed April 19, 2013, www .medicare.gov/your-medicare-costs/help-paying-costs/get-help-paying-costs.html.

11. "How Do Medical Advantage Plans Work?," Medicare.gov, accessed April 19, 2013, www.medicare.gov/sign-up-change-plans/medicare-health-plans/medicare-advantage-plans/how-medicare-advantage-plans-work.html.

12. Centers for Medicare and Medicaid Services, "Your Guide to Medicare Special Needs Plans (SNPs)" (Baltimore, MD: U.S. Department of Health and Human Services, 2011), available online at www.medicare.gov/Publications/Pubs/pdf/11302 .pdf (accessed April 19, 2013).

13. "Drug Coverage (Part D)," Medicare.gov, accessed April 19, 2013, www.medi care.gov/part-d/index.html.

14. "Medicare Costs at a Glance," Medicare.gov, accessed April 19, 2013, www.medi care.gov/your-medicare-costs/costs-at-a-glance/costs-at-glance.html#collapse-4632.

· *16* ·

Health Insurance 101

$\mathcal{T}$his chapter is a speed addict's overview of the medical insurance industry, so caffeine up, and slam your way through it. There are over 1,128 companies licensed for life and/or health insurance in the United States.[1] The reason for the license confusion is insurance companies are subject to each individual state's licensing rules, and some states include medical insurance under its own license, whereas other states incorporate it under the life insurance umbrella. For example, I have been licensed in California, Oregon, and Washington, and here is how medical insurance is licensed in those states:

- California: life, accident, and health, and accident and health;
- Oregon: health, or life and health;
- Washington: life and disability.

Oregon also distinguishes between consultants who work for a fee and agents who receive a commission for products sold or managed.

A single company, like Aetna, can have several different license registrations in each state, so the number of licenses in each state does not mean there are an equal number of separate companies marketing insurance, for many have the same parent company. Additionally, many of the companies who are registered under life and health insurance only market life-insurance plans. Also, some companies, like R & Q Reinsurance Company, only underwrite the stop loss or reinsurance coverage for self-insured medical plans and are not involved in actually paying consumer medical claims directly. Blue Cross and Blue Shield entities, both nonprofit insurance companies, have the greatest market share for health insurance in the United States. Though the registrations may be under names like Regence or WellPoint, they are doing business in multiple states. Regence alone has five corporate registrations in Washington.[2]

Consequently, by the time you account for the duplication and product-specialization licenses, the number of companies selling health or medical insurance contracts is probably more like fifty.

The top twenty-five insurers registered for health insurance represent two-thirds of the marketplace,[3] but the problem with this data is that it is undifferentiated and includes specific loss contracts for cancer as well as regular health insurance policies. Here were the top twenty health insurance companies, by volume:

1. United Health Group
2. Wellpoint Group, Inc.
3. Kaiser Foundation Group
4. Aetna Group
5. Humana Group
6. HCSC Group
7. Coventry Group
8. Highmark Group
9. Independence Blue Cross Group
10. Blue Shield of California
11. Cigna
12. Blue Cross Blue Shield of Michigan
13. Health Net of California
14. Blue Cross Blue Shield of New Jersey
15. Blue Cross Blue Shield of Florida
16. Regence Group (Blue Shield)
17. Blue Cross Blue Shield of Massachusetts
18. Carefirst, Inc., Group
19. Wellcare Group
20. HIP Insurance Group

INDUSTRY TERMS FOR MEDICAL INSURANCE FINANCING

Health insurance has several different product types in the United States. Here are brief descriptions of those models.

Fully insured or community-rated medical plans are prospectively rated, which means the cost per individual/family member is negotiated at the beginning of the contract between the insurance company and the employer and is prospective or future looking. Consequently, no matter what the plan's performance is for that year, the client does not have to pay any additional costs.

Partially self-insured or retention-rated medical plans are retrospectively rated, meaning the company's performance is reviewed at the end of the plan year to determine what they will be paying for medical insurance the next year. The health plan's performance is used to calculate the charges for the contract year in conjunction with the product-line charges for the insurer. Depending on the plan's performance and the degree of risk charged in the contract, the client may owe money at the end of the year or have a partial credit for the next year.

Self-insured or ERISA (Employment Retirement Income Security Act of 1976) exempt plans are not considered traditional insurance plans and as such are exempt from many laws regarding plan design and administration for medical insurance. These plans are required to report annually to the Department of Labor through the filing of form 5500. Under self-insured contracts the elements of an insurance plan include risk, reserves for future claims, administrative charges, and medical claim payments, and are all in separate funding pools. Under some contracts a monthly premium charge is made incorporating all of these factors, but typically, the fixed charges are billed monthly and the risk portion or claims payment is paid via an electronic draft from the employer after a monthly adjudication. The risk portion of the health plan may include dental and vision coverage as well, and is based on the client's group claims activity. Sometimes employers handle this process themselves, but more often than not they work with brokers and consultants to help them find the best administrative arrangements and provider networks for the organization.

Supplemental Medical Plans such as AARP Medicare Supplements are in a separate category from the private-sector employer-sponsored medical plans. All Medicare Supplements and their marketing are strictly controlled by the government, and agents who market the products must undergo additional training to qualify as a representative.

Specific loss contracts like sickness and accident insurance pay a daily dollar amount for a specific medical or accident event and are in another category of insurance. For example, the cancer insurance products that only pay if you get cancer are in this category. I, as the healthpolicymaven™, do not advocate purchasing these types of contracts, as they attempt to combine medical and disability insurance products into a single contract, which is inadequate to protect a person from true financial hardship and only apply under very limited situations. In other words, they are a rip-off.

Special-risk policies are contracts that may be only valid while traveling for a specific period of time, such as medical evacuation, travel medical insurance, or student medical coverage per term of study.

Health maintenance plans are not insurance plans, but they still have to account for their entire plan costs just as retention-rated insurance plans would (similar to the self-insured plans). Also, many of the HMOs today operate as preferred-provider or "open-panel" health plans.

INSURANCE REGULATION

Insurance is primarily regulated through state insurance commissioners, who are elected officials. There is a National Association of Insurance Commissioners, which has recently been advocating for standardization in medical claims processing. However, each state decides how it wants to regulate the insurance business, which is a money maker for the state treasury. This is because the premium taxes paid by insurance companies are included in the rates all insurance purchasers pay and are built into the rate calculations for every product. Insurance commissioners review insurer solvency, approve new insurance products, enforce ethical standards, manage insurance licensing, and provide consumer services. Some states are much more stringent than others in terms of protecting consumers. In any case, it is always a good idea to make sure that the company you are considering purchasing insurance from is an approved carrier in your state and that the agent approaching you is also licensed. Most states have websites where you can review information online.

INSURANCE IS *NOT* HEALTH CARE

Insurance is not health care, but it is a financing vehicle for people to pay for health care services they may not otherwise be able to afford. Approximately half of the population of the United States is covered on private medical insurance. To all of those folks in the insurance industry who still think they are delivering health care, you are simply administering the financing mechanism for some claims payment. And as far as all of the insurance innovation goes, most of the industry is content with collecting increasing premiums as their compensation is built into a percentage of whatever the client has to pay in plan costs. There is minimal incentive for anyone in the insurance industry to concern themselves with the cost and availability of health care, until enough customers bail out of the system and their paychecks become smaller.

EMPLOYER-PROVIDED MEDICAL INSURANCE

Each year at a client's plan anniversary, the insurance company makes an offer, based on the performance of its insurance risk pool and the client's overall risk profile. I remember a conversation with Regence Blue Shield when they came up with an explanation for their huge increase. Here is the breakdown of their offer:

reserves for claims incurred but not yet paid—21 percent;
plan administration—12 percent;
rate stabilization reserve—10 percent;
reinsurance—5 percent;
broker's fee—4 percent.

That left just 48 percent of all of the money collected in a year to pay for actual medical claims. And they wonder why employers started self-insuring.

As a business owner you may be asking yourself: is 3 percent to 5 percent for my agent or broker's commission for overpriced medical insurance too much? Employers are concerned with getting the best value for corporate benefit plans, but their concerns may not mesh with the employees who are enrolled on the plans. This is especially true when the pass-through costs to employees who are covering dependents are so high. When you drill down to the actual value the insured may be getting for their premium payments once the commissions and administrative charges have been extracted, it is easy to see how the public option for medical care has gained momentum in America. The expansion of health insurance through insurance exchanges is seen not as a panacea to health care problems, but as a means to offer medical insurance to those who have been left out of the insurance marketplace.

CHALLENGES IN THE CURRENT INSURANCE MARKET

There are still many roadblocks to obtaining medical insurance, including:

1. obtaining employment with a firm that offers medical insurance to its workforce;
2. earning a living wage and being able to afford your share of the premiums;
3. living in an area where there is an insurance-company network for local doctors;
4. being disabled or otherwise uninsurable, but not necessarily eligible for Medicaid or Medicare/Social Security;
5. finding a clinician who will accept your insurance plan, especially if it is only Medicaid or Medicare Part A and B.

Obviously a lot of employers are not offering medical insurance to their employees prior to the implementation of the 2010 health care reforms, which are slated to be phased in by 2014. As seen in the healthpolicymaven™ scorecards, the states with the lowest level of employer-provided medical insurance for workers were Texas, New Mexico, and Mississippi, where only about half of those firms provided it for their workers.

HEALTHPOLICYMAVEN™ ANALYSIS

An example of an employer shortcoming in the provision of health insurance for the U.S. workforce is the behavior of corporations that look to exclude employees from their medical plans versus including them. Previously I worked up to thirty-six hours a week for a nonprofit organization, which refused to consider that full-time employment, and consequently didn't provide medical insurance. This scenario represents an economic market failure of the private employer sector and encourages public demand for the government to step in and improve the supply of medical insurance or access to health care in some way. The former example of workplace opportunism happens every day in business and is why the mandate for medical insurance was approved by Congress. If employers aren't willing to provide medical insurance, then we as a nation need to adopt a different system of access to health care, through public clinics or individual tax credits. Virtually all other industrialized countries have national health insurance provided through a subsidized program and spend much less per individual than the United States does for its hodge-podge health care financing system.

NOTES

1. "Industry Overview," Insurance Information Institute, accessed March 13, 2013, www.iii.org/media/facts/statsbyissue/industry.

2. National Association of Insurance Commissioners, "Appendix D: Authorized Insurance Companies by Line of Business in Washington 2011," in the 2011 Insurance Commissioner's Annual Report, available online at www.insurance.wa.gov/about-oic/oic-annual-reports/2011-report/documents/2011AppendixD.pdf (accessed April 19, 2013).

3. "Top 25 Health Insurance Companies," U.S. News and World Report, accessed March 13, 2013, http://health.usnews.com/health-plans/national-insurance-companies.

IV

HEALTH MEASURES

Regional and State Results

· 17 ·

Women's Health Care

The Best and the Worst in the United States

$\mathcal{T}$he purpose of this women's health chapter is to review primary components that contribute to a health score, which includes income, as evidenced by the proportion of women qualifying for medical and/or family assistance; the prevalence of insurance coverage, because this is an indicator of health care access; and availability of birth-control options. Birth control and reproductive rights are important health care services for women, and a national survey of these provisions is included in this chapter. The number-one cause of death in the United States is heart failure, so cardiac deaths are compared for each state.[1] Cancer is the number-two cause of death in the United States, so two cancers have been selected for their prevalence in women, breast and ovarian cancer, where state mortality rates are also compared to national levels.

Women's reproductive health is analyzed for the following four components: access to contraception services, including abortion; prescription birth-control options; availability of the morning-after pill (such as RU486); and access to clinics that provide these services.

State-by-state Medicaid enrollment requirements, which indicate the level of poverty a woman must experience in order to enroll on Medicaid medical insurance, are revealed. The ability of a low-income person to obtain medical care and the right to health care access are included as measures of health. Primary health care is supported with the presence of insurance coverage. Additionally, reproductive insurance coverage mandates are analyzed for Medicaid women and contrasted to private-sector insurance provisions.

Since access to health care in America is linked to proof of insurance, the proportion of women with private insurance, as well as the overall levels of coverage for public and private insurance programs for the adult females are shown.

For health care outcomes, death from heart failure and two types of common female cancers—breast and ovarian—are compared state by state to the national CDC average for a health outcome. The health metrics criteria review U.S. adult females over the age of thirty-five for heart failure deaths as well as deaths from ovarian or breast cancer. The top three causes of death in the country for men or women are, in order of precedence, heart failure, cancer, and stroke.[2] These elements are graded and rolled into a scorecard, which shows the best and worst performers in the nation, as well as regional scorecards for all fifty states and the District of Columbia. Though these measures are by no means comprehensive, the intent is to paint a picture of state, regional, and national health care access to primary health services. Additionally, both work-related insurance and overall medical insurance coverage levels are shown to illustrate the proportion of women in each state who have access to employer-sponsored medical insurance. Discussion regarding the levels of insurance coverage are drawn from the annual surveys by the nonprofit Kaiser Family Foundation State Health Facts Annual Surveys for the 2009 calendar year, which was published in 2011 and the 2010 calendar year data, which was published in 2012, as the criteria for national versus state (and the District of Columbia) performance scoring.[3] The health metrics chosen are from the Centers for Disease Control and Prevention and show the difference in the number of deaths, compared to the national average, for heart failure, breast cancer, and ovarian cancer. Again, the thinking here is a lower rate of death from these diseases is an indication of earlier disease treatment, enhanced public education, and better access to medical treatment.

First let's review the reproductive health laws by state, before we move on to Medicaid health benefits for low-income women, the prevalence of insurance for women throughout the nation, and mortality rates from the three illnesses.

REPRODUCTIVE SERVICES

Federal 2010 Medicaid reforms mandate that low-income women shall have the same choices for family planning services as all other women in the federal insurance exchanges. On the surface, this seems perfectly logical since children are expensive, and if you are poor, electing not to have a child may be prudent. However, some groups are opposed to birth control, period, especially if they have to pay for it.

Research Methods

I reviewed legislation for all fifty states and the District of Columbia regarding the 2010 Federal health insurance exchange mandates by reviewing both state legislative sites and the state-by-state legislative data from prochoiceamerica.

org. Reproductive criteria reviewed for analysis include: contraception equity for low-income women, availability of emergency contraception, restrictions on birth-control prescriptions, and state law regarding compliance with the federal health care reform mandates.

Contraception equity: This includes Medicaid-paid birth-control prescriptions, as well as access to abortion. Another aspect of reproductive equity is the level of restriction on various female groups within the state, including state employees, or even those with private insurance plans.

Emergency contraception: Emergency contraception includes the availability of RU486, which prevents fertilization of the egg and hence is not classified as an abortion procedure.

Restrictions on birth control prescriptions: This includes a review of limitations on access to prescription birth control products, such as banning private insurance companies from providing this coverage, limitations on birth control benefits for government employees, and other roadblocks.

Health insurance exchange legislation: An analysis of all state laws regarding federal health insurance exchange legislation was conducted to assess compliance with the 2014 federal health insurance exchange programs, and a complete inventory of these findings is found in chapter 13.

Findings

The vast majority of the fifty states have reviewed legislation repealing the 2010 federal health care reform act, which mandates standardization of coverage for female reproductive health, but only a few have passed exemption laws. The standardization of women's primary health care applies to all health plans to be offered through the 2014 insurance exchanges. Because the insurance exchanges are federally subsidized, the availability of birth control prescriptions, RU 486 (morning-after pill), and pregnancy termination services are scheduled to become standardized women's health benefits throughout the country. Some states are adopting the standards while others are still roiling over the implications for their constituents, so read on for the gritty details.

Most Female-Friendly States for Reproductive Autonomy

Though some of these states have roadblocks to obtaining abortions, in terms of lectures and mandatory delays, if state law provides legal recognition of abortion, it is listed as a female-friendly state.

Current Laws

- Alaska provides constitutional protection for the woman's right to choose, supports emergency contraception, and assures low-income women equal access to family planning options.

- California has an affirmative right to choose in its state law, women are guaranteed access to emergency contraception, and if medical plans cover prescription drugs, they must offer birth control as well. It is also illegal for pharmacists to deny birth control to women.
- Connecticut has a legal affirmative right to choose, assures equity in reproductive options for all women regardless of income, supports emergency contraception, and mandates that health plans that provide prescriptions must also cover contraceptives. Finally, it protects against violence at reproductive clinics.
- Hawaii law protects a woman's right to choose, supports emergency contraception, assures low-income women equal access to family planning, and stipulates that health plans that offer prescription drug benefits must also cover contraceptives.
- Maine guarantees a woman's right to choose in its constitution, supports emergency contraception, protects reproductive service clinics against violence, requires health plans that provide prescription drugs to cover contraceptives, and requires pharmacists to fill birth-control prescriptions.
- Maryland law protects a woman's right to choose, supports access to emergency contraception, requires health plans that cover prescriptions to cover contraceptives, provides equal access to family planning for low-income women, and protects women's health clinics from violence.
- Minnesota state law guarantees a woman's right to choose, provides family planning support for low-income women, protects against violence at family planning clinics, and provides access to emergency contraception. Access to abortion is a problem because 95 percent of the counties in Minnesota do not have a clinician who will perform abortions, but this is a problem throughout the country.[4]
- Montana law protects a woman's right to choose, protects clinicians and clients of reproductive health clinics, assures low-income women of equal access to birth-control options, and requires health plans to offer contraceptives if they cover other prescriptions.
- Nevada law stipulates a woman's right to choose, protects against violence directed at reproductive-rights clinics, requires pharmacists to fill birth-control prescriptions, and mandates that all health plans offering prescription coverage also cover birth control.
- Oregon legally stipulates the woman's right to choose, provides access to abortion for all women, protects against violence for patrons of clinics providing reproductive health services, assures access to emergency contraception, and requires that medical plans offering prescription coverage also cover contraceptives.

- Washington State requires health plans that offer prescription coverage to also cover oral contraceptives, and pharmacists are not allowed to refuse contraceptive prescriptions. State law also protects women's health clinics against violence and provides access to abortion for all Washington women regardless of private insurance or Medicaid status. Finally, the state also supports emergency-contraception services, and state law affirms a woman's right to choose.

Most Restrictive States Regarding Female Reproductive Autonomy

States seeking to criminalize abortion are Alabama,[5] Mississippi,[6] Arkansas,[7] Montana,[8] Nevada,[9] North Dakota,[10] and Oklahoma.[11] These states all seek to give "personhood" status to a fetus, regardless of gestation and have sponsored bills which have made it out of committee. The organization that is championing this legislation is called Personhood USA and is based in Colorado.

Health Care Providers Can Decline to Provide Contraceptive Services

The following states have enacted laws that allow health care providers, including pharmacists or clinicians, to decline to provide birth-control services: Idaho (Senate Bill 1353 was enacted on March 29, 2010) and Oklahoma (Senate Bill 1891 was signed on April 2, 2010).

Abortion Bans under Private Medical Insurance Plans

Under current law, the following states do not allow private insurance funding for abortion services: Kentucky, Missouri, Oklahoma, Idaho, and North Dakota.[12]

Abortions Bans in Health Exchanges

Arizona and Mississippi have enacted laws that restrict abortion and other contraceptive services under state health insurance exchanges. Arizona S-1305,[13] enacted on April 24, 2010, prohibits all insurance companies that participate in the insurance exchanges from offering abortion coverage, and S-1001, signed on April 1, 2010, blocks portions of the federal health care reforms. S-1305 also prohibits insurance companies that insure state employees from offering abortion coverage.[14]

Mississippi Senate L-3214 precludes insurance companies from offering abortion coverage in health insurance exchanges under the 2010 health care reforms.[15]

States That Seek to Limit Birth Control Specifically for Low-Income Women

Virginia passed a bill on May 17, 2010, which limits access to abortion for Medicaid-eligible women.[16] Colorado L-1311 prohibits the payment of abortion for Medicaid participants except for the Hyde Amendment criteria.[17]

States That Seek to Limit Access to Other Elements of Reproductive Autonomy

Additional states that seek to limit access to sex education, contraceptives, and birth control for low-income women (through Medicaid) or to criminalize abortion are: Alabama, Louisiana, Virginia, Colorado, Nevada, and New Mexico.[18]

States with current unenforceable bans on abortion include Virginia, West Virginia, North Carolina, South Carolina, Florida, Texas, Louisiana, Mississippi, Alabama, Georgia, Tennessee, Kansas, Oklahoma, Ohio, Kentucky, Missouri, Utah, Idaho, Massachusetts, Rhode Island, New Jersey, Delaware, Wisconsin, Michigan, Iowa, Nebraska, Arkansas, Indiana, Vermont, New Mexico, North Dakota, and South Dakota.[19]

A word to the wise for people living in these states: If the federal law *Roe v. Wade* is overturned, an era of safe, affordable abortions may be gone for you. It also means more children for people who can't afford them or who may have health factors that impact the health of the fetus. It is unclear at this time if any type of abortion would be allowed if *Roe v. Wade* is overturned. In any case, there are medical reasons for abortion beyond birth control, and it would seem prudent to leave those in the hands of clinicians who are trained to make those assessments.

The attempts to do an "end run" around legal abortions were recently highlighted by the 2011 congressional efforts to redefine rape.[20] This unseemly maneuvering is an effort to avoid covering rape victims' abortions under the Hyde Amendment's federal funding statute for low-income women.[21] In the age of date rape and the drugging of women on college campuses, one wonders about the logic of this unconstitutional effort. It is challenging to keep a civil discourse when the bar has been dropped this low.

WHY SO MANY STATES WANT EXEMPTIONS TO FEDERAL HEALTH STANDARDS FROM THE PATIENT PROTECTION AND AFFORDABLE CARE ACT AND THE AFFORDABLE HEALTH CARE ACT FOR AMERICA

Federal law signed on March 23, 2010, created a mandate to offer family planning services under state Medicaid plans, and this has lit the flames of discontent regarding government health care programs that require state funding.[22] Medicaid is a public health care program for low-income residents that is financed through federal allocations and significant state budget allocations. Another sticking point is the requirement in the Patient Protection and Afford-able Care Act (PPACA) stipulating that free-standing birth-center services are covered under federal Medicaid mandates. This would apply to family planning clinics (Planned Parenthood), which has upset the anti-family-planning lobby.

The PPACA health stipulation allows more people of low-income status to become eligible to receive subsidized insurance through state or regional insurance exchanges. Federal insurance exchange offerings are slated to in-clude a standardized set of benefits, including reproductive and contraceptive services. Small business owners who can't afford group insurance programs will also be eligible for the exchange plans, as well as individuals. This means a lot of people will have access to medical insurance at a more affordable cost. Both the House and Senate bills limited abortion funding in the health insur-ance exchanges to the Hyde Bill criteria, which allows abortion only under the following circumstances: rape, incest, and life-threatening circumstances, such as an ectopic pregnancy. However, each individual state can choose to allow abortion under more liberal circumstances in the exchanges. For ex-ample, state Medicaid plans may opt to treat abortion as any other medically necessary service, and private insurance companies may opt to do the same.

Paying for the Mandates

The federal government is mandating a pay-or-play scenario for medical insurance, requiring all U.S. residents to have it or pay a tax penalty. By es-tablishing the regional insurance exchanges with mandated medical benefits, the government is attempting to standardize health insurance benefits, which have previously been decided by each state insurance commissioner. The insurance mandate is funded through a combination of insurance premium contributions, federal subsidies for working-class and low-income people, and a host of new user taxes as previously reviewed in chapter 13.

Basic Rules of Economics

Insurance 101 dictates that what you pay today does not bear a direct rela-tionship to what you will get back tomorrow or at any time in the future, and this is your opportunity cost. What you are getting is a contract that says you are eligible receive certain benefits should an insurable event occur.

For government programs, what you contribute in the form of taxes equates not to direct individual services but to both direct and indirect programs, like health care research, environmental protections, and the provision of health care.

Does any of this teeth-gnashing really matter when the 1977 Hyde Amendment has continually been ratified, and every federal budget limits payment for abortion procedures except in the case of rape, incest, or a life-threatening situation? Well, for starters, the Hyde Amendment has also been narrowed to exclude federal reimbursement for abortion for any federal employees, for women in the military, or for women covered by Indian Health Services.[23] The latter is a real confounder; American Indian tribes are considered sovereign nations, yet they must obtain health care from the federal government whose mandates are not decided by tribal members.

The 2010 reproductive rights provisions matter because states can choose different provisions for birth-control financing and services available through the private market insurance exchanges and state-run Medicaid programs. There is also specific language to protect clinicians who do not want to provide abortions but no comparable language protecting those who do.[24] States that have laws protecting women's health clinics from violence were noted in the analysis.

The most onerous task in the health care mandates is the requirement to attach a separate premium for abortion costs and to bill it as an addendum to the exchange plans. This seems like a lot of work for the estimated $1 additional cost per eligible woman, per month, but that may be another way for the federal government to discourage abortions.[25]

Building a robust sex-education program and providing contraceptive options to the sexually active population—like RU486, which prevents fertilization after sexual intercourse—and thus meeting the requirement of some religious groups, would seem to be the solution. Since avoiding fertilization prevents pregnancy and thus abortion, why not support legislation to approve this remedy? Even with appropriate sex education, which also includes disease prevention, accidents do happen, prophylactics break, diaphragms aren't always a tight fit, and the rhythm method certainly can sound some discordant notes. The only assured way to avoid pregnancy is abstinence, which is unrealistic for most of the sexually active population.

According to a 2003 survey by the Kaiser Family Foundation on contraceptive care under insurance programs: 87 percent of private employers offered coverage for sterilization, 72 percent covered contraceptives, and 46 percent covered abortion services.[26] As previously mentioned, several states already seek to restrict these legal medical services for private-sector medical-insurance programs, even though they are not paid for by any public funds.

OTHER WOMEN'S HEALTH CARE MEASURES

Insurance Coverage

One of the sources for the women's health insurance citations was the Kaiser Family Foundation State Health Facts Health Insurance Coverage Survey of Adult Women, by State, 2009-2010, which is now archived. Other sources,

including the 2010-2011 Kaiser Family Foundation State Health Facts Insurance Coverage Survey for adult women, which is cited in the end-notes
and is still available online.[27]

Since the U.S. health system relies heavily on private-sector financing
for health care, levels of private employer insurance are examined here on
a statewide basis. Additionally, the total proportion of women with medical insurance, including public sources, is also reviewed, for access to health
care in America is, in many cases, linked to proof of insurance. Here are the
findings for adult women as measured by the Kaiser Foundation 2010-2011
nationwide survey on the uninsured.[28]

Smallest Amount of Uninsured Women.   In the Kaiser Foundation State
Health Facts Annual Survey the national average for adult nonelderly women
without medical insurance, in either a public or, the number of uninsured
women increased to a whopping 20 percent of the entire national population
by the end of the 2010 calendar year.[29]

By the publication of the 2010–2011 Kaiser Foundation's State Health
Facts Survey, Massachusetts was in first place for covering its adult women
for medical insurance with a mere 5% lacking coverage. Massachusetts has a
state mandated medical insurance program which is the model for the insurance exchanges being implemented on a national level. In second place for
the "well covered" status was Hawaii, which boasts only 10% of their adult
women are without medical insurance. Hawaii has a state law requiring most
employers to provide employee medical insurance.[30]

Needless to say, these states and a handful of others outperform the nation in devising ways to bring more of their residents under the umbrella of
medical insurance to increase health care access.

States with the Most Uninsured Women.   By the time the 2010-2011
Kaiser Foundation State Health Facts Insurance Coverage survey results for
adult women was posted in 2012, the bottom three performers for women
without medical insurance were Texas at 30 percent, Louisiana at 28%, and
New Mexico at 27%.[31]

Access to Employer-Sponsored Health Insurance.   The Kaiser Foundation
State Health Facts annual survey methodology for evidence of insurance
includes employer-sponsored medical plans, those covered through military
plans (not active duty), and some on Medicare as a secondary payer in their
calculation for the total employer-provided insurance statistics.[32]

Generous Employers

2011 Survey.   In 2011 New Hampshire still managed to report 72
percent of its women had insurance through employer medical plans, which
also included military-related coverage or Medicare as a secondary payer.
The only other states that even came close to boasting that level of employer
provided medical insurance for their adult women were Minnesota and Utah,
both at 67%.[33]

Tightwad Employers.   Though New Mexico has improved its status for working women with medical insurance, it is still in the bottom three for the 2011 Kaiser Foundation State Health Facts Survey results, posting a mere 48 percent of working women with employer-provided medical insurance. Interestingly enough, Mississippi has also improved, with 55 percent of its adult women reporting medical insurance through their employers. Texas continues to do poorly with just 54 percent of its women reporting employer-related medical insurance.[34]

MEDICAID FUNDING FOR LOW-INCOME WOMEN AND CHILDREN

The U.S. Medicaid program is a federal program that is managed by state governments. Medicaid has an income component and a medical insurance component. Residents who are poor enough qualify to receive this assistance. Several states, like Minnesota, Washington, and Massachusetts, have other programs that provide subsidized medical-insurance programs for people who are often called the working poor—those who don't qualify for Medicaid but are still of low-income status. The total insured versus uninsured calculation takes into consideration these other public insurance programs, if they were disclosed on the Kaiser Family Foundation State Health Facts Insurance Coverage Survey for 2011, as previously indicated.

State Budget Impact

The federal government has been passing more and more Medicaid program costs onto the states to finance, which has caused some states to elect out of traditional Medicaid programs, in the form of a 1115 Waiver Election. Due to the economic recession in the country, some states saw significant increases in their Medicaid population over the past two years, which is a tremendous burden on state budgets, because the federal government does not cover all of the cost for Medicaid program recipients and the states must pick up the difference. Though the national statistic for Medicaid enrollment was listed as 12 percent in 2008 and also for 2009, many states saw increases of 10 percent in this poverty demographic. This means the number of people living in poverty in their states increased by 10 percent or more over that time frame, which is huge. States with this significant increase in their residents falling into poverty status include: California, Colorado, Delaware, Florida, Georgia, Illinois, Indiana, Kentucky, Maine, Maryland, Mississippi, New Jersey, Ohio, Oregon, Rhode Island, South Carolina, Wisconsin, Washington, and Wyoming. The largest increase of residents living in poverty was for the

District of Columbia, going from 18 percent of its population enrolled on Medicaid to 21 percent for Medicaid enrollment as reported in the 2010 Kaiser Foundation State Health Facts Insurance Coverage survey. However, by 2011 Vermont listed 21 percent of its residents on their Medicaid program, so this is a significant change.[35]

Impact on Patient Access

One of the problems with federal programs is that the reimbursement levels are determined at the federal level, and one of the ways to control program cost escalation is to cap reimbursement for services at very low levels. This phenomenon is of particular concern in two areas: for clinicians who provide services to the poor and for urban hospitals with mostly poor populations. This is an acute problem for the "health care safety net" in the United States, because most hospitals must use a variety of funding sources and patient mix in order to work within a solvent budget. In other words, they need the full-pay customers on private insurance to offset the nonpaying or under-paying customers on Medicaid or for the many patients lacking any insurance at all. Unfortunately, the level of payment, particularly for physician services, has been abysmal for years, which means many physicians will not accept Medicaid patients. This partially explains the robust growth in federally qualified health plans and community health centers, which receive federal grants to serve populations who are overlooked. However, these health centers are geared for primary care only and they do not have much impact on the hospital patient mix, hence the safety net in areas of concentrated poverty.

States with the Most Stringent Medicaid Qualifications

The states that provide the least amount of Medicaid support via allowances for women with children are North Dakota, Idaho, Utah, Wyoming, Virginia (although Virginia has a separate program for pregnant women), and Alabama. They all limit eligibility for state Medicaid to 133 percent of the federal poverty level, which was $29,326.50 in 2010 for a family of four.[36] The 133 percent federal poverty level is the federal government's minimum-income level for determining eligibility for Medicaid medical benefits.

States with the Most Generous Medicaid Qualification Standards for Low-Income Women

The following states allow income over 185 percent of the federal poverty threshold to qualify for state Medicaid assistance: California, Colorado, Illinois, Iowa, Indiana, Arkansas, Louisiana, Maine, Connecticut, Rhode Island,

New Jersey, Delaware, Maryland, and the District of Columbia. These are the states with the most generous allowance for low-income women to become eligible for state medical assistance.[37] In addition to the Medicaid financial support, all states except the following also offer nutritional and psychosocial counseling for Medicaid mothers: Connecticut, Florida, Louisiana, Maine, and Kentucky.

HEALTH METRICS

Cardiac Care

According to the Centers for Disease Control and Prevention, the state with the highest rate of cardiac deaths for both men and women was Mississippi, and the state with the lowest was Minnesota.[38] The leading cause of death in the United States in 2006 was cardiac or heart failure, at 26 percent of the 2.4 million deaths that year.[39] American women have myocardial infarctions or heart attacks at about the same rate at men, but often they are not diagnosed with cardiac problems as early as men. According to the American Heart Association, women are less likely to receive cardiac devices to prevent secondary heart attacks than men.[40] The second leading cause of death for men or women was cancer.

Methods of Assessment.   To draw my conclusions, I reviewed by state the CDC data for a five-year period from 2001 to 2006, for deaths attributed to heart disease for people age thirty-five and up.[41] Each state's performance was compared by subtracting the deaths reported per one hundred thousand women from the national average. A negative number indicated that more women died than the average for the nation, and conversely, a positive number meant fewer deaths from heart disease.

Best Places for Women to Avoid Death from Heart Disease.   If you are a woman, the best place to have heart disease is New Mexico, which posted 37 percent fewer deaths from heart disease than the national norm of 351 deaths per 100,000 women over the age of thirty-five.[42] In second place is Minnesota, which had 122 fewer deaths per 100,000 women from this condition.[43] Hawaii came in third place with 33 percent fewer deaths and 115 fewer women who died from heart conditions per 100,000 females.[44]

Worst Places to Live if You Are a Woman with Heart Disease.   The worst place for women to have heart disease is Mississippi, with 150 more deaths per 100,000 women from this condition than the national norm during the same five-year period.[45] The dubious honor for second place goes to the District of Columbia, with 104 more deaths from heart disease per 100,000 women in the same time frame.[46] In third place for the worst female mortality rate from heart disease is Alabama, posting 93 more deaths than the national average, per 100,000 women.[47]

Cancer

Method of Assessment. Breast and ovarian cancer survival information was drawn from the U.S. Centers for Disease Control and Prevention 2006 mortality statistics.[48] All data on the CDC site is age adjusted and drawn from ten primary sites with the highest cancer rates within each state, using the 2000 U.S. Standard Population Census information. I reviewed each state's reported cancer deaths for breast and ovarian cancer for women, subtracting the results from the national average mortality rate for these cancers, to produce the variance. A positive variance indicates the state has fewer deaths from the disease than the national average, and a negative result indicates higher deaths than the average.

Cancer Deaths

States Outperforming the National Average for Breast Cancer Survival. The state with the fewest breast cancer deaths was Hawaii, which reported 19 percent fewer breast cancer deaths than the national average in 2006, according to the most recent cancer statistics from the Centers for Disease Control and Prevention. The metric was 4.5 fewer deaths per 100,000 lives than the national average of 23.4 from breast cancer.[49] The next best state for fewest breast cancer deaths was Montana, outperforming the national average with 4.4 fewer deaths from breast cancer than the average. Minnesota had the third fewest number of deaths, compared to the national average with 3.5 fewer deaths per 100,000 lives.[50]

Worst States for Breast Cancer Deaths. The worst state for breast cancer survival statistics was Alaska, followed by the District of Columbia and New Jersey, which tied for this dubious distinction. Aside from dealing with the snow, women living in the great beyond of Alaska reported 17 percent more breast cancer deaths than the national average of 23.4 deaths per 100,000 women. It is probably harder to get treatment given the distance between urban areas for medical treatment facilities in Alaska.

Ovarian Cancer

States Reporting the Fewest Deaths from Ovarian Cancer. Conversely, it would appear your chances of dying from ovarian cancer are the lowest in Alaska, followed closely by Hawaii and Wyoming, since their reported deaths were well below the national average of 8.5 deaths per 100,000 people. I should also note that the CDC numbers are age-adjusted for a valid statistical calculation.

States Reporting the Highest Deaths from Ovarian Cancer.   Using the same CDC information cited above, the worst states in which to reside and survive ovarian cancer are the District of Columbia, Alabama, and South Dakota, based on their reported deaths compared to the national average for this disease. Amazingly, in D.C., our nation's capital, the death rate from ovarian cancer was 9.8 deaths per 100,000 women, which is 15 percent more than the national average. Sadly, this is only one of many measures where D.C. residents are left with poorer outcomes than elsewhere in the United States. Alabama had 9.7 deaths, and South Dakota posted 9.8 ovarian cancer deaths per 100,000 women.

HEALTHPOLICYMAVEN™ SCORECARD

Global Reporting for the National Scorecard

The Women's Health Scorecards show the high and low fliers for overall health quality for women. A high score is the best because it indicates a positive variance for each of the measures; for example, fewer people dying from heart attacks, as opposed to a lower score, which included states with more deaths than the national average. The scorecard also takes into consideration economics by including levels of income necessary to qualify for state Medicaid assistance, as well as access to health care providers, based on the levels of insurance. Finally, since the District of Columbia is included, there are more than fifty states, so the worst performer is listed at fifty-one.

Fifty-state reporting is done by region, with the country being divided into eight regions labeled as follows: East Coast, Great Lakes, Midwest, Northeast, Outside the 48, Southern, Western, and West Coast. Information on how your state performed follows in the national scorecard found in figure 17.1 for the top 10 percent of the states and figure 17.2 for the bottom 10 percent. For more details on how other states and your region compare for their scorecards, see the appendix at the back of the book.

NOTES

1. "Leading Cause of Death," Centers for Disease Control and Prevention, accessed April 19, 2013, www.cdc.gov/nchs/fastats/lcod.htm.

2. National Center for Health Statistics, *Health, United States, 2010: With Special Feature on Death and Dying* (Hyattsville, MD: National Center for Health Statistics, 2011), available online at www.cdc.gov/nchs/data/hus/hus10.pdf (accessed March 17, 2013).

Women's Health Scorecard-2013 Top Five						
Measures of Health	Nt'l Av.	NM	MN	HI	CO	AK
Ranking		**1**	**2**	**3**	**5**	**4**
Contraception Equity for Birth Control RX	31%	1	0	1	1	1
Abortion coverage for Medicaid women	86%	1	0	1	0	1
Abortion ban for all medical plans	14%	0	0	0	-1	0
Availability of Emergency Contraception	41%	0	0	1	1	1
Women with medical insurance	80%	73%	89%	90%	84%	79%
Women on employer medical plans	58%	48%	67%	67%	60%	60%
Income > FPL for Medicaid	187%	133%	275%	175%	185%	175%
Breast Cancer Deaths	23.4	21.2	20.6	18.4	20.8	27.4
Ovarian Cancer Deaths	8.5	8.5	8.3	7.2	8.3	6.9
Heart Failure Deaths	351	220	229	236	251	260
Total Score		**134**	**126**	**124**	**103**	**92**

Notes: Disease morality is from the CDC 2006 data.
Reproductive data is from NARAL & legislative sites 2010 & 2013.
Insurance & data based on the Kaiser FF 2011 cal. yr. survey.
Health Metrics calculated by comparing state's performance to nt'l av.

Figure 17.1.   Women's Health Scorecard- Top Five

Women's Health Scorecard-2013 Bottom Five						
Measures of Health	Nt'l Av.	WV	AL	OK	DC	MS
Ranking		**47**	**48**	**49**	**50**	**51**
Contraception Equity for Birth Control RX	31%	0	1	1	-1	0
Abortion coverage for Medicaid women	86%	1	1	1	-1	0
Abortion ban for all medical plans	14%	-1	0	-1	0	0
Availability of Emergency Contraception	41%	0	1	0	-1	1
Women with medical insurance	80%	84%	82%	78%	89%	77%
Women on employer medical plans	58%	64%	59%	59%	57%	55%
Income > FPL for Medicaid	187%	150%	162%	133%	185%	185%
Breast Cancer Deaths	23.4	21.6	23.5	24.2	27	25.4
Ovarian Cancer Deaths	8.5	8.7	9.7	8.7	9.8	8
Heart Failure Deaths	351	441	444	453	455	501
Total Score		**-88**	**-91**	**-100**	**-112**	**-151**
Notes: Disease morality is from the CDC 2006 data.						
Reproductive data is from NARAL & legislative sites 2011 & 2013.						
Insurance & Medicaid data based on Kaiser FF 2011 cal. yr. survey.						
Health Metrics calculated by comparing state's performance to nt'l av.						

Figure 17.2.   Women's Health Scorecard- Bottom Five

3. "Health Insurance Coverage of Women 19–64, States (2010–2011), U.S. (2011)," Stateheathfacts.org, Kaiser Family Foundation, accessed April 19, 2013, www.statehealthfacts.org/comparebar.jsp?ind=652&cat=3.

4. "Minnesota: Political Info and Laws in Brief," NARAL Pro-Choice America, accessed March 17, 2013, www.prochoiceamerica.org/government-and-you/state-governments/state-profiles/minnesota.html.

5. Dan Becker, "Abortion Foe Overreaches in Describing Context of Court Ruling," PolitiFact.com, January 14, 2013, accessed April 19, 2013, www.politifact.com/georgia/statements/2013/feb/08/dan-becker/abortion-foe-overreaches-describing-context-court-.

6. "Mississippi Voters Reject Anti-abortion Measure for Fetus Personhood," Reuters, November 9, 2011, accessed April 19, 2013, http://blogs.reuters.com/faithworld/2011/11/09/mississippi-voters-reject-anti-abortion-measure-for-fetus-personhood.

7. "Personhood Bill and Ballot Initiatives," Resolve.org, accessed April 19, 2013, www.resolve.org/get-involved/personhood-bills-and-ballot-initiatives.html#WA.

8. Marnee Banks, "'Personhood' Debated in Montana Legislature," KRTV.com, accessed April 19, 2013, www.krtv.com/news/personhood-debated-in-montana-legislature/#.

9. "Nevada Personhood Amendment (2012)," Ballotpedia.org, accessed April 19, 2013, http://ballotpedia.org/wiki/index.php/Nevada_Personhood_Amendment_(2012).

10. "North Dakota Passes First State Personhood Amendment in US History," PersonhoodUSA.com, March 22, 2013, accessed April 19, 2013, www.personhoodusa.com/press-release/north-dakota-passes-first-state-personhood-amendment-us-history.

11. "Personhood Bill and Ballot Initiatives."

12. Usha Ranji, Alina Salganicoff, and Tina Park, "Access to Abortion Coverage and Health Reform," Kaiser Family Foundation, November 2010, p. 2, available online at www.kff.org/healthreform/upload/8021.pdf (accessed March 17, 2013).

13. "Senate Bill 1305," Arizona State Legislature, 49th legislature, 2nd regular session, 2010, available online at www.arkleg.state.ar.us/healthcare/Insurance/Documents/AZ%20SB%201305.pdf (accessed April 19, 2013).

14. "Senate Bill 1001," Arizona State Legislature, 50th legislature, 1st special session, 2011, available online at www.azleg.gov/legtext/50leg/1s/bills/sb1001s.pdf (accessed April 19, 2013).

15. "Senate Bill 3214," Mississippi State Legislature, 2010 regular session, accessed March 17, 2013, http://billstatus.ls.state.ms.us/2010/pdf/history/SB/SB3214.xml.

16. "State Funding of Abortion under Medicaid," Guttmacher Institute, State Policies in Brief, April 1, 2013, available online at www.guttmacher.org/statecenter/spibs/spib_SFAM.pdf (accessed April 19, 2013).

17. "State Funding of Abortion under Medicaid."

18. "State Governments," NARAL Pro-Choice America, accessed March 17, 2013, www.prochoiceamerica.org/government-and-you/state-governments.

19. "State Governments."

20. "Akins Assault on Women's Health & Dignity," Straight Talk on Health Care blog by Healthpolicymaven™, August 22, 2012, accessed April 19, 2013, http://healthpolicymaven.blogspot.com/2012/08/akins-assault-on-womens-health-dignity.html.

21. Linda Lowen, "What Is the Hyde Amendment?," About.com, accessed April 19, 2013, http://womensissues.about.com/od/reproductiverights/f/HydeAmendment.htm.

22. "Medicaid and CHIP Health Reform Implementation Timeline," Kaiser Family Foundation, accessed March 17, 2013, www.kff.org/healthreform/upload/8064.

23. Ranji, Salganicoff, and Park, "Access to Abortion Coverage and Health Reform," p. 2.

24. Government Is Not God PAC, "PAC Ad Says Obama Will Force Christian Groups to Pay for Abortions," PolitiFact.com, September 23, 2012, accessed April 19, 2013, www.politifact.com/truth-o-meter/statements/2012/sep/26/government-not-god-pac/pac-ad-says-obama-will-force-christian-groups-pay-.

25. "Does Barack Obama's Health Care Bill Include $1 Abortions?," PolitiFact.com, March 12, 2012, accessed April 19, 2013, www.politifact.com/truth-o-meter/statements/2012/mar/21/blog-posting/does-barack-obamas-health-care-bill-include-1-abor.

26. A. Sonfield, J. J. Frost, R. B. Gold, "U.S. Insurance Coverage of Contraceptives and the Impact of Contraceptive Coverage Mandates, 2002," *Perspectives on Sexual and Reproductive Health* 236, no. 2 (2004): 1.

27. "Women's Health Insurance Coverage for Women 19-64, by State, 2010-2011," Kaiser Family Foundation State Health Facts, accessed April 19, 2013, http://statehealthfacts.org/comparetable.jsp?ind=652&cat=3&sub=178&yr=274&typ=2

28. "Women's Health Insurance Coverage for Women 19-64, by State, 2010-2011," Kaiser Family Foundation State Health Facts, accessed April 19, 2013. http://statehealthfacts.org/comparetable.jsp?ind=652&cat=3&sub=178&yr=274&typ=2

29. "Women's Health Insurance Coverage for Women 19-64, by State, 2010-2011," Kaiser Family Foundation State Health Facts, accessed April 19, 2013, http://statehealthfacts.org/comparetable.jsp?ind=652&cat=3&sub=178&yr=274&typ=2

30. "Health Insurance Coverage of Nonelderly Women 19-64, States 2010-2011," Kaiser Family Foundation State Health Facts, accessed April 5, 2013, http://statehealthfacts.org/comparemaptable.jsp?ind=132&cat=3&sub=178&yr=274&typ=2

31. "Women's Health Insurance Coverage for Women 19-64, by State, 2010-2011," Kaiser Family Foundation State Health Facts, accessed April 19, 2013, http://statehealthfacts.org/comparetable.jsp?ind=652&cat=3&sub=178&yr=274&typ=2

32. "Health Insurance Coverage of Women 19-64, States 2010-2011," Kaiser Family Foundation State Health Facts, accessed April 5, 2013, http://statehealthfacts.org/comparemaptable.jsp?ind=652&cat=3&sub=178&yr=274&typ=2,

33. "Women's Health Insurance Coverage for Women 19-64, by State, 2010-2011," Kaiser Family Foundation State Health Facts, accessed April 19, 2013, http://statehealthfacts.org/comparetable.jsp?ind=652&cat=3&sub=178&yr=274&typ=2

34. "Women's Health Insurance Coverage for Women 19-64, by State, 2010-2011," Kaiser Family Foundation State Health Facts, accessed April 19, 2013, http://statehealthfacts.org/comparetable.jsp?ind=652&cat=3&sub=178&yr=274&typ=2

35. "Women's Health Insurance Coverage for Women 19-64, by State, 2010-2011," Kaiser Family Foundation State Health Facts, accessed April 19, 2013, http://statehealthfacts.org/comparetable.jsp?ind=652&cat=3&sub=178&yr=274&typ=2

36. "Medicaid and CHIP Eligibility Table by State," National Conference of State Legislatures, accessed April 19, 2013, www.ncsl.org/issues-research/health/medicaid-eligibility-table-by-state-state-activit.aspx.

37. Usha Ranji, Alina Salganicoff, Alexandra M. Stewart, Marisa Cox, and Lauren Doamekpor "State Medicaid Coverage of Perinatal Services: Summary of State Survey Findings, November 2009," Kaiser Family Foundation and George Washington University School of Public Health and Health Services, p. 7, accessed March 17, 2013, www.kff.org/womenshealth/upload/8014.pdf.

38. Melonie Heron, Donna L. Hoyert, Sherry L. Murphy, Jiaquan Xu, Kenneth D. Kochanek, and Betzaida Tejada-Vera, "Deaths: Final Data for 2006," *National Vital Statistics Reports* 57, no. 14 (2009), available online at www.cdc.gov/nchs/data/nvsr/nvsr57/nvsr57_14.pdf (accessed March 17, 2013).

39. Heron et al., "Deaths: Final Data for 2006."

40. Donald Lloyd Jones, Robert Adams, Mercedes Carnethon et al., "Heart Disease and Stroke Statistics—2009 Update. A Report from the American Heart Association Statistics Committee and Stroke Statistics Subcommittee," *Circulation*, December 15, 2008, available online at http://circ.ahajournals.org/cgi/reprint/CIRCULATIONAHA.108.191261v1 (accessed March 17, 2013).

41. National Center for Health Statistics, "Heart Failure Mortality Statistics, 2001–2006," available online at ftp://ftp.cdc.gov/pub/Health_Statistics/NCHS/Datasets/DVS/mortality/mort2006ps.zip (accessed April 8, 2013).

42. National Center for Health Statistics, Department of Vital Statistics, Centers for Disease Control. Heart Failure Mortality Statisitics, five year age-adjusted, 2001–2006, ftp://ftp.cdc.gov/pub/Health_Statistics/NCHS/Datasets/DVS/mortality/mort2006ps.zip

43. National Center for Health Statistics, Department of Vital Statistics, Centers for Disease Control. Heart Failure Mortality Statistics, five year age-adjusted, 2001–2006, ftp://ftp.cdc.gov/pub/Health_Statistics/NCHS/Datasets/DVS/mortality/mort2006ps.zip

44. National Center for Health Statistics, Department of Vital Statistics, Centers for Disease Control. Heart Failure Mortality Statistics, five year age-adjusted, 2001–2006, ftp://ftp.cdc.gov/pub/Health_Statistics/NCHS/Datasets/DVS/mortality/mort2006ps.zip

45. National Center for Health Statistics, Department of Vital Statistics, Centers for Disease Control. Heart Failure Mortality Statisitics, five year age-adjusted, 2001–2006, ftp://ftp.cdc.gov/pub/Health_Statistics/NCHS/Datasets/DVS/mortality/mort2006ps.zip

46. National Center for Health Statistics, Department of Vital Statistics, Centers for Disease Control. Heart Failure Mortality Statisitics, five year age-adjusted, 2001–2006, ftp://ftp.cdc.gov/pub/Health_Statistics/NCHS/Datasets/DVS/mortality/mort2006ps.zip

47. National Center for Health Statistics, Department of Vital Statistics, Centers for Disease Control. Heart Failure Mortality Statistics, five year age-adjusted,

2001–2006, ftp://ftp.cdc.gov/pub/Health_Statistics/NCHS/Datasets/DVS/mortality/mort2006ps.zip

48. "United States Cancer Statistics (USCS): 2009 State vs. National Comparisons," Centers for Disease Control and Prevention, accessed April 4, 2013, http://apps.nccd.cdc.gov/uscs/statevsnational.aspx.

49. "United States Cancer Statistics (USCS): 2009 State vs. National Comparisons," accessed March 27, 2013, http://wonder.cdc.gov/controller/datarequest/D51.

50. "United States Cancer Statistics (USCS): 2009 State vs. National Comparisons," Cancer Mortality-Ovarian Cancer, accessed 3/27/2013, http://wonder.cdc.gov/controller/datarequest/D51.

Men's Health Care

The Best and the Worst in the United States

In reviewing criteria for male health care, I looked at heart disease, because it is the number-one cause of death in the United States, so cardiac deaths are one of the health measures. I then took the Centers for Disease Control and Prevention cardiac death data for adult males for each state and compared it to the national average. If the state had fewer deaths from heart failure than the national average, it generated a positive number, and more deaths than the national average created a negative scoring factor for the state rankings.

The second-greatest cause of death in the country is now cancer, which includes many different types of cancer, but for purposes of this analysis only prostate cancer deaths were analyzed. Prostate cancer is highly treatable if found early, and therefore this is also an indication of decent primary health care.

Finally, because the ability to pay for health care services and evidence of health insurance have a strong correlation with health care access, the overall levels of insurance coverage, including employer-provided health care programs, state Medicaid levels, and uninsured statistics were also evaluated. States with higher levels of an insured population scored better than states that reported low levels of insurance. The state levels were compared to the national average for insurance coverage to develop the measurement benchmark.

INSURED/UNINSURED STATISTICS

Please refer to the Kaiser State Health Facts Mens Health Policy Insurance Survey for 2010-2011, for adult males between the ages of 19 and 64, unless otherwise noted.[1]

Based on the Kaiser Foundation's State Insurance Facts Comparison, for the 2009 calendar year the uninsured population of the United States was 24 percent for all adult men between the ages of nineteen and sixty-four. Reviewing the same data for the 2010 calendar year report, the level of uninsured adult men in the country was 26 percent.[2] This change reflects the steep job losses across the country, in the worst economic collapse since the Great Depression. However, by the following year, 2011, uninsured men totaled only 23% of the adult male population in the country. By examining state-wide data (and the District of Columbia) I assessed changes in the type of health insurance and found that most states experienced an increase in men enrolled on Medicaid or other state-subsidized health care programs.

Least Insured

Using the Kaiser Family Foundation State Health Facts Men's Health Insurance Survey for 2010-2011, to determine state rankings, I found that the state with the most uninsured adult men was Texas with 33 percent of its adult males lacking medical insurance. By 2011, 5 percent of Texas men were enrolled on Medicaid[3] and another 4 percent on other subsidized state health care programs. This was followed closely by New Mexico, where 32 percent of adult males lacked any medical insurance and 12 percent were enrolled on Medicaid and other public programs. Though previously Louisiana was in the bottom group for men without medical insurance, it has been usurped by Nevada, which reports that 31 percent of its men lacked insurance in the 2010-2011 calendar year.[4] Additionally, 5% of Nevada men were enrolled on Medicaid and another 4% on other subsidized medical plans.

Though nationally, the level of women enrolled on state Medicaid programs, as revealed in chapter 17 is greater than men, as you can see, there are many millions of men in the country who also rely on this coverage for health care access. One wonders at what point the number of uninsured citizens becomes the tipping point for the health care safety net. In other words, how much more "free health care" can hospitals provide and still remain solvent? Second, how much more can the private-sector medical-insurance plans continue to subsidize the losses the hospitals take on the uninsured population? Obviously, this was a consideration in the federal insurance exchanges and the subsidies the federal government plans to pay to increase the number of Americans with health insurance, which increases their ability to buy health services.

Most Insured

The state with the fewest uninsured adult men under sixty-five was Massachusetts with just 7 percent of its adult men lacking health insurance in

2011. Massachusetts also reported 18 percent of its adult men were enrolled on Medicaid.[5] In second place with a high level of health insurance for men was Hawaii with 13 percent lacking health insurance by 2011. Hawaii reports that 10 percent of its men were on subsidized public health-insurance programs in the same time frame. In third place for top honors was Minnesota with 14 percent of its adult males without health insurance by 2011. Minnesota indicates that 10 percent of its men were also covered on Medicaid and another 2% on other subsidized public medical programs for the 2010-2011 period. These citations were all drawn from the previously mentioned Kaiser Foundation 2011 Men's Health Insurance Survey.

States that reported the fewest number of uninsured men also reported substantial populations on state-subsidized medical programs. What is that economic adage—the government steps in when the private sector fails?

Availability of Employer-Sponsored Medical Insurance

Access to health care is related to the levels of clinical reimbursement, and based on the extent that an individual is insured, more clinicians will be available to provide treatment. I reviewed the statehealthfacts.org data for employers providing health insurance. Here are the best and worst in that category, according to the 2010 Kaiser Foundation Survey.[6]

States with the Most Generous Employers. The state boasting the most men covered through employer medical plans at 71% was none other than New Hampshire, the "Live free or die" state.[7] Hawaii continues to maintain a high level of employer provided insurance for its men at 69%, followed by Massachusetts with 68% of its men showing work-related insurance coverage. The citations were all drawn from the same Kaiser Foundation State Health Facts Men's Health Insurance Survey for 2010-2011, as cited above.

States with Tightwad Employers. New Mexico employers provided medical insurance to their male employees only 46.5 (rounded to 47%) percent of the time by 2011. In second place for low marks was Montana, with just 49 percent of its employers providing insurance by 2011.[8] Tied for third place are Florida and California, both showing adult men receive employer based medical insurance only 52% of the time.[9] This is quite a reversal of fortune for California, which used to boast a high level of employer-based medical insurance. Meanwhile, states that used to be at the bottom for providing medical insurance through the workplace, such as Texas and Mississippi have moved upward on Maslow's Scale of the Hierarchy of Human Needs, reporting 55% and 54% respectively for men covered by work place insurance plans.[10] These states place an extreme burden on their hospitals, which are mandated by the federal Emergency Medical Treatment and Active Labor[11] Act to treat all patients regardless of their ability to pay. It is also sad to see so many people working without basic health insurance.

HEALTH MEASURES

Cardiac Care

Methods for Health Assessment.   I reviewed the Centers for Disease Control and Prevention mortality data for heart disease during a fiveyear period from 2001 to 2006 by state, broken down by sex for those age thirty-five and up, to arrive at my conclusions for state rankings on heart disease.[12] The District of Columbia is included as well.

Best Places for Men to Avoid Death from Heart Disease.   If you are a man, the best place to have heart disease is New Mexico, which had 64 percent fewer deaths from heart disease than the national norm of 529 deaths per 100,000 males above the age of thirty-five. In second place we have the usually healthy Colorado, which had 38 percent fewer deaths from this condition than the nation's average. Utah came in third place, with 33 percent fewer deaths caused by heart conditions for males. Gee guys, it looks like the great wide open is the place to be for a healthy heart.[13]

Worst Places to Live if You Are a Man with Heart Disease.   The worst place for men to have heart disease is none other than Mississippi, with 27 percent more deaths from heart disease than the national norm during the same five-year period. The roll call for the second-worst performer for heart-disease management goes to the District of Columbia, with 22 percent more deaths from heart disease than the nation's average. In third place for the worst mortality from heart disease for men is Oklahoma, posting 149 more deaths than the national average of 529 per 100,000 men.[14]

Cancer

Methods for Health Assessment.   For men's cancer-survival conclusions, I used the 2006 Centers for Disease Control and Prevention age-adjusted cancer rates from ten primary sites with the highest disease incidence within each state. I reviewed the state's data for cancer mortality and compared it to the national average of deaths per 100,000 men.[15]

Prostate Cancer Survival.   In case men don't already want to move to Hawaii, here is another reason to book your passage; this state has the least number of deaths from prostate cancer. According to the Centers for Disease Control and Prevention 2006 data, the Aloha State had a mere 13.4 deaths from prostate cancer per 100,000 men, which was 43 percent less than the national average! Alaska, another end destination for the testosterone set, posted 22 percent fewer prostate-cancer deaths than the national average of 23.6 deaths per 100,000 men. And in third place, we find Florida, with 19.6 fewer deaths per 100,000 men, 17 percent lower than the national mean.

Worst Places for Prostate Cancer.   Unfortunately, the District of Columbia once again has the worst performance metric, with 73 percent more prostate cancer deaths than the national average, a whopping 40.8 versus 23.6 for every 100,000 men in 2006. If it is not tough enough living in this expensive crime-infested city, your chances of dying from cancer are significantly higher as well. Also, to acknowledge the reality of disparity in health care, the majority of residents of Washington, D.C., are minority populations. However, not to be outdone, Louisiana has the second-worst death statistic for prostate cancer, 19 percent above the national average with 29 deaths per 100,000 men. And again, the population of Louisiana has many poor black Americans, especially in New Orleans. In third place for this dubious honor, we have Alabama with a prostate cancer death rate that was 16 percent higher than the national average in 2006. This seems to be a southern phenomenon, as these other states also posted a death rate for prostate cancer that was significantly higher than the national average: Georgia, North Carolina, and South Carolina.

HEALTHPOLICYMAVEN™ SCORECARD

The scorecard in figure 18.1 shows the top 10 percent and bottom 10 percent of health performers throughout the country in 2011. For information on how the other states performed, go to the Kaiser Foundation State Health Facts Mens Insurance Survey, adult men 19-64, state-by-state for 2010-2011.

Men's Health Scorecard-2013											
Measures	Nat'l Av.	NM	CO	MN	UT	AZ	KY	AL	OK	D.C.	MS
Ranking		1	2	3	4	5	47	48	49	50	51
Men with any medical insurance	77%	68%	78%	86%	81%	76%	77%	79%	73%	84%	78%
Men covered by employer medical plans	58%	47%	60%	67%	68%	54%	56%	60%	57%	58%	54%
Medicaid enrollment	12%	12%	7%	10%	5%	12%	14%	6%	6%	16%	7%
Prostate Cancer Deaths	23.6	26	22.5	23.3	26.7	19.1	25.8	28.8	22.8	40.8	32.6
Heart Failure Deaths	529	322	382	400	398	418	647	660	678	681	720
Total Score		205	148	129	128	115	-120	-136	-148	-169	-200
Notes:											

High score means the state had lower mortality figures & a high level of insurance statewide.
Insurance and Medicaid eligibility based on the Kaiser Foundation 2011 Calendar year Survey.
Mortality data is from the Centers for Disease Control 2006 reports per 100,000 lives for both prostate cancer and heart failure deaths.

Figure 18.1.   Men's Health Scorecard

NOTES

1. Kaiser Family Foundation State Health Facts, Mens Health Policy, Mens Insurance Survey for 2010-2011, accessed April 19, 2013, http://www.statehealthfacts.org/comparetable.jsp?ind=653&cat=3&sub=178&yr=274&typ=2.

2. "Health Insurance Coverage of Men 19–64, States (2010–2011), U.S. (2011)," Statehealthfacts.org, accessed March 17, 2013, www.statehealthfacts.org/comparebar.jsp?ind=653&cat=3.

3. http://www.statehealthfacts.org/profileind.jsp?cmprgn=45&cat=4&rgn=1& sub=52 as of 4/5/2013 as of April 5, 2013.

4. Kaiser Family Foundation State Health Facts, Mens Health Policy, Mens Insurance Survey for 2010-2011, accessed April 19, 2013, http://www.statehealthfacts.org/comparetable.jsp?ind=653&cat=3&sub=178&yr=274&typ=2.

5. Kaiser Family Foundation State Health Facts, Mens Health Policy, Mens Insurance Survey for 2010-2011, accessed April 19, 2013.

6. www.statehealthfacts.org/comparemaptable.jsp?ind=653&cat=3&sub=178&yr=252&typ=2.

7. Kaiser Family Foundation State Health Facts, Mens Health Policy, Mens Insurance Survey for 2010-2011, accessed April 19, 2013, http://www.statehealthfacts.org/comparetable.jsp?ind=653&cat=3&sub=178&yr=274&typ=2.

8. Kaiser Family Foundation State Health Facts, Mens Health Policy, Mens Insurance Survey for 2010-2011, accessed April 19, 2013, http://www.statehealthfacts.org/comparetable.jsp?ind=653&cat=3&sub=178&yr=274&typ=2.

9. Kaiser Family Foundation State Health Facts, Mens Health Policy, Mens Insurance Survey for 2010-2011, accessed April 19, 2013, http://www.statehealthfacts.org/comparetable.jsp?ind=653&cat=3&sub=178&yr=274&typ=2.

10. Kaiser Family Foundation State Health Facts, Mens Health Policy, Mens Insurance Survey for 2010-2011, accessed April 19, 2013, http://www.statehealthfacts.org/comparetable.jsp?ind=653&cat=3&sub=178&yr=274&typ=2.

11. http://www.cms.gov/Regulations-and Guidance/Legislation/EMTALA/index.html?redirect=/emtala/

12. "Interactive Atlas of Heart Disease and Stroke," Centers for Disease Control and Prevention, accessed March 17, 2013, http://apps.nccd.cdc.gov/giscvh2/Default.aspx.

13. CDC, National Center for Health Statistics, Department of Vital Statistics, Mortality Tables, 2006, accessed April 8, 2013, ftp://ftp.cdc.gov/pub/Health_Statistics/NCHS/Datasets/DVS/mortality/mort2006ps.zip.

14. CDC, National Center for Health Statistics, Department of Vital Statistics, Mortality Tables, 2006, accessed April 8, 2013, ftp://ftp.cdc.gov/pub/Health_Statistics/NCHS/Datasets/DVS/mortality/mort2006ps.zip.

15. "United States Cancer Statistics (USCS): 2009 State vs. National Comparisons," Centers for Disease Control and Prevention, accessed March 17, 2013, http://apps.nccd.cdc.gov/uscs/statevsnational.aspx.

· *19* ·

Children's Health Care

The Best and the Worst in the United States

$\mathcal{C}$hildren are our most precious resource, and the states that do the most to provide for their children's health are acknowledged in this analysis, along with the laggards. In my algorithm of children's health, the following criteria were built into the scoring metrics: access to primary care as reinforced by prevalence of medical insurance coverage, prenatal and postnatal care as indicated by low infant-mortality rates, and routine care follow-up as evidenced by immunization records. Also, due to the obesity epidemic in America, statewide obesity rates are compared against the appalling national average of 31.6 percent of American kids who are obese.

Thanks to the wildly successful Supplemental Children's Health Insurance Program or SCHIP, which is a federally subsidized expansion of state Medicaid programs, most of the nation's children now have health insurance. The national rate of children with health insurance is 89.56 (rounded up to 90%) percent according to the nonprofit Kaiser Foundation's survey on children's health insurance for the calendar year 2010, which was posted in October of 2012.[1] The national proportion of children's insurance provided by employers or through privately purchased insurance is now only 50 percent, with the balance provided through state Medicaid programs and other publicly funded programs, as shown in the most recent 2011 Kaiser Foundation State Health Facts survey.[2] For example, Washington State's Basic Health Plan covers families with a higher income threshold than just the Medicaid program. Many other states also have programs like this, including Hawaii's state-subsidized insurance plan, Oregon's Family Health Insurance Assistance, Minnesota Cares, and Massachusetts Medical Security Plan.

Insurance Coverage Citations

Citations on levels of insurance coverage by state were derived from the Kaiser Family Foundation's State Health Facts Survey for the 2010 calendar year, which results were posted in 2012,[3] as revealed in the introduction above and cited in chapter the end notes, unless otherwise specified.

Childhood Immunization Citations

Immunization rates come from the Centers for Disease Control 2010 survey for children to thirty-months of age and exhibits 19.1 and 19.2 show the specific findings for the high and low immunization rates. This data also comes from chapter 1.[4]

Childhood Obesity Citations

The following national childhood obesity rankings and statewide performance measures come from the Kaiser Foundation's State Health Facts Survey of Childhood Obesity from 2007.[5]

FIRST PLACE: MASSACHUSETTS

Based on the 2011 survey data, Massachusetts is proud to be the state with the highest level of children covered by medical plans at 97%. The abbreviated version of their state motto is "peace under liberty" and 87.55% of their children received the recommended early childhood vaccinations.[6] And they have the lowest infant mortality rate in the country, at 4.9 deaths per 1,000 live births, equal to many European countries.[7] As far as obese children, the birthplace of our revolution for emancipation manages to squeak in just below the national average at 30 percent.[8]

SECOND PLACE: NORTH DAKOTA

North Dakota is now in second place for children's health with 92 percent of all children enrolled on medical plans by 2011.[9] In the "liberty and union, now, and forever," state, their children have an immunization rate of 87.75 percent, an infant-mortality rate of 5.9 babies per 1,000 live births, and only 25.7 percent of their children ranked as obese.[10]

THIRD PLACE: NEW HAMPSHIRE

In third place for children's overall health care is New Hampshire, the "live free or die" state," reporting that 93 percent of their children have health insurance,[11] an immunization rate of 89.55 percent,[12] a low infant-mortality rate of 5.6 deaths per 1,000 babies,[13] and it also just squeaked under the national average for childhood obesity with 29.40 percent of its child population ranked as obese.[14]

BEST STATES FOR CHILDREN'S HEALTH-INSURANCE COVERAGE

This measure of insurance coverage represents two things: the prevalence of employer-provided health care plans coupled with the degree of coverage provided through state medical programs for lower-income families. California used to be in first place for providing insurance for its children, reporting 97 percent in 2008, but that fell to 89 percent in 2009,[15] as reported in the Kaiser Family Foundation 2010 survey.

Many of the people who are enrolled in government-subsidized Medicaid insurance plans are working either full or part time. I can recall learning of these families when I used to conduct annual benefit plan enrollments for corporate clients. There is something wrong with the health care infrastructure when someone works full time and cannot afford their employer's medical insurance. Or worse yet, there are those working full time that don't even have an employer-based medical insurance plan. If this is how the country provides health care access, should it be so laissez-faire?

Lest we become overly confident on our provision of children's health care, the increases in levels of insurance primarily came as their families dropped into poverty status, qualifying them for Medicaid and other state programs for low-income families, as cited by the Kaiser Foundation's report, "Rising Unemployment, Medicaid, and the Uninsured," which was published in 2009.[16] According to the University of Michigan, 24 percent of the country's children live in poverty.[17] This statistic includes only those poor enough to qualify for federal or state subsidies for health insurance, food assistance, housing, or other means to live. It does not include the near-poor or the working poor in the country. The number of children living in poverty in the United States has increased from 10 percent in 1980 to nearly 25 percent now, which is an astounding statistic for one of the wealthiest countries in the world.[18]

Gold–Medal Winners

In the current Kaiser Foundation State Health Facts annual health insurance survey,[19] the following states all continue to have at least 95 percent of their children covered by insurance: Maine, Vermont, and Massachusetts. So once again the race is neck-and-neck between the Northeastern states for best-in-class health care awards.

Silver–Medal Winners

States continuing to report between 90 percent and 95 percent of their children are covered on health insurance, besting the national average of 90 percent, include[20]: Connecticut, Delaware, Illinois, Indiana, Iowa, Kentucky, Maryland, Minnesota, New York, North Dakota, Ohio, Oregon, Pennsylvania, Rhode Island, South Dakota, Tennessee, Virginia, and Washington.

It should be noted that there has been a significant increase in federally subsidized children's health insurance because of the national financial melt down and subsequent high unemployment rates in the United States since the fourth quarter of 2007. Not all states benefited from the children's health insurance plan because their poverty levels weren't low enough, such as California, which reports that 89 percent of its children have insurance.

WORST STATES FOR CHILDREN'S HEALTH INSURANCE

Texas has the lowest percentage of its children covered by insurance in the nation at just 83 percent.[21] Next for the low-scoring group is Florida, which tied with Nevada, reporting that only 84 percent of its youth were covered by insurance. Arizona is in third place, with 85 percent of its children covered by insurance.[22]

INFANT DEATHS

As cited in chapter 1 of the book, the United States spends 25 percent more than any other industrialized country for health care, and it does not have the lowest infant death rates,[23] which has long been a bone of contention for public health advocates. Infant mortality is an indicator of a variety of behavioral and public health choices, including adequate prenatal and postnatal care on the one end and the high rate of premature births on the other. The latter increases the incidence of multiple births and the likelihood of low-birth-weight babies. Also, as a former insurance broker, whenever a client had an employee who gave birth to a premature baby, we knew that was an automatic $50,000 first-year claim, with a lifetime cost of easily $600,000 to $1,000,000 for the corporate client, and this was thirteen years ago. Most severely premature babies have chronic medical problems, including under developed lungs, vision problems, and developmental disabilities.[24]

According to the Library of Medicine from the National Institutes of Health (NIH), the cost of premature births in the United States was an average of $51,600 in 2005,[25] versus the average newborn expense of approximately $4,500. Very preterm infants are considered those born between twenty-eight and thirty-one weeks versus the normal gestation range of thirty-seven to thirty-nine weeks. If the country could reduce the number of very preterm infants, it was estimated it would save 10.2 billion dollars for Medicaid and other public funding programs. This figure is based the NIH comprehensive report on premature births in the United States for 2005, as cited above. The report reveals that 38 percent of premature birth costs are born by the private insurance sector, but 39 percent of that total cost of preemie health care comes from government programs and charity care. Certainly this is one of the areas where the country should focus in order to reduce the cost of health care while simultaneously improving infant health outcomes.

The United States does not have a standard health policy for assessing birth viability in terms of weight or organ function, nor does it provide routine standards of care for all pregnant mothers across the country. In fact, with the "green card" requirements enacted in 2007, only immigrants who can show proof of legal residency can enroll on Medicaid or other government programs. This restriction also applies to their children, who may be born here, but because their parents may not be able to show proof of legal residency, will be denied access to primary health care. This also means that more immigrant mothers, almost all of whom are here to work, will be forced to go without health care during pregnancy because they are not eligible for Medicaid. That said, federal law requires all hospitals in the United States to treat any patient who is in need of urgent care, until stabilized, and able to be discharged, regardless of their ability to pay. But this is hardly an optimal method for maternity care.

We are all paying for this uncoordinated prenatal approach with our high health care premiums, diminished resources available for the allocation of health care for other patients, and the cost of our public programs. Because U.S. medical policy is largely driven by reimbursement through private-sector insurance, residents who lack this coverage do not have the same access to health care. For example, if you are a non-English-speaking person in Washington, D.C., you will not have the same access to primary health care for two reasons: Medicaid pays so little to doctors that many doctors will not accept Medicaid patients with language barriers. Thus, covering more people on Medicaid does not mean they will have access to primary care. Though federally qualified health plans seek to remedy this problem through community health centers, it is a patchwork of health care and not a cohesive remedy.

How the United States Compares to the World

As previously cited in chapter 1, the World Bank's Development Indicators, show the United States had an infant-mortality rate of 6.7 lives per 1,000 births in 2009, whereas the CIA World Facts Book for 2009 results lists 6.22 deaths per 1,000 live births. This places the United States just ahead of Poland and the Faroe Islands (Danish property in the Atlantic) but behind Croatia and the U.S. territory of Guam, in 46th place in the world. Yes, that is 46th, behind so many countries that have much fewer resources and spend less money on health care than Americans.[26] Here is a partial list of countries that have lower infant mortality than the United States: Cuba, Taiwan, and Canada, pretty much all of Europe, all of Scandinavia, New Zealand, Japan, Bermuda, and Singapore. Singapore was number 1 for the lowest infant death rate with only 2.3 deaths per 1,000 live births, a third of the U.S. infant mortality! It is not surprising that Singapore is also a leader in medical tourism; apparently people there know how to deliver quality health care on a budget.[27,28]

Best States for Low Infant Mortality

Number 1 in keeping infants alive is Massachusetts, with a mortality rate of 4.9 for every 1,000 live births. This places it equal to the United Kingdom and New Zealand. In second place it's a dead heat between Minnesota and Utah, with a mortality rate of 5 deaths per 1,000 infants. In third place for this performance honor is Washington State with 5.1 deaths per 1,000 babies. Thanks, guys, for raising the standards in the United States.[29]

Worst States for Infant Mortality

Fifty-first: District of Columbia.   The absolute worst place in the union if you are looking to keep your baby alive is none other than the District of Columbia, with an infant-mortality rate of 12.6 deaths per 1,000 births! Those poor residents of D.C. sure seem to show up in the worst places for health measures. This is double the national average for infant deaths and makes this performance equal to those of many developing countries, including Panama, Qatar, and Botswana. Surely the United States can do a better job of preventing infant mortality than this!

Fiftieth: Mississippi. Coming in second for the worst infant-mortality rate in the United States is none other than Mississippi with 10.6 deaths per 1,000 infants.

Forty-ninth: Louisiana. Louisiana has the third-worst infant-mortality rate, with 10 deaths per 1,000 babies.

These statistics were all taken from the nonprofit Kaiser Foundation's state-healthfacts.org survey on infant mortality and births from 2004–2006[30] and also fact-checked for 2009 data.

Taking a deeper look into these troubling statistics, I reviewed potential causes for these deaths including low birth weight, and none of these states were in the top group for low-birth-weight babies. I then looked at preterm births, and 16 percent of all births in the District of Columbia were premature, 16.3 percent for Louisiana, and 18.7 percent in Mississippi.[31] What is going on in Mississippi? When you compare these metrics with the national average for low-birth-weight infants of 12.8 percent, this is troubling.

Finally, I viewed the rankings of premature births by ethnicity, finding black Americans experienced premature births 19 percent of the time in the District of Columbia. In other states with large populations of black persons, I found 21.5 percent of babies were born prematurely in Louisiana and 22.9 percent in Mississippi. Here are the rates of Hispanics born prematurely in the same locations: D.C., 13.8 percent, Louisiana, 11.7 percent, and 16.6 percent of Mississippi infants. The white population premature births were: D.C., 10.8 percent, Louisiana, 13.3 percent, and Mississippi, 15 percent. The difference in patient outcomes is a disparity in health care. So when you hear the term *health disparity*, it means not everyone is getting the same services in a given region, hence, the differences in outcomes, which are most pronounced when you have children dying of preventive causes. Though there has been some movement to correct these differences, especially with the Obama protocols, it will be a number of years before the new programs will show an impact, certainly later than 2014.

PREVALENCE OF CHILDHOOD IMMUNIZATIONS

Based on the Centers for Disease Control and Prevention survey for 2010, here are the U.S. vaccination rates for children to thirty-five months of age:

diphtheria and pertussis (whooping cough); polio; measles, mumps, and rubella; (Hib) influenza B; hepatitis B; chickenpox or varicella; PCV or childhood pneumonia; and hepatitis.[32]

States with the Highest Degree of Childhood Immunizations

Top states for childhood immunizations are: (1) New Hampshire at 89.55 percent, (2) Virginia at 89.01 percent, (3) North Dakota at 87.75 percent, followed closely by (4) Massachusetts, with 87.25 percent of its children receiving all recommended early childhood vaccinations.[33] Figure 19.2 (below) shows the proportion of children nineteen months to thirty-five months of age who received all of the vaccinations shown. For the statistical layperson, immediately next to the percentage is a statistical term indicating the degree of confidence level for the calculation. What this indicates is the width of the confidence interval in terms of a data measure to statistically repeat the findings.

States with the Lowest Degree of Childhood Immunizations

States in the bottom percentile for levels of children receiving the recommended childhood vaccination are: (51) Missouri at 73.66 percent, (50) Montana at 75.95 percent, (49) Idaho at 77.38 percent, and (48) Indiana at 77.87 percent. The dearth of childhood immunizations could reflect the limited access to primary care in some rural areas. It may also indicate less sense of urgency to vaccinate for diseases they have never heard of in their locale. I am not going to get into the concept of *herd immunity* here except to say that if enough of a given population is not vaccinated, the *entire* population becomes at risk for a disease outbreak, which only takes one infected person.

HEALTHPOLICYMAVEN™ SCORECARD

This scorecard (see figure 19.3) incorporates all the data for the four criteria: insurance coverage, infant mortality, rate of immunization compliance for children's health measures, and obesity levels. The ranking includes the best and the worst for an overall ranking. This is not meant to be a comprehensive statement but rather a snapshot with a few pearls of wisdom thrown in from a policymaking perspective. I compared the state proportion of insured children to the national average in order to rank levels of insurance. I also subtracted the state infant-mortality rate from the national

2010	US, National Immunization Survey, Q1/2010-Q4/2010[†]													
Immuniza	3+DTaP	4+DTaP[‡]	3+Polio[§]	1+MMR[‖]	3+Hib[¶]	Hib-PS[**]	Hib-FS[††]	3+HepB[‡‡]	Hep B Birth dose[§§]	1+Var[‖‖]	3+PCV[¶¶]	4+PCV[***]	2+HepA[†††]	Complianc e Totals
US National	95.0±0.6	84.4±1.0	93.3±0.7	91.5±0.7	90.4±0.9	92.2±0.8	66.8±1.3	91.8±0.7	64.1±1.3	90.4±0.8	92.6±0.8	83.3±1.0	49.7±1.4	83.50
Idaho	90.8±4.5	77.9±5.7	89.2±4.7	87.2±5.0	77.7±6.2	82.3±5.9	53.3±6.9	86.8±4.9	65.2±6.4	83.7±5.1	88.0±4.9	79.7±5.5	44.2±6.8	77.38
Indiana	93.2±3.4	81.6±5.2	92.1±3.5	92.3±3.5	87.8±4.3	89.0±4.2	65.1±6.0	91.7±3.4	77.9±5.1	88.5±4.2	91.1±3.7	80.2±5.3	46.9±6.5	77.87
Missouri	92.6±3.4	80.3±5.2	89.9±3.8	90.4±3.9	87.8±4.4	90.8±3.7	64.1±6.4	89.2±4.0	64.8±6.5	86.7±4.4	87.8±4.3	76.2±5.6	44.4±6.5	73.66
Montana	88.0±5.0	76.6±6.2	84.3±5.4	85.1±5.6	80.8±5.8	84.0±5.4	60.5±7.0	87.0±4.4	67.8±6.4	80.6±5.9	84.5±5.3	72.6±6.5	35.5±6.6	75.95

Figure 19.1.   US, National Immunization Survey-Lowest States

2010

US, National Immunization Survey, Q1/2010-Q4/2010[I]

Immunization	3+DTaP[v]	4+DTaP[‡]	3+Polio[§]	1+MMR[||]	3+Hib[¶]	Hib-PS[**]	Hib-FS[††]	3+HepB[‡‡]	Hep B Birth dose[§§]	1+Var[||||]	3+PCV[¶¶]	4+PCV[***]	2+HepA[†††]	Compliance Totals
US National	95.0±0.6	84.4±1.0	93.3±0.7	91.5±0.7	90.4±0.9	92.2±0.8	66.8±1.3	91.8±0.7	64.1±1.3	90.4±0.8	92.6±0.8	83.3±1.0	49.7±1.4	83.50
Massachusetts	97.7±2.9	91.0±4.3	95.6±3.4	92.3±4.3	95.7±3.3	96.2±3.3	73.7±6.4	95.8±2.5	67.3±6.5	91.5±3.9	95.9±3.3	90.4±4.2	51.1±7.3	87.25
New Hampshire	99.5±0.7	92.0±5.1	97.8±2.0	95.8±3.0	99.5±0.8	99.5±0.8	75.1±6.7	97.2±1.8	62.8±7.8	92.8±4.5	99.2±1.0	93.2±4.0	59.7±8.2	89.55
North Dakota	96.8±2.4	85.3±4.8	96.1±2.8	92.6±3.5	90.6±3.7	93.0±3.3	70.4±5.9	98.3±1.5	79.5±5.6	90.5±3.8	97.2±2.3	89.4±4.2	61.1±6.5	87.75
Virginia	96.4±2.6	88.3±4.5	93.5±3.3	92.3±3.5	91.8±3.7	93.3±3.5	68.1±6.3	87.0±4.9	58.3±6.7	91.6±3.3	93.6±3.3	84.9±4.8	50.0±6.8	89.01

Figure 19.2. US, National Immunization Survey-Top States

average, which produced either a positive or negative result. Massachusetts had the lowest infant-mortality rate, reporting only 4.9 deaths per 1,000 births. And finally, for the immunization score, I compared the state's proportion to the national average for each vaccine. The state's immunization level was based on its reported compliance for each vaccine and then averaged for a total compliance score per state.

HEALTHPOLICYMAVEN™ SCORECARD

Healthpolicymaven™ statistics as cited above were drawn from the Kaiser Family Foundation State Health Facts Survey results for the 2010 calendar year that was published in 2012, the Centers for Disease Control 2010 Immunization data for children, and the Kaiser State Health Facts Surveys Survey on Childhood Obesity of 2007, all previously cited in this chapter. Additionally, the following sources were used to cite Infant Mortality rates; The CIA World Factbook Infant Mortality Rankings for 2009 and the Kaiser Family Foundation State Health Facts Report on Infant Mortality for 2006-2008 as previously cited. The scorecard includes the top and bottom 10 percent of states based on their overall performance compared to the reported national averages for the following criteria: levels of insurance, infant deaths, immunization rates, and childhood obesity. Rankings include the District of Columbia. Refer to figure 19.3 for details.

Childrens Health Scorecard-2013											
Measures	Ntl Average	MA	ND	NH	MN	WI	TX	SC	MO	NV	MS
Ranking		**1**	**2**	**3**	**4**	**5**	**47**	**48**	**49**	**50**	**51**
Insured percentile	90.00	97.00	92.00	93.00	93.00	95.00	83.00	86.00	90.00	81.00	88.00
Infant Deaths	6.8	4.9	5.9	5.6	5	6.3	6.3	9.0	7.5	6.2	10.6
Immuniza tion rate	83.30	87.25	87.75	89.55	82.60	85.09	83.78	84.78	73.66	78.82	84.21
Obesity Rate	31.60	30.00	25.70	29.40	23.10	27.90	32.20	33.70	31.00	34.20	44.40
Final Score		**14.45**	**13.25**	**12.65**	**12.60**	**10.99**	**-6.62**	**-6.82**	**-9.74**	**-15.48**	**-17.69**
Immunization rate is recommended childhood vaccinations except rhotovirus for CDC 2010.											
Data for insured children comes from the Kaiser Family Foundation for 2011 Cal. Yr.											
Infant mortality rates come from 2009 Kaiser Foundation State health facts.											

Figure 19.3. Children's' Health Scorecard

Top 10 percent

The best places to live for children's overall health in the United States are none other than New Hampshire, Massachusetts, North Dakota, and Wisconsin.

Bottom 10 percent

The worst places to live in terms of children's health care are Mississippi, Nevada, Missouri, Texas, and South Carolina.

NOTES

1. "Health Insurance Coverage of Children 0–18, States (2010–2011), U.S. (2011)," Statehealthfacts.org, accessed March 17, 2013, www.statehealthfacts.org/comparetable.jsp?ind=127&cat=3.

2. http://www.statehealthfacts.org/comparecat.jsp?cat=3&rgn=6&rgn=1

3. Kaiser Foundation State Health Facts Children's Health Insurance Survey posted February of 2010, accessed February of 2011 http://www.statehealthfacts.org/comparetable.jsp?ind=127&cat=3

4. Centers for Disease Control, Childhood Immunization Statistics for 2010, accessed 4/7/3013, http://www.cdc.gov/vaccines/stats-surv/nis/data/tables_2010.htm

5. Kaiser State Health Facts Childhood Obesity Survey, data from 2007, accessed April 7, 2013, http://www.statehealthfacts.org/comparetable.jsp?ind=51&cat=2&sub=14&yr=62&typ=2

6. Centers for Disease Control, Childhood Immunization Statistics for 2010, accessed 4/7/3013, http://www.cdc.gov/vaccines/stats-surv/nis/data/tables_2010.htm

7. "Infant Mortality Rate (Deaths per 1,000 Live Births), Linked Files, 2006–2008," Statehealthfacts.org, accessed March 17, 2013, www.statehealthfacts.org/comparemaptable.jsp?ind=47&cat=2.

8. Kaiser State Health Facts Childhood Obesity Survey, data from 2007, accessed April 7, 2013, http://www.statehealthfacts.org/comparetable.jsp?ind=51&cat=2&sub=14&yr=62&typ=2

9. http://www.statehealthfacts.org/comparetable.jsp?ind=127&cat=3.accessed April 8, 2013.

10. Kaiser State Health Facts Childhood Obesity Survey, data from 2007, accessed April 7, 2013, http://www.statehealthfacts.org/comparetable.jsp?ind=51&cat=2&sub=14&yr=62&typ=2

11. "Health Insurance Coverage of Children 0–18, states (2010–2011), U.S. (2011)," Statehealthfacts.org, accessed March 17, 2013, www.statehealthfacts.org/comparetable.jsp?ind=127&cat

12. Centers for Disease Control, Childhood Immunization Statistics for 2010, accessed 4/7/3013, http://www.cdc.gov/vaccines/stats-surv/nis/data/tables_2010.htm

13. "Infant Mortality Rate (Deaths per 1,000 Live Births), Linked Files, 2006–2008," Statehealthfacts.org, accessed March 17, 2013, www.statehealthfacts.org/comparemaptable.jsp?ind=47&cat=2

14. Kaiser State Health Facts Childhood Obesity Survey, data from 2007, accessed April 7, 2013, http://www.statehealthfacts.org/comparetable.jsp?ind=51&cat=2&sub=14&yr=62&typ=2

15. "California," Statehealthfacts.org, accessed March 17, 2013, www.statehealthfacts.org/profileglance.jsp?rgn=6&rgn=1.

16. http://www.kff.org/uninsured/upload/7850.pdf.

17. "Poverty in the United States, Frequently Asked Questions," National Poverty Center, accessed March 17, 2013, www.npc.umich.edu/poverty/#5.

18. U.S. Bureau of the Census, "Income Alternative Poverty Estimates in the United States: 2003," Report P60, n. 227, tables B-1 and B-3, pp. 18, 20.

19. http://www.statehealthfacts.org/comparetable.jsp?ind=127&cat=3., accessed April 8, 2013.

20. http://www.statehealthfacts.org/comparetable.jsp?ind=127&cat=3., accessed April 8, 2013.

21. http://www.statehealthfacts.org/comparetable.jsp?ind=127&cat=3., accessed April 8, 2013.

22. "Health Insurance Coverage of Children 0–18, states (2010–2011), U.S. (2011)."

23. 37th-Measuring the U.S. Health Care System, Health Policy and Reform, New England Journal of Medicine, Jan 14, 2010, 363:98-99 and can be found on line at: http://www.who.int/healthinfo/paper30.pdf, accessed April 7, 1013.

24. Science News, Effect of Premature Birth Can Reach Into Adulthood, June 16, 2011, accessed April 7, 2013, http://www.sciencedaily.com/releases/2011/06/110615171408.htm.

25. "Institute of Medicine (U.S.) Committee on Understanding Premature Birth and Assuring Healthy Outcomes," R. E. Behrman, and A. S. Butler, eds., "Societal Costs of Preterm Birth," in *Preterm Birth: Causes, Consequences, and Prevention* (Washington, D.C.: National Academies Press, 2007), available online at www.ncbi.nlm.nih.gov/books/NBK11358 (accessed March 17, 2013).

26. "List of Countries by Infant Mortality Rate," Wikipedia, accessed March 17, 2013, http://en.wikipedia.org/wiki/List_of_countries_by_infant_mortality_rate.

27. "Country Comparison: Infant Mortality Rate," Indexmundi.com, accessed March 17, 2013, www.indexmundi.com/g/r.aspx?c=us&v=29.

28. "Country Comparison: Infant Mortality Rate," CIA—The World Factbook, accessed March 17, 2013, www.cia.gov/library/publications/the-world-factbook/rankorder/2091rank.html.

29. "Infant Mortality Rate (Deaths per 1,000 Live Births), Linked Files, 2006–2008," Statehealthfacts.org, accessed March 17, 2013, www.statehealthfacts.org/comparemaptable.jsp?ind=47&cat=2.

30. "Infant Mortality Rate (Deaths per 1,000 Live Births), Linked Files, 2006–2008."

31. "Preterm Births as a Percent of All Births, 2010," Statehealthfacts.org, accessed March 17, 2013, www.statehealthfacts.org/comparemaptable.jsp?ind=39&cat=2.

32. "Statistics and Surveillance: 2008 Table Data," Centers for Disease Control and Prevention, accessed March 17, 2013, www.cdc.gov/vaccines/stats-surv/nis/data/tables_2008.htm.

33. "Statistics and Surveillance: 2010 Table Data," Centers for Disease Control and Prevention, accessed March 17, 2013, www.cdc.gov/vaccines/stats-surv/nis/data/tables_2010.htm#overall.

Strategies for Reducing the Cost of Health Care in the United States

$\mathcal{D}$espite the plethora of books and media coverage on the U.S. health system and what is needed for reform, I think it is beneficial to decide what inequities and inefficiencies we want to target first. In my take on a health care fix, I am addressing the improvement of primary or basic health care for the nation, by analyzing access to care, both fiscally and physically in terms of the availability of the necessary clinicians. Secondly, since the United States spends double what other countries do for health care, based on a measurement of the percent of Gross Domestic Product spent, as shown in chapter 4, let's analyze how we can cut costs and optimize purchasing power. Thirdly, are we paying clinicians and other purveyors of health care services appropriately? There is no question that primary-care doctors are getting the squeeze, but what about some of the other providers? Fourthly, in terms of efficiency, what can be done to streamline the tremendously fragmented U.S. health care system? And finally, let's review our financing of health care for adequacy and equity. Based on these objectives, I have outlined these five fundamental questions for their importance in creating a more effective health care system for Americans.[1]

1. Does everyone have access to some type of primary care?
2. Is the U.S. government optimizing its purchasing power for public programs?
3. Are provider reimbursements in line with health care goals?
4. Is there a mechanism for eliminating unnecessary and costly redundancies in a fragmented delivery system?
5. Is the financing of health care for the country adequate and equitable?

ACCESS TO CARE

First of all, access to care is not the same as access to health insurance. Health insurance is one of the financing mechanisms for health care; it does not provide care. Second, access means adequacy of supply in relation to the demand for services, especially primary-care services. Presently, there are significant shortages of nurses, obstetricians, pediatricians, and other primary-care health professionals in the United States. Increasing the demand for health care services without provisions for stemming shortages of providers will only exacerbate the lack of access for patient care.

The United States could improve access for its residents by increasing funding to universities, thereby enabling more professionals to be developed in areas of shortages. Since many universities are publicly funded, it is incumbent on state legislatures to have the political will to act. Do we have to wait until facilities close before we address the supply issue? Another critical element for access is alignment of reimbursements with social needs, such as pediatrics. Presently, medical schools throughout the United States indirectly encourage doctors to pursue specialty practices because of the high cost of a medical education and the ability to earn more money in specialty care. This disparity can be addressed in two ways: by reducing tuition costs for professionals going into areas of need and by increasing Medicare and Medicaid reimbursements for targeted services.

OPTIMIZING GOVERNMENT PURCHASING

Based on my analysis of the federal budget and the health care programs it funds, the largest single provider of health care in the United States is the government, through its Medicare, Medicaid, Veterans Health Administration, and various Health and Human Services Agency–funded programs, such as the federally qualified community centers. In addition, the federal government funds all kinds of initiatives at universities and private health care groups through grants and program reimbursements that advance science and public programs. As such, the federal government has the greatest influence on reimbursements for providers and, ultimately, what the health care consumer pays for services. Changes in Medicare drive changes in private health care plans as well. One of the areas where the government failed to utilize its mass purchasing power was in the Medicare prescription drug program, which was enacted in 2006. Medicare subscribers now have a limited prescription-drug benefit, but at market prices. This is a failure of a monopoly to exert its purchasing power, which has cost the taxpayers millions. Is it unreasonable to expect the prescription-drug industry to offer a group discount to its largest customer base? This contracting practice is used in private industry all the time, where large customers get preferential pricing for products. When I worked for a large hospital network, one of my performance-improvement projects was to optimize bulk purchasing for pharmaceuticals. The Bush and Obama administrations both failed to negotiate effectively with the pharmacy industry. A better health care value for the country would be obtaining deep discounts for government-purchased Medicare pharmaceuticals. As an enticement to lower prices, there is also room for increased efficiency in the Federal Drug Administration's review process for approval of new drugs.

REIMBURSEMENT ALIGNMENT
WITH DESIRED OUTCOMES

One of the key problems with health care access is that the federal government is the main financier for health care, and it has not reinforced primary care with adequate financial reimbursements. The 2010 changes in Medicare, as cited in chapter 13, seek to increase clinician compensation in primary-care health services. Until compensation levels are adequate, we will not see a major increase in the supply of pediatricians, obstetricians, and other primary-care providers. The entire Medicare reimbursement system has been based on paying for transactions, like surgical procedures, and not for wellness or even disease-management promoting processes. However, the pay-for-performance initiatives for Accountable Care Organizations do provide higher compensation for clinics that generate better clinical results through patient management and safety. Also, the 2010 *medical-home* designation allows a clinic to obtain chronic-disease-management fees for serving as a patient's care manager. It is not fair to expect physicians and other providers to offer health services for free or at a financial loss. There is no other sector of the economy that is expected to offer services in a nonviable manner into perpetuity. This problem drives family practitioners out of business. My ideas (as the healthpolicymaven™) for improving clinician reimbursement include paying a stipend for continuity of care over a period of years, not just per visit, thereby enhancing the long-term patient-management experience. Also, let's recognize best practices and incorporate that into the financial allocations, which, thankfully, Medicare is now starting to do. Medicare is conducting demonstration projects for optimizing diabetic care and other chronic disease management programs differently, which is a step in the right direction. It should be noted that the national goal to make diabetics healthier or to reduce the incidence of diabetes may be at odds with some medical suppliers who make money off this demographic. And this is an example of how profit-taking distorts health care outcomes in the United States.

STREAMLINING THE HEALTH CARE SYSTEM

The United States has fifty-one different health care systems because each state (plus Washington, D.C.) has its own private insurance oversight and Medicaid practices. This creates unnecessary burdens on benefit administrators in the private and public sectors. One way to streamline health care is to establish common templates for claims processes, as has been done by the nonprofit Health Care Forum in Washington State, a consortium of health care providers who work toward process improvements. Several insurance commissioners are also working toward a standardized medical-insurance claim form as well. Another method is to encourage the adoption of electronic processes, which all major health care entities are already doing; the 2010 health reforms provide some funding for the initiative. The question is, How many different standards do we need? For private-sector suppliers of electronic medical records and insurance claims administration, market differentiation in services is essential to their success. However, this is not in the best interest of the consumer, as it adds to the ultimate cost for national health care administration. But nothing compares to the irony of fifty differing state Medicaid programs to administer. However, since these programs are increasingly financed through state and not federal tax revenues, it is difficult to imagine relief without a major systemic change for Medicaid. Perhaps someday Medicaid patients will be covered under one national health care pool.

It would be more effective to create regional purchasing pools for health care, where the electronic platform, claims process, and deployment will be standardized, which is what the 2010 health care reforms attempt. Standardization saves time, reduces errors, and is a common element of effective business practices. However, it should come as no surprise that many states do not want standardization, and more than 80 percent have filed for some type of exemption to the insurance exchanges rules, which directly impact their Medicaid programs. However, by 2012 half of the states had adopted legislation for the implementation of insurance exchanges, as cited in chapter 13.

States' rights are a coveted privilege, and most states are reluctant to cede any of their own governance and administrative powers to the federal government. That said, I think many states would gladly give the expensive Medicaid program back to the federal government.

All health care purchasing cooperative gains should be cycled through to residents of each state participating in a health care purchasing cooperative through lower rates for health insurance. Financial success through regional purchasing pools would include the following elements:

1. saving money in health care administration expenditures;
2. reduced volatility in health-insurance premiums;
3. reductions in program expenses from mass purchasing;
4. simplified claims processing, because we do not need fifty different claims adjudication systems, and the National Association of Insurance Commissioners has recognized this issue;
5. ultimately, reducing unnecessary plan differentiation will optimize administrative simplification and administrative efficiency, without sacrificing patient care; and
6. private payers, such as insurance companies and third-party administrators, would have an opportunity to administer these regional contracts through a competitive bid process. This assures a private-sector influence on service delivery and innovation, which is a good thing. The California company Molina administers Medicaid contracts successfully.

OTHER CONSIDERATIONS

The changes in Medicare reimbursements in 2010 will directly impact imaging and other medical diagnostic services. These medical services respond to a complex system that encourages certain procedures due to higher reimbursements, creates hypersensitivity to avoidance of malpractice claims in our litigious society, responds to consumer demands, and features a highly incentivized medical-supply sector. With the public-private composition of the health care system, it is difficult to control all elements for optimizing efficacy. There are lots of excellent health care organizations that already have good practices, but more effort needs to go into reforming those entities that don't, because one way or another we are all paying for it.

Malpractice Insurance Issues

You can't pick up a newspaper without reading some story about an insurance settlement in this litigious country of ours. According to the Robert Wood Johnson Foundation, it is very difficult to determine the true cost of malpractice concerns in the American health care system. The foundation estimates that the hard costs for malpractice insurance break down into the following factors: claim costs of $4.4 billion, legal defense costs of $1.4 billion, and $700 million for insurance administration.[2] Malpractice insurance is less frequently provided by traditional insurance companies, and instead is usually provided by mutually owned physician groups that are nonprofit groups. What is more difficult to calculate is the cost of defensive medicine including extra tests, extra images, diagnostic surgeries, and other procedures. Because of the clinical concern for missing some disease clue, a high level of scrutiny is placed on redundancies in medical diagnostics, which increases costs throughout the health care system. It is very difficult to assign a value for this indirect cost of the current medical liability climate. Even if we knew these costs, it is still difficult to calculate how this breaks down into a per-person unit cost, which is how people pay for medical insurance. I took a stab at calculating the cost per person, by using U.S. Census data from 2008.[3] At that time, there were 228 million adults in the country, so that would work out to be $28.51 per adult each year for the direct costs. At least that is a start for understanding what we are all paying for this aspect of the health care system. Defensive medicine costs would probably double or triple that figure. All medical plans—public or private—bear the burden of this health care cost.

Other concerns are the lack of uniformity for medical malpractice insurance requirements by state. For example, 5 percent of Florida physicians practice without this insurance, because it is not required.[4] These doctors probably have their bank accounts off-shore as well, along with their homes titled in the name of someone else because they could lose everything if they are found liable for an adverse medical event. I personally would not contract with a physician who does not have malpractice liability insurance. One wonders how easy it is for a patient to find out about the insurance for his doctor. The National Practitioner Databank collects information on malpractice claims paid by insurance companies, and it reports significant differences among states for severity of claims.[5] This suggests that political and regulatory influences are impacting malpractice settlements and ultimately the costs.

Only about 40 percent of every dollar paid for malpractice settlements goes to the patient who was injured, because litigation costs (lawyers' fees) are so high. Awards for damages are inequitable as well, and there is increasing evidence that malpractice awards are not a successful deterrent to future medical claims. Malpractice claims often occur from a systemic failure and not the actions of a single clinician. To that extent, the malpractice system does not help advance patient safety as much as other nonpunitive measures, like National Quality Agency reporting.

Tort reform or medical malpractice costs are of concern in the current health system, but the dialogue should switch from the polarizing prolitigation or antilitigation mantras to figuring out a systemic way to offer more affordable malpractice insurance for clinicians in primary care. This included practitioners in obstetrics, gynecology, and other areas deeply impacted by the dearth of affordable malpractice insurance. For example, the U.S. government could underwrite the stop-loss coverage beyond a fixed level of insured liability for these medical practitioners. This would make the government the reinsurance provider only in areas where there are shortages of essential clinicians. Essentially, these professionals would be covered in one insurance pool across the country rather than the piecemeal approach with the private insurance sector. This insurance support would really help the rural providers with small practices. This method of providing affordable professional insurance has been successful with community health center innovators. Also, the government could contract for very specific loss controls, which would have a ripple effect on the rest of the insurance industry.

FINANCING HEALTH CARE

Presently the United States has a fragmented method of financing health care services for its residents, including government programs, private insurance plans ($13,770 is the average medical insurance premium for a family according to the nonprofit Kaiser Family Foundation[6]), individual contributions, and unpaid services. Services that are paid with payroll taxes include Medicare and state workers' compensation taxes. Other government programs like Medicaid are funded through state general funds, federal allowances, and sin taxes from alcohol and cigarette consumption. Ways to finance a national health care mandate to cover all residents include increasing the FICA/FUTA payroll tax, creating a new tax like the Canadian Value Added Tax, or using an income-tax method. The Patient Protection and Affordable Care Act of 2010 applies a complex combination of user fees, taxes, and penalties to finance medical-insurance purchasing for individuals and small businesses.

According to the Kaiser Foundation 2007 primer on health care costs, premiums for private-sector health care grew 87 percent between 2000 and 2006, which was four times the rate of wage growth.[7] Every person covered on a private health insurance plan is paying for services that are not reimbursed to hospitals and other clinical providers because of gaps in Medicaid reimbursement and charges for the uninsured. The current method of paying for health care in America is not sustainable. The question that should be asked isn't how much more will a national health care mandate cost, but how will we deploy our resources? We are already spending the money, just not effectively or fairly. How much longer are Americans willing to spend 25 percent more for health care than any other country, with 12 percent of the national population lacking basic access to health care and millions of people without primary care? The present health care delivery system uses resources from both the private and public sector disproportionately to the actual benefits for most residents. It is time for a change in health care delivery, but let's make sound systemic changes, not just add-ons to a poorly designed system.

NOTES

1. "Five Things You Need to Ask Yourself about Health Care Reforms," Straight Talk on Health Care blog by Healthpolicymaven™, January 19, 2008, accessed March 17, 2013, http://healthpolicymaven.blogspot.com/2008/01/five-things-you-need-to-ask-yourself.html.

2. Michelle M. Mello, "Understanding Medical Malpractice Insurance: A Primer," Research Synthesis Report no. 8, the Synthesis Project, Robert Wood Johnson Foundation, January 2006, available online at www.rwjf.org/content/dam/farm/reports/reports/2006/rwjf17974 (accessed April 18, 2013).

3. "Self-Described Religious Identification of Adult Population: 1990 to 2008," U.S. Census Bureau, accessed March 17, 2013, www.census.gov/compendia/statab/2010/tables/10s0075.pdf.

4. Mello, "Understanding Medical Malpractice Insurance."

5. Mello, "Understanding Medical Malpractice Insurance."

6. Kaiser Family Foundation, "Health Care Costs: A Primer," March 2009, p. 12, available online at www.kff.org/insurance/upload/7670_02.pdf (accessed March 17, 2013).

7. "Health Care Costs: A Primer, Key Information on Health Care Costs and Their Impact," Kaiser Family Foundation, August 2007, p. 12.

Epilogue

$\mathcal{T}$his book has been my truth telling about the state of affairs of our health care system and our inglorious waste of resources. I have tried to keep the rhetoric to a minimum and reveal useful health care performance measurements and relationships among the various health care silos of government programs, employer-sponsored medical plans, and individual health insurance. According to the nonprofit Kaiser Foundation 2010 Employer Health Plan Survey, only 69 percent of employers offered medical insurance for their employees.[1] In the 2009 Kaiser Foundation health care cost primer, the private sector, including individual and corporate contributions, paid for 54 percent of the total health care spend in the country.[2] It is interesting to note that in just two years since the Kaiser Foundation conducted the previous health care cost survey, the private sector contribution has decreased by 1 percent of the total health care spend for the nation. This is significant and is reflective of the long-term trend that health care is a growing part of the federal budget obligation and not the private sector. However, this figure did not include the federal investment in the Veterans Health Administration or the Bureau of Indian Health, as previously pointed out in chapter 1. Taking this into consideration, that number represents about 46 percent of the total health care spending for the country, as the rest is paid by our government for Medicare, Medicaid, and other health care programs like the Veterans Health Administration. This relationship will change somewhat in 2014 after the health care mandates are in place, assuming they survive congressional machinations and lobbyist influences, which have already weakened some of the teeth in the patient-safety aspects of the Accountable Care Act.[3] Hospitals that do not meet targeted outcomes for certain diseases are to receive lower reimbursements from CMS, but this performance threshold to receive the "Shared Savings Dollars" has already been lowered thanks to enterprising hospital lobbyists. A good portion of the insurance mandates will be financed by the federal government through direct premium-payment subsidies. Through existing public programs and tax subsidies, the primary provider of health care in the United States will continue to be the government.

Conversely, many academics and clinicians think that health care should not be a for-profit enterprise or even called a business. Personally, I don't have a problem with that, as long as the value is produced within the guidelines of a regulated model. The private sector can innovate more quickly than public groups, and we need that innovation. Also, because private-sector operations are leaner and hiring practices differ, a for-profit company may offer solid value to the health care community and still be profitable. After all, that is how our capital market is created. There is nothing wrong with making a profit, as long as regulations are in place to encourage and enforce systemic goals for the greatest efficacy in national health care. *Efficacy* means clinical and financial optimization, not one or the other.

And finally, let's talk about our collective resources, because a health care system, whether it is public or private, is a community resource. I am speaking of sharing our resources to optimize the greatest good for our society, not necessarily for every individual. It is not *the government* but rather *our government*, as it belongs to the people in our democracy. Perhaps if we change how we label things, we will come closer to resolving some health care delivery problems. At least that is my hope. Even though I have been called foolish by many, I continue to believe in the democratic process. We can achieve much more collectively than individually, so let us work in concert to improve health care clinical outcomes and value for everyone in the country. This is the healthpolicymaven™ signing off for now.

NOTES

1. Kaiser Family Foundation and Health Research and Educational Trust, "Employer Health Benefits: 2010 Summary of Findings," p. 4, available online at http://ehbs.kff.org/pdf/2010/8086.pdf (accessed March 11, 2013).

2. Kaiser Family Foundation, "Health Care Costs: A Primer," March 2009, p. 11, available online at www.kff.org/insurance/upload/7670_02.pdf (accessed March 13, 2013).

3. "Quality Measures and Performance Standards," Centers for Medicare and Medicaid Services, accessed April 18, 2013, www.cms.gov/Medicare/Medicare-Fee-for-Service-Payment/sharedsavingsprogram/Quality_Measures_Standards.html.

Acknowledgments

$\mathscr{I}$ want to give a special thanks to the following people who served as my "focus group" agreeing to read chapters. I am listing them in alphabetical order.

Mel Belding, MD, hospital quality

Steve Carwin, men's health and coming up with the title *Unraveling U.S. Health Care*

Bethlyn Gerard, naturopathic and alternative health care

Michael Hamerly, men's health

Anne Matthiesen, children's health

Wendy O'Shaughnessy, patient safety

Beth Perry, Medicare

Authonomy.com—thanks to all of the terrific and insightful writers who read and commented on the early galleys of the book. Praevalere!

All Ivy Editors, thanks for really putting your back into this, my first book.

Primary Sources, Kim Pearson for early stewardship to this endeavor.

Brianna Shepherd for wrestling the final product into something doable.

To all of the people at Seton Family of Hospitals who still take my calls, but especially Dr. Frank Mazza for his cogent responses and support for my post-Seton endeavors.

Thanks to all of the people who take time out of their hectic lives to read my blog posts, which are sometimes kind of chunky.

And to Dr. Hank Kaplan, my oncologist for nearly twenty years, who has always been willing to find the creative solution to patient care—thanks for modeling patient-centered care before the phrase was coined.

To the University of Washington, thanks for letting me enter graduate school for my mid-career change; maybe I'll make enough royalties off the book to make a donation to the school. Of note are: Will Welton (former MHA program director), Jon Brock (Evans School, retired), Steve Page (professor, MPA program), and Cindy Watts (now at VCU)—thank you for going the extra mile.

I want to acknowledge the early teachers that made a big impact in my life—Keith (social studies) and Kay (art) Rosengren, Miss Bryant (English), and Mrs. Ericksen (heartfelt awareness)—as my life would have been a lot harder without you.

To all of my former clients for sharing their wisdom with me, not just about business, but also about life, especially Peter Mathisen and Dick and Fran Sherwood.

And last but certainly not least, to family members who supported me even if you wondered what the heck I was doing.

Saving the best for last, my fabulously handsome and talented son, Nathan Patrick Winter—thanks for accepting me as the eccentric and irregular mom that I am.

Appendix

For the Informed Health Care Purchaser

$\mathscr{H}$ere are some good resources for future inquiries and updates.

UNDERSTANDING HEALTH CARE REGULATIONS

The Commonwealth Fund: www.commonwealthfund.org
Kaiser Family Foundation: www.kff.org, www.kff.org/kaiserpolls, www.state
  healthfacts.org, www.kaiseredu.org

NATIONWIDE COMPARISONS ON
HEALTH CARE MEASURES

Kaiser Family Foundation: www.statehealthfacts.org

PATIENT SAFETY AND HOSPITAL QUALITY

Centers for Disease Control: www.cdc.gov, www.cdc.gov/traumacare
Leapfrog Group: www.leapfroggroup.org
American College of Surgeons: www.facs.org/trauma/verifiedfaq.html
Health and Human Services: www.hospitalcompare.hhs.gov
Centers for Medicare & Medicaid Services: www.cms.gov/Certificationand
  Complianc/Downloads/ApprovedTransplantPrograms.pdf, www.medicare
  .gov/MedicareEligibility

RESEARCH AND CLINICAL OUTCOME DATA

Agency for Healthcare Research and Quality: www.ahrq.gov
Centers for Disease Control: www.cdc.gov

HEALTH POLICY ORGANIZATIONS

Robert Wood Johnson Foundation: www.rwjf.org
The Commonwealth Fund: www.commonwealthfund.org
Kaiser Family Foundation: www.kff.org

SCORECARDS FOR FIFTY STATE PERFORMANCE MEASURES

Women's Health Scorecard Eastern Region									
Measures of Health	Avg.	CT	DE	D.C.	MD	NJ	NY	PA	VI
Contraception Equity for Birth Control RX	31%	0	1	-1	0	1	1	-1	0
Abortion coverage for Medicaid women	86%	0	0	-1	0	0	1	-1	0
Abortion ban for all medical plans	14%	0	0	0	0	0	-1	-2	-1
Availability of Emergency Contraception Pill	41%	0	1	-1	1	1	0	1	0
Women with Medical Insurance	80%	88%	87%	89%	84%	81%	84%	87%	83%
Women covered by employer medical plans	58%	69%	66%	57%	68%	63%	58%	65%	63%
Medicaid Eligibility: Income >FPL	133%	175%	200%	185%	185%	185%	133%	185%	185%
Breast Cancer Deaths	23.4	23.8	21.3	27	25	27	22.8	24.8	25.2
Ovarian Cancer Deaths	8.5	8.2	7.2	9.8	8.6	9.3	8.7	9.3	9.1
Heart Failure Deaths	351	315	378	455	375	367	413	381	343
Total Score for Women		36	-22	-112	-25	-18	-61	-35	5
Notes: Disease morality is from the CDC 2006 data.									
Reproductive data is from NARAL & legislative sites 2010 & 2011.									
Insurance & Medicaid eligibility based on the Kaiser FF 2011 Survey.									
Health Metrics calculated by comparing state's performance to nt'l av.									

Appendix Figure 1.   Eastern States

Women's Health Scorecard Northeastern Region						
Measures of Health	Nt'l Average	ME	MA	NH	RI	VT
Contraception Equity for Birth Control RX	31%	1	1	0	0	1
Abortion coverage for Medicaid women	86%	1	1	1	1	1
Abortion ban for all medical plans	14%	0	-1	0	0	0
Availability of Emergency Contraception Pill	41%	1	1	1	1	1
Women with Medical Insurance	80%	89%	95%	86%	86%	89%
Women covered by employer medical plans	58%	59%	67%	72%	61%	60%
Medicaid Eligibility: Income >FPL	187%	200%	200%	185%	181%	200%
Breast Cancer Deaths	23.4	21.4	23.3	20.7	21.3	21.9
Ovarian Cancer Deaths	8.5	8.1	9.6	7.3	9.1	7.7
Heart Failure Deaths	351	314	303	329	366	321
Total Score for Women		42	49	28	-11	35
Notes: Disease morality is from the CDC 2006 data.						
Reproductive data is from NARAL & legislative sites 2010 & 2013.						
Insurance & Medicaid data from the Kaiser FF 2011 Cal. Yr. Survey.						
Health Metrics calculated by comparing state's performance to nt'l av.						

Appendix Figure 2.   Northeastern States

Women's Health Scorecard Midwestern Region							
Measures of Health	Nt'l Average	IN	IA	KS	MO	NE	OK
Contraception Equity for Birth Control RX	31%	0	1	-1	1	0	1
Abortion coverage for Medicaid women	86%	0	0	-1	-1	0	1
Abortion ban for all medical plans	14%	0	0	0	-1	0	-1
Availability of Emergency Contraception Pill	41%	0	1	-1	0	1	0
Women with Medical Insurance	80%	82%	86%	84%	82%	84%	78%
Women covered by employer medical plans	58%	62%	66%	63%	59%	62%	59%
Medicaid Eligibility: Income >FPL	133%	200%	300%	150%	185%	185%	133%
Breast Cancer Deaths	23.4	25.5	22.6	23.9	25.3	25.2	24.2
Ovarian Cancer Deaths	8.5	9.2	8.7	9	8.7	8.7	8.7
Heart Failure Deaths	351	379	319	324	405	301	453
Total Score for Women		-29	37	24	-56	50	-100

Notes: Disease morality is from the CDC 2006 data.

Reproductive data is from NARAL & legislative sites 2010 & 2011.

Insurance & Medicaid eligibility based on the Kaiser FF 2011 Survey.

Health Metrics calculated by comparing state's performance to nt'l av.

Appendix Figure 3.   Midwestern States

Women's Health Scorecard Great Lakes Region & the Dakotas								
Measures of Health	Nt'l Average	IL	MI	MN	ND	OH	SD	WI
Contraception Equity for Birth Control RX	31%	0	-1	0	-1	1	-1	1
Abortion coverage for Medicaid women	86%	0	-1	0	-1	-1	-1	1
Abortion ban for all medical plans	14%	0	0	0	-1	0	0	-1
Availability of Emergency Contraception Pill	41%	0	-1	0	0	1	0	0
Women with Medical Insurance	80%	82%	84%	89%	86%	83%	83%	89%
Women covered by employer medical plans	58%	61%	60%	67%	65%	62%	60%	64%
Medicaid Eligibility: Income >FPL	187%	200%	185%	275%	133%	200%	133%	300%
Breast Cancer Deaths	23.4	24.1	25	20.6	20.4	26.5	19.6	22.6
Ovarian Cancer Deaths	8.5	8.6	5.6	8.3	9.1	7.9	9.8	9.7
Heart Failure Deaths	351	364	409	229	284	393	298	316
Total Score for Women		-14	-60	126	66	-43	54	36

Notes: Disease morality is from the CDC 2006 data.

Reproductive data is from NARAL & legislative sites 2010 & 2013.

Insurance & Medicaid eligibility based on the Kaiser FF 2011 cal. yr. survey.

Health Metrics calculated by comparing state's performance to nt'l av.

Appendix Figure 4. Great Lakes & the Dakotas States

Women's Health Scorecard-Southern Region											
Measures of Health	**Avg.**	**AL**	**AR**	**FL**	**GA**	**KY**	**MS**	**NC**	**SC**	**TN**	**WV**
Contraception Equity for Birth Control RX	31%	1	0	1	0	1	0	1	-1	0	0
Abortion coverage for Medicaid women	86%	1	1	1	0	0	0	1	-1	1	1
Abortion ban for all medical plans	14%	0	0	0	0	0	0	-1	-2	0	-1
Availability of Emergency Contraception Pill	41%	1	1	1	0	1	1	0	1	0	0
Women with Medical Insurance	80%	82%	75%	74%	75%	81%	77%	78%	76%	84%	80%
Women covered by employer medical plans	58%	59%	54%	54%	55%	59%	55%	57%	54%	58%	59%
Medicaid Eligibility: Income % >FPL	187	162	133	185	200	185	185	185	185	185	150
Breast Cancer Deaths	23.4	23.5	23.7	21.5	23.6	23.8	25.4	24.2	24.4	24.6	21.6
Deaths	8.5	9.7	7.5	7.6	8.1	8.7	8	8.1	8	8.6	8.7
Heart Failure Deaths	351	444	410	293	387	430	501	353	355	419	441
Total Score for Women		**-91**	**-56**	**64**	**-36**	**-78**	**-151**	**-1**	**-8**	**-68**	**-88**
Notes: Disease morality is from the CDC 2006 data.											
Reproductive data is from NARAL & legislative sites 2010 & 2011.											
Insurance & Medicaid eligibility based on the Kaiser FF 2011 Survey.											
Health Metrics calculated by comparing state's performance to nt'l av.											

Appendix Figure 5. Southern States

Women's Health Scorecard Western States										
Measures of Health	Avg.	AZ	CO	ID	MT	NV	NM	TX	UT	WY
Contraception Equity for Birth Control RX	31%	0	1	0	1	1	1	0	0	0
Abortion coverage for Medicaid women	86%	1	0	1	1	0	1	0	1	1
Abortion ban for all medical plans	14%	-1	-1	-1	0	0	0	-1	0	0
Availability of Emergency Contraception	41%	0	1	0	0	1	0	0	1	0
Women with Medical Insurance	80%	79%	84%	75%	75%	74%	73%	70%	82%	76%
Women covered by employer plans	58%	55%	60%	56%	51%	57%	48%	54%	67%	60%
Eligibility: % Income >FPL	187	133	185	185	133	275	133	185	133	133
Breast Cancer Deaths	23.4	27.4	20.8	20.7	19	20.5	21.2	22.5	25.2	24.2
Ovarian Cancer Deaths	7.6	8.4	8.3	8.4	8.4	7.3	8.5	8.1	8	7.2
Heart Failure Deaths	351	270	251	297	276	357	220	321	281	307
Total Score for Women		76.19	102.94	55.85	80.55	-0.86	134.23	29.47	69.82	44.56

Notes: Disease morality is from the CDC 2006 data.

Reproductive data is from NARAL & legislative sites 2010 & 2013.

Insurance & Medicaid eligibility based on the Kaiser FF 2011 Survey.

Health Metrics calculated by comparing state's performance to nt'l av.

Appendix Figure 6. Western States

Women's Health Scorecard West Coast				
Measures of Health	Nt'l Average	CA	OR	WA
Contraception Equity for Birth Control RX	31%	1	1	1
Abortion coverage for Medicaid women	86%	1	1	1
Abortion ban for all medical plans	14%	0	0	0
Availability of Emergency Contraception Pill	41%	1	1	1
Women with Medical Insurance	80%	77%	82%	81%
Women covered by employer medical plans	58%	53%	59%	61%
Medicaid Eligibility: Income >FPL	187%	200%	185%	185%
Breast Cancer Deaths	23.4	22.3	23.1	22.8
Ovarian Cancer Deaths	8.5	8.3	9.6	9.7
Heart Failure Deaths	351	310	276	287
Total Score for Women		45	77	66

Notes: Disease morality is from the CDC 2006 data.

Reproductive data is from NARAL & legislative sites 2010 & 2011.

Insurance & Medicaid eligibility based on the Kaiser FF 2011 Survey.

Health Metrics calculated by comparing state's performance to nt'l av.

Appendix Figure 7.   West Coast States

Women's Health Scorecard Outside the 48 States			
Measures of Health	Nt'l Average	AK	HI
Contraception Equity for Birth Control RX	31%	1	1
Abortion coverage for Medicaid women	86%	1	1
Abortion ban for all medical plans	14%	0	0
Availability of Emergency Contraception Pill	41%	1	1
Women with Medical Insurance	80%	79%	90%
Women covered by employer medical plans	58%	69%	74%
Medicaid Eligibility: Income >FPL	187%	175%	175%
Breast Cancer Deaths	23.4	27.4	18.4
Ovarian Cancer Deaths	8.5	6.9	7.2
Heart Failure Deaths	351	260	236
Total Score for Women		92	124
Notes: Disease morality is from the CDC 2006 data.			
Reproductive data is from NARAL & legislative sites 2010 & 2011.			
Insurance & Medicaid eligibility based on the Kaiser FF 2011 Survey.			
Health Metrics calculated by comparing state's performance to nt'l av.			

Appendix Figure 8.   Outside the 48 States

Men's Health Scorecard-Eastern States									
Health Measures	Nt'l Average	CT	DE	DC	MD	NJ	NY	PA	VA
Men with medical insurance	77%	85%	83%	84%	81%	77%	79%	84%	79%
Men covered by employer medical plans	58%	68%	64%	58%	67%	65%	57%	65%	64%
Medicaid enrollment	12%	11%	14%	16%	8%	6%	17%	11%	9%
Prostate cancer deaths	23.6	24.3	21.7	40.8	26.4	21.2	21.8	24.1	25.7
Heart failure deaths	529	487	555	681	549	540	586	583	521
Total Score		41	-24	-169	-23	-9	-55	-54	6
Notes:									
Medicaid enrollment includes other state subsidized medical insurance too.									
Insurance & Medicaid eligibility based on the Kaiser FF 2011 cal. yr. data.									
Mortality data is from the CDC for 2006 mortality per 100,000 lives.									
High score means lower deaths & a high level of insurance statewide for men.									

Appendix Figure 9.   Eastern States

Men's Health Scorecard-Northeastern Region						
Health Measures	Nt'l Av.	ME	MA	NH	RI	VT
Men with medical insurance	77%	84%	93%	83%	81%	86%
Men covered by employer medical plans	58%	57%	68%	71%	61%	59%
Medicaid enrollment	12%	22%	18%	7%	11%	19%
Prostate cancer deaths	23.6	23.9	24.6	24.6	23.6	21.4
Heart failure deaths	529	489	475	503	366	484
Total Score		40	53	25	163	47
Notes:						
Medicaid figure includes other state subidized medical insurance plans.						
Insurance/Medicaid eligibility from the Kaiser FF 2011 cal.yr survey.						
Mortality data is from the CDC for 2006 mortality per 100,000 lives.						
High score means lower deaths & a high level of insurance statewide.						

Appendix Figure 10.   Northeastern States

Health Measures	Nt'l Average	IN	IA	KS	MO	NE	OK
Men's Health Scorecard-Midwestern Region							
Men with medical insurance	77%	81%	83%	79%	79%	82%	73%
covered by employer medical plans	58%	65%	66%	63%	60%	65%	57%
Medicaid enrollment	12%	11%	8%	9%	12%	7%	11%
Prostate cancer deaths	23.6	23.4	25.3	21	23.7	23.5	22.8
Heart failure deaths	529	588	504	504	612	477	678
Total Score		**-59**	**23**	**28**	**-83**	**52**	**-148**

Medicaid enrollment includes other state subsidized medical insurance too.

Insurance & Medicaid eligibility based on the Kaiser FF 2011 cal. yr. data.

Mortality data is from the CDC for 2006 mortality per 100,000 lives.

High score means lower deaths & a high level of insurance statewide for men.

Appendix Figure 11. Midwestern States

Men's Health Scorecard-Great Lakes & the Dakotas								
Health Measures	Nt'l Average	IL	MI	MN	ND	OH	SD	WI
Men with medical insurance	76%	77%	79%	86%	83%	80%	80%	87%
Men covered by employer medical plans	58%	60%	60%	67%	63%	63%	59%	64%
Medicaid enrollment	11%	11%	11%	13%	4%	11%	10%	9%
Prostate cancer deaths	23.6	25.3	22.3	23.3	26.7	24.9	26.4	24
Heart failure deaths	529	557	602	400	498	599	505	516
Total Score		-30	-72	129	28	-71	21	13
Notes:								
Medicaid enrollment includes other state subsidized medical insurance too.								
Insurance & Medicaid eligibility based on the Kaiser FF 2011 cal. yr. survey.								
Mortality data is from the CDC for 2006 mortality per 100,000 lives.								
High score means lower deaths & a high level of insurance statewide for men.								

Appendix Figure 12.   Great Lakes & the Dakotas States

Health Measures	Nt'l Average	AL	AR	FL	GA	KT	LA	MS	NC	SC	TN	WV
Men's Health Scorecard-Southern States												
Men with medical insurance	77%	79%	72%	70%	73%	77%	71%	72%	75%	70%	77%	81%
Men covered by employer medical	58%	60%	55%	52%	56%	58%	53%	54%	58%	54%	57%	59%
Medicaid enrollment	12%	15%	13%	12%	11%	14%	14%	12%	11%	13%	15%	21%
Prostate cancer deaths	23.6	28.8	25.2	20	28.7	25.8	29	32.6	28	27.9	22.3	21.1
Heart failure deaths	529	660	616	451	593	647	635	720	554	572	636	651
Total Score		-136	-88	82	-69	-120	-111	-200	-29	-47	-105	-119

Notes:

Medicaid enrollment includes other state subidized medical insurance too.

Insurance & Medicaid eligibility based on the Kaiser FF 2011 cal. yr. data.

Mortality data is from the CDC for 2006 mortality per 100,000 lives.

High score means lower deaths & a high level of insurance statewide for men.

Appendix Figure 13.   Southern States

Men's Health Scorecard-Western States										
Measures	Nt'l Avg.	AZ	CO	ID	MT	NV	NM	TX	UT	WY
Men with medical insurance	77%	76%	78%	74%	72%	72%	68%	67%	81%	77%
Men on employer medical plans	60%	54%	60%	56%	49%	57%	47%	55%	68%	62%
Medicaid enrollment	12%	16%	9%	5%	6%	9%	12%	7%	5%	5%
Prostate cancer deaths	23.6	19.1	22.5	24.5	28.2	23.9	26	22.3	26.7	21.4
Heart failure deaths	529	418	382	457	460	550	322	472	398	466
Total Score		115	148	71	64	-21	205	58	128	65
Notes:										
Medicaid enrollment includes other state subsidized medical insurance too.										
Insurance & Medicaid eligibility based on the Kaiser FF 2011 cal. yr. data.										
Mortality data is from the CDC for 2006 mortality per 100,000 lives.										
High score means lower deaths & a high level of insurance statewide for men.										

Appendix Figure 14.   Western States

Men's Health Scorecard-West Coast				
Health Measures	Nt'l Average	CA	OR	WA
Men with medical insurance	77%	71%	77%	79%
Men covered by employer medical plans	58%	52%	60%	60%
Medicaid enrollment	14%	13%	11%	12%
Prostate cancer deaths	23.6	22.2	25.6	24.5
Heart failure deaths	529	458	442	456
Total Score		72	85	72
Notes:				
Medicaid enrollment includes other state subsidized medical insurance too.				
Insurance & Medicaid eligibility based on the Kaiser FF 2011 cal. yr. data.				
Mortality data is from the CDC for 2006 mortality per 100,000 lives.				
High score means lower deaths & a high level of insurance for men.				

Appendix Figure 15.   West Coast States

Men's Health Scorecard-Outside the 48 States			
Health Measures	Nt'l Average	AK	HI
Men with medical insurance	77%	75%	88%
Men covered by employer medical plans	58%	59%	69%
Medicaid enrollment	11%	12%	14%
Prostate cancer deaths	23.6	18.5	13.4
Heart failure deaths	529	423	425
Total Score		**111**	**114**
Notes:			
Medicaid enrollment includes other state subsidized medical insurance too.			
Insurance & Medicaid eligibility based on Kaiser FF 2011 cal. yr. survey.			
Mortality data is from the CDC for 2006 mortality per 100,000 lives.			
High score means lower deaths & a high level of insurance for men.			

Appendix Figure 16.   Outside the 48 States

CHAPTER 19 EXHIBITS FOR CHILDREN'S HEALTH

Childrens Health Scorecard-Eastern States									
Health Measures	Nt'l Avg.	CT	DE	DC	MD	NJ	NY	PA	VI
Percent with health insurance	90%	94%	94%	95%	90%	90%	92%	92%	92%
Public Health Plan	36%	26%	33%	49%	26%	27%	38%	32%	26%
Private Insurance	54%	68%	60%	40%	63%	62%	54%	60%	66%
Infant Mortality	6.8	5.8	8.6	12.6	7.9	5.4	5.9	7.4	7.3
Immunization Rate	83.34%	86.38%	86.93%	86.86%	82.62%	80.02%	78.32%	87.18%	89.01%
Obesity Rate	31.60%	25.70%	33.20%	35.40%	28.80%	31.00%	32.90%	29.70%	31.00%
Score		1.13	-1.74	-5.75	-1.08	1.37	0.86	-0.52	-0.42
Immunization rate includes recommendations except Rotovirus and from the CDC 2010 data.									
Obesity rates come from the Kaiser State Health Facts Obesity Survey in 2007.									
Data for insured children comes from the Kaiser Family Foundation 2011 data.									
Infant mortality rates come from the 2009 Kaiser Foundation State Health Facts.									

Appendix Figure 17.   Eastern States

Childrens Health Scorecard-Northeastern Region						
Health Measures	Nt'l Average	ME	MA	NH	RI	VT
Percent with health insurance	90%	94%	97%	93%	94%	96%
Public Sector Ins.	36%	37%	29%	18%	35%	49%
Private ins ER & Indiv	54%	55%	68%	74%	59%	53%
Infant Mortality	6.8	6.3	4.9	5.6	6.5	5.6
Immunizatio n Rate	83.34%	80.02%	87.25%	89.55%	85.86%	77.92%
Obesity Rate	31.60%	28.20%	30.00%	29.40%	30.10%	26.70%
Score		4.58	14.45	12.65	8.32	6.68
Notes						
Immunizations inc. all recommended except Rotovirus from CDC 2010 data.						
Obesity rates come from the Kaiser State Health Facts 2007 Obesity Survey.						
Data for insured children from the Kaiser FF 2011 Cal. Yr. data.						
Infant mortality rates from the 2009 Kaiser Foundation State Health Facts.						

Appendix Figure 18.   Northeastern States

Childrens Health Scorecard-Midwestern Region							
Health Measures	Nt'l Average	IN	IA	KS	MO	NB	OK
Percent with health insurance	90%	94%	94%	91%	90%	91%	90%
Public Sector	36%	36%	30%	31%	29%	26%	40%
Private ins ER & Indiv	54%	57%	61%	58%	53%	63%	48%
Infant Mortality	6.8	7.9	5.2	7.3	7.5	5.9	8
Immunizatio n Rate	83.34%	77.87%	84.12%	84.93%	73.66%	86.68%	81.70%
Obesity Rate	31.60%	29.90%	26.50%	31.10%	31.00%	31.50%	29.50%
Score		-0.87	8.48	0.59	-9.74	5.34	1.66

Immunizations includes all recommendations except Rotovirus from 2010 CDC data.

Obesity rates come from the Kaiser State Health Facts Obesity Survey in 2007.

Data for insured children comes from the Kaiser Family Foundation 2011 yr. data.

Infant mortality rates come from the 2009 Kaiser Foundation State Health Facts.

Appendix Figure 19. Midwestern States

Childrens Health Scorecard-Great Lakes & the Dakotas								
Health Measures	Nt'l Average	IL	MI	MN	ND	OH	SD	WI
Percent with health insurance	90%	93%	95%	93%	92%	91%	93%	95%
Public Sector	36%	39%	33%	25%	22%	34%	34%	32%
Private ins ER & Indiv	54%	53%	58%	69%	69%	57%	57%	61%
Infant Mortality	6.8	7.4	7.6	5	5.9	7.8	7.3	6.3
Immunizatio n Rate	83.3%	84.6%	86.6%	82.6%	87.8%	84.9%	80.7%	85.1%
Obesity Rate	31.6%	34.9%	30.6%	23.1%	25.7%	33.3%	28.4%	27.9%
Score		0.40	8.50	12.60	13.25	-0.10	4.10	11.00

Immunization rate includes all recommendations except Rotovirus from the CDC 2010 data.

Obesity rates come from the Kaiser State Health Facts Obesity Survey in 2007.

Data for insured children comes from the Kaiser FF 2011 Cal. Yr. data.

Infant mortality rates come from the 2009 Kaiser Foundation State Health Facts.

Appendix Figure 20.   Great Lakes & the Dakotas States

Childrens Health Scorecard-Southern States												
Health Measures	Nt'l Average	AL	AR	FL	GA	KY	LA	MS	NC	SC	TN	WV
Percent with health insurance	90%	92%	92%	86%	89%	93%	90%	88%	90%	86%	93%	94%
Public Sector Health Ins.	36%	37%	49%	37%	39%	40%	47%	44%	41%	35%	41%	39%
Private ins ER or Indiv	54%	51%	38%	49%	51%	52%	47%	38%	50%	49%	51%	51%
Infant Mortality	6.8	9.1	8.2	7.2	8.2	7	10	10.6	8.5	9	8.7	7.6
Immunization Rate	83.34%	86.72%	82.64%	86.21%	86.11%	82.88%	84.21%	84.21%	85.49%	84.78%	85.67%	83.59%
Obesity Rate	31.60%	36.10%	37.50%	33.10%	37.30%	37.10%	35.90%	44.40%	33.50%	33.70%	36.50%	35.50%
Score		-1.42	-6.00	-3.03	-5.33	-4.36	-6.63	-17.69	-1.45	-6.82	-1.47	-0.45

Immunization rate includes all recommendations except Rotovirus and are from the CDC 2010 data.

Obesity rates come from the Kaiser State Health Facts Obesity Survey in 2007.

Data for insured children comes from the Kaiser Family Foundation 2011 Cal. Yr. data.

Infant mortality rates come from the 2009 Kaiser Foundation State Health Facts.

Appendix Figure 21.   Southern States

Childrens Health Scorecard-Western States										
Health Measures	Nt'l Avg.	AZ	CO	ID	MT	NV	NM	TX	UT	WY
Percent with health insurance	90%	85%	90%	89%	89%	81%	88%	83%	89%	89%
Public Sector	36%	33%	27%	33%	34%	22%	47%	38%	18%	30%
Private ins ER & Indiv	54%	51%	63%	55%	53%	57%	37%	45%	69%	57%
Infant Mortality	6.8	6.6	6.1	6.3	6	6.2	6.1	6.3	5	7.4
Immunizatio n Rate	83.34%	84.15%	81.29%	77.38%	75.95%	78.82%	81.12%	83.78%	81.72%	81.62%
Obesity Rate	31.60%	30.60%	27.20%	27.50%	25.60%	34.20%	32.70%	32.20%	23.10%	25.70%
Score		-2.99	3.05	-2.36	-1.59	-15.48	-4.62	-6.62	7.68	2.58

Immunization rate includes all recommendations except Rotovirus and are from the CDC 2010 data.

Obesity rates come from the Kaiser State Health Facts Obesity Survey in 2007.

Data for insured children comes from the Kaiser Family Foundation 2011 Cal. Yr. data.

Infant mortality rates come from the 2009 Kaiser Foundation State Health Facts.

Appendix Figure 22.   Western States

Childrens Health Scorecard-West Coast				
Health Measures	**Nt'l Average**	**CA**	**OR**	**WA**
Percent with health insurance	90%	89%	91%	93%
Public Sector	36%	39%	35%	41%
Private ins ER & Indiv	54%	50%	56%	51%
Infant Mortality	6.8	5.2	5.6	5.1
Immunization Rate	83.34%	80.02%	83.64%	82.72%
Obesity Rate	31.60%	30.50%	24.30%	29.50%
Score		**1.57**	**1.29**	**1.74**

Immunization rate for all recommendations except Rotovirus 2010 CDC 2010.

Obesity rates come from the Kaiser State Health Facts Obesity 2007 Survey.

Data for insured children comes from the Kaiser FF 2011 Cal. Yr. data.

Infant mortality rates come from the 2009 Kaiser FF State Health Facts.

Appendix Figure 23.   West Coast States

Childrens Health Scorecard-Outside the 48 States			
Health Measures	Nt'l Average	AK	HI
Percent With Health insurance	90%	87%	97%
Public Sector	36%	36%	42%
Private Ins ER & Indiv	54%	49%	51%
Infant Mortality	6.8	6.5	6.1
Immunization Rate	83.34%	81.82%	83.38%
Obesity Rates	31.60%	33.90%	28.50%
Score		0.23	0.80
Immunization rate for all 2010 CDC recommendations except Rotovirus.			
Obesity rates come from the Kaiser State Health Facts Obesity Survey in 2007.			
Insured children data comes from the Kaiser Family Foundation 2011 year data.			
Infant mortality rates come from the 2009 Kaiser Foundation State Health Facts.			

Appendix Figure 24.   Outside the 48 States

Bibliography

"37th-Measuring the U.S. Health Care System," Health Policy and Reform, New England Journal of Medicine, Jan 14, 2010, 363:98-99 and can be found on line at: http://www.who.int/healthinfo/paper30.pdf, Accessed April 7, 2013.

"2009 Marks the 150th Anniversary of the Queen's Medical Center." The Queen's Medical Center. Accessed March 12, 2013. www.queensmedicalcenter.net/index .php?option=com_content&view=article&id=290:2009-marks-the-150th-anniversary-of-the-queens-medical-center&catid=37:2009-news-stories&Itemid=144.

"2009 Summary of Oregon's Death with Dignity Act." Oregon Health Authority. Accessed March 16, 2013. http://public.health.oregon.gov/ProviderPartner Resources/EvaluationResearch/DeathwithDignityAct/Documents/year12.pdf.

"2010 United States Federal Budget." Statistic Brain. Accessed April 17, 2013. www .statisticbrain.com/2010-united-states-federal-budget.

"2010 United States Federal Budget." Wikipedia. Accessed March 11, 2013. http:// en.wikipedia.org/wiki/2010_United_States_federal_budget.

"2012 HHS Poverty Guidelines." U.S. Department of Health & Human Services. Accessed April 18, 2013. http://aspe.hhs.gov/poverty/12poverty.shtml.

"2013 Summary of Oregon's Death with Dignity Act." Oregon Health Authority, p. 4. Accessed April 4, 2013. http://public.health.oregon.gov/ProviderPartner Resources/EvaluationResearch/DeathwithDignityAct/Documents/year15.pdf.

American Association of Naturopathic Medicine Licensure Map, Accessed April 1, 2013. http://www.aanmc.org/images/licensuremap-shaded_October 2012.gif Politifact.com, Abortion Foe Overreaching in Describing the Context of a Court Ruling, Dan Becker, posted 1/14/2013, accessed March 25, 2013.

"A Policy Statement on Naturopathy." Iowa Board of Medicine. Accessed March 15, 2013. http://medicalboard.iowa.gov/policies/naturopathy.html#.

"About Flagstaff Medical Center." Flagstaff Medical Center. Accessed March 15, 2013. www.flagstaffmedicalcenter.com/AboutFMC/default.

"About Leapfrog." The Leapfrog Group. Accessed March 12, 2013. www.leapfrog group.org/about_us.

"About Mount Sinai." Mount Sinai Hospital. Accessed March 15, 2013. www
.mountsinaihospital.org/about-us.

"About Us." Vanderbilt University Medical Center. Accessed April 18, 2013. www
.mc.vanderbilt.edu/about.

Abubakar, I., D. Kanka, B. Arch, J. Porter, and P. Weissberg. "Outcomes after Acute
Myocardial Infarction: A Comparison of Patients Seen by Cardiologists and General
Physicians." *British Medical Journal Cardiovascular Disorders* 4 (August 2004): 14.

"Act 25 & the Palliative Care and Pain Management Task Force." Vermont Ethics
Network. Accessed April 19, 2013. www.vtethicsnetwork.org/act25_task_force.html.

"Acute Care Surgery & Adult Trauma." Johns Hopkins Medicine. Accessed March 12,
2013. www.hopkinsmedicine.org/surgery/div/Acute_Care_Surgery_and_Adult_
Trauma.html.

"Adverse Event Reporting Tools by State." National Academy for State Health
Policy. Accessed March 12, 2013. www.nashp.org/pst-state-list.

"Affiliated Hospitals." The University of Tennessee Health Science Center. Accessed
March 12, 2013. www.uthsc.edu/hospitals.

"Affordable Care Act." Medicaid.gov. Accessed April 18, 2013. www.medicaid.gov/
AffordableCareAct/Affordable-Care-Act.html.

"Affordable Care Act-Implementing Medicare Cost Savings." Centers for Medicare and Medicaid, Accessed April 6, 2013. http://www.cms.gov/apps/docs/aca-
update-implementing-medicare-costs-savings.pdf.

"Affordable Care Act—Pragmatic Implementation." Straight Talk on Health Care
blog by Healthpolicymaven™, March 6, 2013. Accessed April 18, 2013. http://
healthpolicymaven.blogspot.com/2013/03/affordable-care-act-pragmatic.html.

"Affordable Care Act Tax Provisions." Internal Revenue Service. Accessed April 18,
2013. www.irs.gov/uac/Affordable-Care-Act-Tax-Provisions.

"AHRQ's Patient Safety Initiative: Building Foundations, Reducing Risk." Agency
for Healthcare Research and Quality, December 2003, appendix 2. Accessed
March 12, 2013. www.ahrq.gov/qual/pscongrpt/psiniapp2.htm.

"Akins Assault on Women's Health & Dignity." Straight Talk on Health Care
blog by Healthpolicymaven™, August 22, 2012. Accessed April 19, 2013. http://
healthpolicymaven.blogspot.com/2012/08/akins-assault-on-womens-health-
dignity.html.

Allen, Martha. "What Is Naturopathic Medicine." Athens Natural Medicine. Accessed March 15, 2013. www.drmarthaallen.com/naturopathicmedicine.html.

American Hospital Association. "Uncompensated Hospital Care Cost Fact Sheet: December 2010." Available online at www.aha.org/content/00-10/10uncompensatedcare
.pdf (accessed April 17, 2013).

"Arizona State Legislature, Bills, SB 1001s." Accessed March 25, 2013. http://www.
azleg.gov/legtext/50leg/1s/bills/sb1001s.pdf.

Arizona State Naturopathic Physicians Medical Board, Accessed March 25, 2013.
http://www.aznd.gov/agency/pages/home.asp.

"Arkansas State Legislature, Healthcare Insurance Documents," 201305. Accessed
March 25, 2013. http://www.arkleg.state.ar.us/healthcare/Insurance/Documents/
AZ%20SB%201305.pdf.

"Arkansas Trauma System Designates the Med as Level I Center." *Memphis Business Journal*, September 28, 2010. Available online at http://memphis.bizjournals.com/memphis/stories/2010/09/27/daily9.html (accessed March 12, 2013).

"Average Single Premium per Enrolled Employee For Employer-Based Health Insurance, 2011." statehealthfacts.org, Kaiser Family Foundation. Accessed March 11, 2013. www.statehealthfacts.org/comparetable.jsp?ind=270&cat=5.

Banks, Marnee. "'Personhood' Debated in Montana Legislature." KRTV.com. Accessed April 19, 2013. www.krtv.com/news/personhood-debated-in-montana-legislature/#.

Becker, Dan. "Abortion Foe Overreaches in Describing Context of Court Ruling." PolitiFact.com, January 14, 2013. Accessed April 19, 2013. www.politifact.com/georgia/statements/2013/feb/08/dan-becker/abortion-foe-overreaches-describing-context-court-.

Bergner, Daniel. "Death in a Family." *New York Times*, December 2, 2007, p. 1.

"Best Hospitals." *U.S. News and World Report*. Accessed March 14, 2013. www.usnews.com/besthospitals/rankings.

Birkhead, John, R. M. Norris, T. Quinn, et al. *Acute Myocardial Infarction: A Core Data Set for Monitoring Standards of Care.* London: Clinical Effectiveness & Evaluation Unit, Royal College of Physicians, 1999.

Brumley, Richard, S. Enguidanos, P. Jamison, R. Seitz, N. Morgenstern, S. Saito, J. McIlwane, K. Hillary, and J. Gonzalez. "Increased Satisfaction with Care and Lower Costs: Results of a Randomized Trial of In-Home Palliative Care." *Journal of American Geriatrics Society* 55, no. 7 (July 2007): 993–1000.

"Burn and Trauma Services Renamed to Honor Devoted Benefactors." University of Rochester Medical Center. Accessed March 15, 2013. www.urmc.rochester.edu/news/story/index.cfm?id=3007.

"Business and Professions Code, Section 3630-3637." Legislative Council, State of California. Accessed April 18, 2013. www.leginfo.ca.gov/cgi-bin/displaycode?section=bpc&group=03001-04000&file=3630-3637.

"California." Statehealthfacts.org. Accessed March 17, 2013. www.statehealthfacts.org/profileglance.jsp?rgn=6&rgn=1.

"Care and Services." Pen Bay Medical Center. Accessed March 12, 2013. www.penbayhealthcare.org/penbaymedicalcenter/services/Care_and_Services.

Centers for Disease Control, Childhood Immunization Statistics for 2010, Accessed April 7, 2013. http://www.cdc.gov/vaccines/stats-surv/nis/data/tables_2010.htm.

Centers for Disease Control, National Center for Health Statistics, Fastats, Accessed March 25, 2013. http://www.cdc.gov/nchs/fastats/lcod.htm.

Centers for Medicare and Medicaid Services. "Your Guide to Medicare Special Needs Plans (SNPs)." Baltimore, MD: U.S. Department of Health and Human Services, 2011. Available online at www.medicare.gov/Publications/Pubs/pdf/11302.pdf (accessed April 19, 2013).

"Chapter 70.245 RCW: The Washington Death with Dignity Act." Washington State Legislature. Accessed April 19, 2008. http://apps.leg.wa.gov/rcw/default.aspx?cite=70.245.

"CMS 1500 Claim Form." EMR Consultant. Accessed April 18, 2013. www.emrconsultant.com/education/cms-1500-claim-form.

"Comparative Summary of States' Adverse Event Reporting and Performance Experiences." Quality and Patient Safety. Accessed March 12, 2013. www.qups.org/med_errors.php?c=state_comparison&t=17.

"Compare Visitors Medical Insurance." American Visitor Insurance. Accessed April 18, 2013. www.americanvisitorinsurance.com/insurance/visitors-medical-summary.asp.

Compendia Statistics Tables 12s0075, U.S. Census Bureau. Accessed March 25, 2013. http://www.census.gov/compendia/statab/2012/tables/12s0075.pdf, http://www.cdc.gov/nchs/data/nvsr/nvsr57/nvsr57_14.pdf. Accessed March 25, 2013.

"Compilation of Title XXVII of the Public Health Service Act (and Related Provisions)." 111th Congress, 2nd session. Available online at www.nadp.org/libraries/hcr_documents/phsa027.sflb.ashx (accessed April 18, 2013).

"The Cost to Die; an Insiders View on Terminally Ill Patients and Advanced Directives." Straight Talk on Health Care blog by Healthpolicymaven™, January 3, 2008. Accessed April 19, 2013. http://healthpolicymaven.blogspot.com/2008/01/cost-to-die-insiders-view-on-terminally.html.

"Country Comparison: Infant Mortality Rate." CIA—The World Factbook. Accessed March 17, 2013. www.cia.gov/library/publications/the-world-factbook/rankorder/2091rank.html.

"Country Comparison: Infant Mortality Rate." Indexmundi.com. Accessed March 17, 2013. www.indexmundi.com/g/r.aspx?c=us&v=29.

"Creating a New Competitive Health Insurance Marketplace." The Center for Consumer Information & Insurance Oversight. Accessed April 18, 2013. http://cciio.cms.gov/Archive/Grants/exchanges-map.html.

"Death with Dignity Act." Oregon Health Authority. Accessed April 19, 2013. http://public.health.oregon.gov/ProviderPartnerResources/Evaluationresearch/deathwithdignityact/Pages/index.aspx.

"Death with Dignity Acts." Death with Dignity National Center. Accessed April 19, 2013. www.deathwithdignity.org/acts.

Delaware Board of Licensure and Medical Discipline, Licensure of Physicians and Healthcare Professionals. Accessed April 10, 2013. http://dpr.delaware.gov/boards/medicalpractice/index.shtml.

Deloitte Center for Health Solutions. "Medical Tourism: Emerging Phenomenon in Health Care Industry—2008 Report." Available online at www.deloitte.com/us/2008medicaltourism (accessed April 18, 2013).

"Delta Health Center Receives Major Grant." Bolivar Medica Center, December 2, 2012. Accessed March 12, 2013. www.bolivarcom.com/view/full_story/18464032/article-Delta-Health-Center-receives-major-grant-.

"Department of Neurosurgery." University of South Carolina School of Medicine. Accessed March 12, 2013. http://neurosurgery.med.sc.edu.

"Direct-Entry Midwifery State-by-State Legal Status." Midwives Alliance of North America, May 11, 2011. Accessed March 15, 2013. http://mana.org/statechart.html.

"Distribution of the Nonelderly Uninsured by Age, States (2010–2011), U.S. (2011)." Statehealthfacts.org. Accessed March 17, 2013. www.statehealthfacts.org/compare bar.jsp?ind=134&cat=3.

"District of Columbia Municipal Regulations for Naturopathic Medicine." District of Columbia Department of Health, May 1, 2012. Accessed April 18, 2013. http://doh.dc.gov/sites/default/files/dc/sites/doh/publication/attachments/naturopathic_regulations.pdf.

"Division of Traumatology and Surgical Critical Care." Penn Medicine. Accessed March 12, 2013. www.pennmedicine.org/surgery/cpup/divisions/trauma.html.

"Do All Doctors Have Insurance." Florida Medical Malpractice. Accessed March 12, 2013. www.floridamalpractice.com/med20.htm.

"Does Barack Obama's Health Care Bill Include $1 Abortions?" PolitiFact.com, March 12, 2012. Accessed April 19, 2013. www.politifact.com/truth-o-meter/statements/2012/mar/21/blog-posting/does-barack-obamas-health-care-bill-include-1-abor.

"Drug Coverage (Part D)." Medicare.gov. Accessed April 19, 2013. www.medicare.gov/part-d/index.html.

Drummond, Michael, and Deborah Marshall. "Putting a Price on Life." *The Globe and Mail*, December 8, 2006, p. A25.

"Effects of Premature Birth Can Reach into Adulthood." Science Daily, June 16, 2011. Accessed April 19, 2013. www.sciencedaily.com/releases/2011/06/110615171408.htm.

Einhorn, Bruce. "Outsourcing the Patients." *Businessweek*, March 12, 2008. Available online at www.businessweek.com/stories/2008-03-12/outsourcing-the-patients. Accessed March 12, 2013.

Electronic Medical Record, Education, Centers for Medicare and Medicaid 1500 Claim Form. Accessed, April 10, 2013. http://www.emrconsultant.com/education/cms-1500-claim-form.

"Emergency Medical Treatment & Labor Act (EMTALA)." Centers for Medicare and Medicaid Services. Accessed April 19, 2013. www.cms.gov/Regulations-and-Guidance/Legislation/EMTALA/index.html?redirect=/emtala.

"Employer Health Benefits 2009 Annual Survey." Kaiser Family Foundation. Accessed March 11, 2013. http://ehbs.kff.org/2009.html.

"Employer Health Benefits 2012 Annual Survey." Kaiser Family Foundation. Accessed April 17, 2013. http://ehbs.kff.org/?page=charts&id=1&sn=6&p=1.

"Employer-Sponsored Coverage Rates for the Nonelderly by Gender, States (2010–2011), U.S. (2011)." Statehealthfacts.org. Accessed March 17, 2013. www.statehealthfacts.org/comparetable.jsp?ind=152&cat=3.

Eskridge, Carey. "Disproportionate Share Hospital (DSH) Program: Your Questions Answered." TLC Research Division. Accessed March 12, 2013. www.tlc.state.tx.us/pubspol/dshprogram.pdf.

"Establishing Health Insurance Exchanges: An Overview of State Efforts." Kaiser Family Foundation. Accessed April 18, 2013. www.kff.org/healthreform/8213.cfm.

Federal Register volume 75, no. 123, June 28, 2010, Rules and Regulations, pp. 37187–37241. Available online at www.gpo.gov/fdsys/pkg/FR-2010-06-28/html/2010-15278.htm (accessed April 18, 2013).

"Fees for Visa Services." Travel.State.Gov. Accessed March 14, 2013. http://travel
.state.gov/visa/temp/types/types_1263.html#special.

"Financial Information." MD Anderson Cancer Center. Accessed March 15, 2013.
www.mdanderson.org/patient-and-cancer-information/guide-to-md-anderson/
international-center/financial-information/index.html.

Fitzgerald, William. "Paving Way for International Patients." *Conquest* (fall 2010).
Available online at www.mdanderson.org/publications/conquest/issues/2010-fall/
international-patients.html (accessed March 15, 2013).

"Five Things You Need to Ask Yourself about Health Care Reforms." Straight Talk on
Health Care blog by Healthpolicymaven™, January 19, 2008. Accessed March 17,
2013. http://healthpolicymaven.blogspot.com/2008/01/five-things-you-need-to-ask-
yourself.html.

Florida Department of Health, Office of Trauma, Division of Emergency Medical
Operations. "Florida's Trauma Care System 2003 Annual Report." July 2004.
Available online at www.doh.state.fl.us/demo/trauma/pdfs/emstraumarept11_04.
pdf (accessed April 18, 2013).

"Florida: Health Insurance Exchanges." Statehealthfacts.org. Accessed April 18,
2013. www.statehealthfacts.org/profileind.jsp?cat=17&sub=205&rgn=11.

"Florida Trauma Centers Contact Information." Florida Department of Health.
Accessed March 12, 2013. www.doh.state.fl.us/demo/trauma/PDFs/FLTrauma
CntrContactInfo7-09.pdf.

"For International Patients." Memorial Sloan-Kettering Cancer Center. Accessed
March 15, 2013. www.mskcc.org/mskcc/html/3226.cfm.

"Former Governor's Death with Dignity Initiative Booth Gardner." Straight Talk on
Health Care blog by Healthpolicymaven™, January 11, 2008. Accessed April 19,
2013. www.healthpolicymaven.com/?p=47 and http://healthpolicymaven.blogspot
.com/2008/01/former-governors-death-with-dignity.html.

"Frequently Asked Questions, Nursing Homes." Oregon Patient Safety Commission, summer 2007. Accessed March 12, 2013. http://library.state.or.us/repository/
2007/200710171149033/index.pdf.

Galland, Zoe. "Medical Tourism: The Insurance Debate." *Businessweek*, November
9, 2008. Available online at www.businessweek.com/stories/2008-11-09/medical-
tourism-the-insurance-debatebusinessweek-business-news-stock-market-and-
financial-advice (accessed March 12, 2013).

"General Assembly of North Carolina: Session 2011." North Carolina General Assembly. Accessed March 15, 2013. www.ncleg.net/Sessions/2011/Bills/Senate/PDF/
S467v1.pdf.

"Get Help Paying Costs." Medicare.gov. Accessed April 19, 2013. www.medicare
.gov/your-medicare-costs/help-paying-costs/get-help-paying-costs.html.

"Global Health Observatory Data Repository." World Health Organization. Accessed March 11, 2013. http://apps.who.int/ghodata.

"Global Health Sites." Duke Global Health Institute. Accessed March 15, 2013.
http://globalhealth.duke.edu/whos-involved/field-sites.

Government Is Not God PAC. "PAC Ad Says Obama Will Force Christian Groups
to Pay for Abortions." PolitiFact.com, September 23, 2012. Accessed April 19,
2013. www.politifact.com/truth-o-meter/statements/2012/sep/26/government-
not-god-pac/pac-ad-says-obama-will-force-christian-groups-pay-.

"Government Spending Details." Usgovernmentspending.com. Accessed April 18, 2013. www.usgovernmentspending.com/year_spending_2013USbt_13bs1n_0010 #usgs302.

"H. B. 3089." West Virginia Legislature. Accessed March 15, 2013. www.legis.state .wv.us/Bill_Status/bills_text.cfm?billdoc=hb3089%20intr.htm&yr=2001&sess type=RS&i=3089.

Hammer, Bethany. "Mandatory Reporting of Hospital-Acquired Infections." Thesis Presentation, Loyola University, 2009. Available online at http://healthlawonline .luc.edu/documents/Hammer_ThesisPresentation.pdf (accessed March 12, 2013).

"Harborview Medical Center UW Diversity Appraisal." The University of Washington, October 2004. Accessed March 12, 2013. www.washington.edu/diversity/ divpdfs/Harborview_Medical_Center.pdf.

Hawaii Department of Health, Office of Health Care Assurance, Hospital Accreditation Status, Posted February 20, Accessed April 11, 2013. http://hawaii.gov/ health/elder-care/health-assurance/medicare-facilities/directory-hospital.html

"Health Care Costs: A Primer, Key Information on Health Care Costs and Their Impact." Kaiser Family Foundation, August 2007, p. 12.

"Health Care Spending in the United States and Selected OECD Countries: April 2011." Kaiser Family Foundation. Accessed March 11, 2013. www.kff.org/insurance/ snapshot/oecd042111.cfm.

"Health Costs and Budgets." Statehealthfacts.org. Accessed March 15, 2013. www .statehealthfacts.org/comparecat.jsp?cat=5&rgn=6&rgn=1.

"Health Coverage and Uninsured." Statehealthfacts.org, Kaiser Family Foundation. Accessed April 17, 2013. www.statehealthfacts.org/comparecat.jsp?cat=3&rgn=6&rgn=1.

"Health Insurance Coverage of Children 0–18, states (2010–2011), U.S. (2011)." Statehealthfacts.org. Accessed March 17, 2013. www.statehealthfacts.org/compare table.jsp?ind=127&cat=3.

"Health Insurance Coverage of Men 19–64, States (2010–2011), U.S. (2011)." Statehealthfacts.org. Accessed March 17, 2013. www.statehealthfacts.org/comparebar .jsp?ind=653&cat=3.

"Health Insurance Coverage of Nonelderly Women 0–64, States (2010–2011), U.S. (2011)." Statehealthfacts.org, Kaiser Family Foundation. Accessed April 19, 2013. http://statehealthfacts.org/comparemaptable.jsp?ind=132&cat=3&sub=178&yr=2 74&typ=2.

"Health Insurance Coverage of Women 19–64, States (2010–2011), U.S. (2011)." Stateheathfacts.org, Kaiser Family Foundation. Accessed April 19, 2013. www.state healthfacts.org/comparebar.jsp?ind=652&cat=3.

"Healthcare Costs Around the World." Visual Economics, March 1, 2010. Accessed March 11, 2013. www.visualeconomics.com/healthcare-costs-around-the-world_2010-03-01.

Heron, Melonie, Donna L. Hoyert, Sherry L. Murphy, Jiaquan Xu, Kenneth D. Kochanek, and Betzaida Tejada-Vera. "Deaths: Final Data for 2006." *National Vital Statistics Reports* 57, no. 14 (2009). Available online at www.cdc.gov/nchs/data/ nvsr/nvsr57/nvsr57_14.pdf (accessed March 17, 2013).

Hinda Chaikind. "Medicare Secondary Payer—Coordination of Benefits." Congressional Research Service, July 10, 2008. Available online at http://aging.senate.gov/ crs/medicare11.pdf (accessed April 19, 2013).

Holahan, John, A. Bowen Garrett, and the Urban Institute. "Rising Unemployment, Medicaid and the Uninsured." Kaiser Commission on Medicaid and the Uninsured. Available online at www.kff.org/uninsured/upload/7850.pdf (accessed April 17, 2013).

"Home." Penn State Hershey Children's Hospital. Accessed March 12, 2013. www.pennstatehershey.org/web/childrens/home.

"Homeopathy: An Introduction." National Center for Complementary and Alternative Medicine. Accessed March 15, 2013. http://nccam.nih.gov/health/homeopathy#keys.

Home page. Cleveland Clinic, Florida. Accessed March 15, 2013. http://my.cleveland clinic.org/florida/default.aspx.

Home page. Kansas State Board of Healing Arts. Accessed March 15, 2013. www.ksbha.org.

Home page. Maryland Association of Naturopathic Physicians. Accessed March 15, 2013. www.mdanp.org.

Home page. Massachusetts Society of Naturopathic Doctors. Accessed March 15, 2013. http://msnd.org.

Home page. Partners Harvard Medical International. Accessed March 15, 2013. www.phmi.partners.org.

Home page. Pennsylvania Association of Naturopathic Physicians. Accessed April 18, 2013. www.panp.org.

Home page. State of Arizona Naturopathic Physicians Medical Board. Accessed April 18, 2013. www.aznd.gov/agency/pages/home.asp.

Home page. Statehealthfacts.org, Kaiser Family Foundation. Accessed April 19, 2013. www.statehealthfacts.org.

Horowitz, Michael D., Jeffrey A. Rosensweig, and Christopher A. Jones. "Medical Tourism: Globalization of the Healthcare Marketplace." *MedGenMed* 9, no. 4 (2007): 33. Available online at www.ncbi.nlm.nih.gov/pmc/articles/PMC2234298 (accessed April 18, 2013).

"Hospitals." State of Hawaii Department of Health, Office of Health Care Assurance, Medicare Section. Accessed April 18, 2013. http://hawaii.gov/health/elder-care/health-assurance/medicare-facilities/directory-hospital.html.

"How Do Medical Advantage Plans Work?" Medicare.gov. Accessed April 19, 2013. www.medicare.gov/sign-up-change-plans/medicare-health-plans/medicare-advantage-plans/how-medicare-advantage-plans-work.html.

"How Hospitals Will Fare Under the 2010 Public Health Service Act," posted March 23, 2010. Accessed April 6, 2013. http://healthpolicymaven.blogspot.com/2010/03/how-hospitals-will-fare-under-2010.html.

Humphry, Derek. "Tread Carefully When You Help to Die: Assisted Suicide Laws around the World." Euthanasia Research and Guidance Organization, March 1, 2005. Accessed March 16, 2013. www.assistedsuicide.org/suicide_laws.html.

Hussey, Peter S., Gerard F. Anderson, Robin Osborn, Colin Feek, Vivienne McLaughlin, John Millar, and Arnold Epstein. "How Does the Quality of Care Compare in Five Countries?" *Health Affairs* 23, no. 3 (May 2004): 89–99. Available online at http://content.healthaffairs.org/content/23/3/89.full (accessed March 11, 2013).

"Idaho: Health Insurance Exchanges." Statehealthfacts.org. Accessed April 18, 2013. www.statehealthfacts.org/profileind.jsp?cat=17&sub=205&rgn=14.

"Indiana: Health Insurance Exchanges." Statehealthfacts.org. Accessed April 18, 2013. www.statehealthfacts.org/profileind.jsp?cat=17&sub=205&rgn=16.

"Indiana Reports Fewer Preventable Medical Errors; Kansas Struggles to Meet Oral Health Needs." Kaiser Health News, August 31, 2010. Accessed March 12, 2013. www.kaiserhealthnews.org/Daily-Reports/2010/August/31/State-Round-Up.aspx.

Indiana State Department of Health. *Indiana Medical Error Reporting System: Final Report for 2009*. Indianapolis: Indiana State Department of Health, 2010. Available online at www.in.gov/isdh/files/2009_MERS_Report.pdf (accessed March 12, 2013).

"Industry Overview." Insurance Information Institute. Accessed March 13, 2013. www.iii.org/media/facts/statsbyissue/industry.

"Infant Mortality Rate (Deaths per 1,000 Live Births), Linked Files, 2006–2008." Statehealthfacts.org. Accessed March 17, 2013. www.statehealthfacts.org/compare maptable.jsp?ind=47&cat=2.

Institute of Medicine (U.S.) Committee on Understanding Premature Birth and Assuring Healthy Outcomes, R. E. Behrman, and A. S. Butler, eds. "Societal Costs of Preterm Birth." In *Preterm Birth: Causes, Consequences, and Prevention*. Washington, D.C.: National Academies Press, 2007. Available online at www.ncbi.nlm.nih.gov/books/NBK11358 (accessed March 17, 2013).

"Insurance Changes from the Patient Protection and Affordable Care Act." Straight Talk on Health Care blog by Healthpolicymaven™, March 26, 2010. Accessed March 15, 2013. http://healthpolicymaven.blogspot.com/2010/03/insurance-changes-from-patient.html.

"Interactive Atlas of Heart Disease and Stroke." Centers for Disease Control and Prevention. Accessed March 17, 2013. http://apps.nccd.cdc.gov/giscvh2/Default.aspx.

Internal Revenue Service. "Health Insurance Premium Tax Credit." Federal Register 77, no. 100 (May 2012). Available online at www.gpo.gov/fdsys/pkg/FR-2012-05-23/pdf/2012-12421.pdf (accessed March 15, 2013).

"International Services." Baptist Health, South Florida. Accessed April 18, 2013. http://baptisthealth.net/en/international/Pages/default.aspx.

"International Services." Mayo Clinic. Accessed March 15, 2013. www.mayoclinic.org/international.

"International Services." Memorial Hermann. Accessed March 15, 2013. www.memorial-hermann.org/international.

"International Services." UCSF Medical Center. Accessed April 18, 2013. www.ucsfhealth.org/services/international_services.

"Iowa: Health Insurance Exchanges." Statehealthfacts.org. Accessed April 18, 2013. www.statehealthfacts.org/profileind.jsp?cat=17&sub=205&rgn=17.

"JCI Accredited Organizations." Joint Commission International. Accessed April 18, 2013. www.jointcommissioninternational.org/JCI-Accredited-Organizations.

Johnson, Toni. "Healthcare Costs and U.S. Competitiveness." Council on Foreign Relations, March 26, 2012. Accessed March 11, 2013. www.cfr.org.health-science-and-technology/healthcare-costs-us-competiveness.

Joint Commission International Accredited Organizations, Accessed April 10, 2013. www.jointcommissioninternational.org/JCI-Accredited-Organizations/

Jones, Donald Lloyd, Robert Adams, Mercedes Carnethon et al. "Heart Disease and Stroke Statistics—2009 Update. A Report from the American Heart Association Statistics Committee and Stroke Statistics Subcommittee." *Circulation*, December 15, 2008. Available online at http://circ.ahajournals.org/cgi/reprint/CIRCULATIONAHA.108.191261v1 (accessed March 17, 2013).

Kaiser Family Foundation. "Explaining Health Care Reform: Questions about Health Insurance Subsidies." Kaiser Family Foundation Focus on Health Reform, July 2012. Accessed March 15, 2013. www.kff.org/healthreform/upload/7962-02.pdf.

———. "Health Care Costs: A Primer." March 2009. Available online at www.kff .org/insurance/upload/7670_02.pdf (accessed March 13, 2013).

———. "State Health Facts Women's Health Insurance Coverage for Women 19-64, 2010–2011." Accessed April 19, 2013. http://statehealthfacts.org/comparetable.jsp?ind=652&cat=3&sub=178&yr=274&typ=2

———. "Survey of People Who Purchase Their Own Insurance." June 2010. Available online at www.kff.org/kaiserpolls/upload/8077-R.pdf (accessed March 11, 2013).

Kaiser Family Foundation and Health Research and Educational Trust. "Employer Health Benefits: 2010 Summary of Findings." Available online at http://ehbs.kff.org/pdf/2010/8086.pdf (accessed March 11, 2013).

———. "Employer Health Benefits: 2012 Summary of Findings." Available online at http://ehbs.kff.org/pdf/2012/8346.pdf (accessed April 18, 2013).

"Kansas: Health Insurance Exchanges." Statehealthfacts.org. Accessed April 18, 2013. www.statehealthfacts.org/profileind.jsp?cat=17&sub=205&rgn=18.

"Kidney Transplantation Services." Stony Brook Medicine. Accessed March 15, 2013. www.stonybrookmedicalcenter.org/transplant.

"Language Assistance." Cleveland Clinic. Accessed March 15, 2013. http://my.cleveland clinic.org/global_patient_services/patients/international/languages.aspx.

"Leading Cause of Death." Centers for Disease Control and Prevention. Accessed April 19, 2013. www.cdc.gov/nchs/fastats/lcod.htm.

Leapfrog Group hospital comparison tool. Accessed March 12, 2013. www.leapfrog group.org/cp.

Legislature of the State of Idaho. House Bill no. 220, 61st Legislature, 1st regular session, 2011. Available online at http://legislature.idaho.gov/legislation/2011/H0220.pdf (accessed April 18, 2013).

Legislative Info, State of California, Business and Professional Licensing Code, Section 3630–3637, Application for Licensure for a Naturopathic Doctor, Accessed April 12, 2013. http://www.leginfo.ca.gov/cgi-bin/displaycode?section=bpc&group=03001-04000&file=3630-3637

Lenhart, Maria, and Marilee Crocker. "Walmart Offers Medical Travel Coverage to Employees." Travel Market Report, November 15, 2013. Accessed April 18, 2013. www.travelmarketreport.com/articles/Walmart-Offers-Medical-Travel-Coverage-to-Employees.

Leyden, Christine G. "Coming to America—What Medical Tourists Need to Know." Medvoy, August 4, 2009. Accessed March 14, 2013. www.medvoy.com/resource.php?industrynews_id=4.

"Licensed States & Licensing Authorities." American Association of Naturopathic Physicians. Accessed April 18, 2013. www.naturopathic.org/content.asp?contentid=57.

"Licensing." Indiana Association of Naturopathic Physicians. Accessed March 15, 2013. www.inanp.com/?page_id=25.

"Licensing Area: Naturopathic Medicine." Hawaii Department of Commerce and Consumer Affairs. Accessed March 15, 2013. http://hawaii.gov/dcca/pvl/boards/naturopathy.

"Licensing States and Licensing Authorities." American Association of Naturopathic Physicians. Accessed March 15, 2013. www.naturopathic.org/content.asp?contentid=57.

Licensure map. Association of Accredited Naturopathic Medical Colleges. Accessed April 18, 2013. www.aanmc.org/images/licensuremap-shaded_October2012.gif.

"Links and Resources." Vermont Association of Naturopathic Physicians. Accessed March 15, 2013. www.vanp.org/links.php.

"List of Countries by Infant Mortality Rate." Wikipedia. Accessed March 17, 2013. http://en.wikipedia.org/wiki/List_of_countries_by_infant_mortality_rate.

Lobosky, Jeffrey M. *It's Enough to Make You Sick.* Lanham, MD: Rowman & Littlefield, 2012.

Lowen, Linda. "What Is the Hyde Amendment?" About.com. Accessed April 19, 2013. http://womensissues.about.com/od/reproductiverights/f/HydeAmendment.htm.

"Luxembourg." World Bank. Accessed March 11, 2013. http://data.worldbank.org/country/Luxembourg.

"Maine: Health Insurance Exchanges." Statehealthfacts.org. Accessed April 18, 2013. www.statehealthfacts.org/profileind.jsp?cat=17&sub=205&rgn=21.

"Massage Therapy Certification." Natural Healers. Accessed March 15, 2013. www.naturalhealers.com/qa/massage.html.

"Mayo Clinic in Rochester, Minnesota." Mayo Clinic. Accessed March 15, 2013. www.mayoclinic.org/Rochester.

"Medicaid and Children's Health Insurance Program Provisions in the New Health Reform Law." Kaiser Family Foundation. Accessed March 15, 2013. www.kff.org/healthreform/7952.cfm.

"Medicaid and CHIP Eligibility Table by State." National Conference of State Legislatures. Accessed April 19, 2013. www.ncsl.org/issues-research/health/medicaid-eligibility-table-by-state-state-activit.aspx.

"Medicaid and CHIP Health Reform Implementation Timeline." Kaiser Family Foundation. Accessed March 17, 2013. www.kff.org/healthreform/upload/8064.

"Medicaid Enrollment by State." Medicaid. Accessed March 11, 2013. www.medicaid.gov/Medicaid-CHIP-Program-Information/By-State/By-State.html.

"Medicaid Payments per Enrollee, FY2009." Statehealthfacts.org. Accessed March 11, 2013. www.statehealthfacts.org/comparemaptable.jsp?ind=183&cat=4.

"Medical Tourism: Emerging Phenomenon in Health Care Industry—2008 Report." Deloitte, May 14, 2012. Accessed March 14, 2013. www.deloitte.com/us/2008medicaltourism.

"Medical Tourism Facility: Johns Hopkins Medicine International." Online Medical Tourism. Accessed March 15, 2013. www.onlinemedicaltourism.com/Johns-Hopkins-Medicine-International.html.

"Medicare-Approved Transplant Programs." Centers for Medicare & Medicaid Services, January 31, 2013. Accessed March 14, 2013. www.cms.gov/Certification andComplianc/Downloads/ApprovedTransplantPrograms.pdf.

"Medicare Costs at a Glance." Medicare.gov. Accessed April 19, 2013. www.medicare .gov/your-medicare-costs/costs-at-a-glance/costs-at-glance.html#collapse-4632.

"Medicare Eligibility Tool." Medicare.gov. Accessed April 19, 2013. www.medicare .gov/MedicareEligibility/home.asp?version=default&browser=Chrome%7C25%7 CWindows+7&language=English.

"Medicare Prescription Drug, Improvement, and Modernization Act of 2003." Public Law 108–173, 108th Congress, December 8, 2003. www.gpo.gov/fdsys/pkg/PLAW-108publ173/pdf/PLAW-108publ173.pdf (accessed April 28, 2013).

"Medicare Spending and Financing." Kaiser Family Foundation, June 2007. Accessed March 16, 2013. www.kff.org/medicare/upload/7305-02.pdf.

Meier, Diane E., Carol-Ann Emmons, Sylvan Wallenstein, Timothy Quill, R. Sean Morrison, and Christine K. Cassel. "A National Survey of Physician-Assisted Suicide and Euthanasia in the United States." *N Engl J Med* 338 (1998): 1193–1201. Available online at www.nejm.org/doi/full/10.1056/NEJM199804233381706 (accessed April 19, 2013).

Mello, Michelle M. "Understanding Medical Malpractice Insurance: A Primer." Research Synthesis Report no. 8, the Synthesis Project, Robert Wood Johnson Foundation, January 2006. Available online at www.rwjf.org/content/dam/farm/reports/reports/2006/rwjf17974 (accessed April 18, 2013).

"Methodist J. C. Walter Jr. Transplant Center—Houston, TX." The Methodist Hospital System. Accessed March 15, 2013. www.methodisthealth.com/mtc.cfm?id=35448.

Minnesota Licenses, Naturopathic Doctor Registry, Minnesota.gov, Accessed 4/10/2013. http://mn.gov/elicense/licenses/licensedetail.jsp?URI=tcm:29-3569&CT_URI=tcm:27-117-32

"Minnesota: Political Info and Laws in Brief." NARAL Pro-Choice America. Accessed March 17, 2013. www.prochoiceamerica.org/government-and-you/state-governments/state-profiles/minnesota.html.

"Mississippi: Health Insurance Exchanges." Statehealthfacts.org. Accessed April 18, 2013. www.statehealthfacts.org/profileind.jsp?cat=17&sub=205&rgn=26.

"Mississippi Voters Reject Anti-abortion Measure for Fetus Personhood." Reuters, November 9, 2011. Accessed April 19, 2013. http://blogs.reuters.com/faithworld/2011/11/09/mississippi-voters-reject-anti-abortion-measure-for-fetus-personhood.

"Missouri Nosocomial Infection Reporting Data: Report to the Governor and General Assembly—2011." Missouri Department of Health and Senior Services. Accessed March 12, 2013. http://health.mo.gov/data/pdf/2011NosocomialReport.pdf.

"Montana Licensing Information." Montana Association of Naturopathic Physicians. Accessed March 15, 2013. www.mtnd.org/licensing.htm.

"Montana: Public and Private Policy Medical Errors and Patient Safety." Quality and Patient Safety. Accessed March 12, 2013. http://qups.org/med_errors .php?c=individual_state&s=27&t=1.

Murphy, Jarrett. "Trauma Treatment: New York's Level 1 Centers." City Limits, October 7, 2010. Accessed March 15, 2013. www.citylimits.org/news/articles/4202/ trauma-treatment-new-york-s-level-1-centers.

Murray, Christopher. "WHO Issues New Healthy Life Expectancy Rankings: Japan Number One in New 'Healthy Life' System." World Health Organization press release. Available online at www.who.int/inf-pr-2000/en/pr2000-life.html (accessed March 11, 2013).

Murray, Christopher J. L., and Julio Frenk. "Ranking 37th—Measuring the Performance of the U.S. Health Care System." *New England Journal of Medicine* 362 (January 2010): 98–99. Available online at http://healthpolicyandreform.nejm .org/?p=2610 (accessed March 11, 2013).

National Association of Insurance Commissioners. "Appendix D: Authorized Insurance Companies by Line of Business in Washington 2011." In the 2011 Insurance Commissioner's Annual Report. Available online at www.insurance.wa.gov/ about-oic/oic-annual-reports/2011-report/documents/2011AppendixD.pdf (accessed April 19, 2013).

National Center for Health Statistics. *Health, United States, 2010: With Special Feature on Death and Dying.* Hyattsville, MD: National Center for Health Statistics, 2011. Available online at www.cdc.gov/nchs/data/hus/hus10.pdf (accessed March 17, 2013).

———. "Heart Failure Mortality Statistics, 2001–2006." Available online at ftp:// ftp.cdc.gov/pub/Health_Statistics/NCHS/Datasets/DVS/mortality/mort2006ps .zip (accessed April 8, 2013).

"National Health Expenditure Data." Centers for Medicare and Medicaid Services. Accessed March 11, 2013. www.cms.gov/NationalHealthExpendData/25_NHE_ Fact_Sheet.asp.

National Highway Transportation Safety Administration, U.S. Department of Transportation. "Highlights of 2009 Motor Vehicle Crashes." Washington, DC: NHTSA's National Center for Statistics and Analysis, 2010. Available online at www-nrd.nhtsa.dot.gov/Pubs/811363.PDF (accessed March 11, 2013).

"Naturopathic Doctor Licensure." Association of Accredited Naturopathic Colleges. Accessed March 15, 2013. www.aanmc.org/careers/naturopathic-doctor-licensure .php.

"Naturopathic Doctor." Maine Office of Professional and Occupational Regulation. Accessed March 15, 2013. http://maine.gov/pfr/professionallicensing/professions/ complementary/naturopathic_doctor.htm.

"Naturopathic Doctor Registry." License Minnesota. Accessed April 18, 2013. http://mn.gov/elicense/licenses/licensedetail.jsp?URI=tcm:29-3569&CT_ URI=tcm:27-117-32.

"Naturopathic Examiner." New Hampshire Department of Health and Human Services. Accessed March 15, 2013. www.dhhs.nh.gov/oos/blc/naturopath.

"Naturopathic Licensing Jurisdictions in the United States/Canada." Oregon Board of Naturopathic Medicine. Accessed March 15, 2013. www.oregon.gov/OBNM/PopDocs/NaturopathicBoardsOfAmerica.pdf?ga=t.

"Naturopathic Physician Continuing Education Requirements." OnlineCE. Accessed March 15, 2013. www.onlinece.com/pages/naturopathic_requirements.php.

"Naturopathic Physician Licensing Requirements." Connecticut Department of Public Health. Accessed April 18, 2013. www.ct.gov/dph/cwp/view.asp?a=3121&q=389384.

"Naturopathic Physician Practice Act." Utah Division of Occupational and Professional Licensing. Accessed March 15, 2013. www.dopl.utah.gov/laws/58-71.pdf.

"Naturopaths." Florida Department of Health, August 31, 2012. Accessed March 15, 2013. http://doh.state.fl.us/mqa/naturopath/index.html.

"Nebraska: Public and Private Policy Medical Errors and Patient Safety." Quality and Patient Safety. Accessed March 12, 2013. http://qups.org/med_errors.php?c=individual_state&s=28&t=1.

"Nevada Personhood Amendment (2012)." Ballotpedia.org. Accessed April 19, 2013. http://ballotpedia.org/wiki/index.php/Nevada_Personhood_Amendment_(2012).

"New York State Trauma Centers." New York State Department of Health. Accessed March 12, 2013. www.health.state.ny.us/nysdoh/ems/trauma2.htm.

"North Dakota Passes First State Personhood Amendment in US History." PersonhoodUSA.com, March 22, 2013. Accessed April 19, 2013. www.personhoodusa.com/press-release/north-dakota-passes-first-state-personhood-amendment-us-history.

"North Dakota: Public and Private Policy Medical Errors and Patient Safety." Quality and Patient Safety. Accessed March 12, 2013. http://qups.org/med_errors.php?c=individual_state&s=35&t=1.

"Oregon Formulary & Jurisprudence Exams—Applications, Requirements, Dates." Oregon Board of Naturopathic Medicine. Accessed March 15, 2013. www.oregon.gov/OBNM/Exams.shtml.

"Overview." The University of Mississippi Medical Center. Accessed April 18, 2013. www.umc.edu/Overview.aspx.

"Overview of Naturopathic Regulation." NaturoWatch. Accessed April 18, 2013. www.naturowatch.org/licensure/laws.shtml.

"Overview of the Patient-Centered Outcomes Research Institute." Center for Medical Technology Policy. Accessed March 11, 2013. www.cmtpnet.org/comparative-effectiveness/overview-of-the-patient-centered-outcomes-research-institute.

"Palliative Care Information Act." New York State Department of Health. Accessed April 19, 2013. www.health.ny.gov/professionals/patients/patient_rights/palliative_care/information_act.htm.

"Part A Costs." Medicare.gov. Accessed April 19, 2013. www.medicare.gov/your-medicare-costs/part-a-costs/part-a-costs.html.

"Part B Costs." Medicare.gov. Accessed March 17, 2013. www.medicare.gov/your-medicare-costs/part-b-costs/part-b-costs.html.

"Patient Care at Its Best." Baylor College of Medicine. Accessed March 15, 2013. www.bcm.edu/patientcare.

"The Patient Protection and Affordable Care Act." Public Law 111–148, 111th Congress, March 23, 2010. Available online at www.gpo.gov/fdsys/pkg/PLAW-111publ148/pdf/PLAW-111publ148.pdf (accessed April 18, 2013).

"Patient Protection and Affordable Care Act; Standards Related to Essential Health Benefits, Actuarial Value, and Accreditation; Proposed Rule." Federal Register volume 77, no. 227, November 26, 2012. Available online at www.gpo.gov/fdsys/pkg/FR-2012-11-26/pdf/2012-28362.pdf (accessed April 18, 2013).

"Patient Safety Event Reporting Systems Reviewed." Agency for Healthcare Research and Quality. Accessed March 12, 2013. www.pso.ahrq.gov/formats/psersys.htm.

"Patient Services." UCSF Medical Center. Accessed March 14, 2013. www.ucsfhealth.org/services/index.html.

"Penn Medicine Announces New Advanced Care Hospital Pavilion and Trauma Center at Penn Presbyterian Medical Center." News release, Penn Medicine, November 2, 2012. Available online at www.uphs.upenn.edu/news/News_Releases/2012/11/expansion (accessed April 18, 2013).

"Percent of Children (10–17) Who Are Overweight or Obese, 2007." Statehealthfacts.org, Kaiser Family Foundation. Accessed April 17, 2013. www.statehealthfacts.org/comparetable.jsp?ind=51&cat=2&sub=14&yr=62&typ=2.

"Personalized Services." UCLA Health System. Accessed March 14, 2013. www.uclahealth.org/site.cfm?id=169.

"Personhood Bill and Ballot Initiatives." Resolve.org. Accessed April 19, 2013. www.resolve.org/get-involved/personhood-bills-and-ballot-initiatives.html#WA.

"Personhood Debated in Montana Legislature," KRTV News.com, accessed March 25, 2013, http://www.krtv.com/news/personhood-debated-in-montana-legislature/#_

"Poverty in the United States, Frequently Asked Questions." National Poverty Center. Accessed March 17, 2013. www.npc.umich.edu/poverty/#5.

"Preterm Births as a Percent of All Births, 2010." Statehealthfacts.org. Accessed March 17, 2013. www.statehealthfacts.org/comparemaptable.jsp?ind=39&cat=2.

"Preventive and Screening Services." Medicare.gov. Accessed April 19, 2013. www.medicare.gov/coverage/preventive-and-screening-services.html.

"Professional Services for Patients." The Methodist Hospital System. Accessed March 15, 2013. www.methodisthealth.com/basic.cfm?id=37113.

"Public Health Service Act XXVII, as amended, May 1, 2010", Accessed April 12, 2013. http://www.nadp.org/libraries/hcr_documents/phsa027.sflb.ashx

"Quality Measures and Performance Standards." Centers for Medicare and Medicaid Services. Accessed April 18, 2013. www.cms.gov/Medicare/Medicare-Fee-for-Service-Payment/sharedsavingsprogram/Quality_Measures_Standards.html.

"R Adams Cowley Shock Trauma Center." University of Maryland. Accessed March 12, 2013. www.umm.edu/shocktrauma.

Ranji, Usha, Alina Salganicoff, and Tina Park. "Access to Abortion Coverage and Health Reform." Kaiser Family Foundation, November 2010. Available online at www.kff.org/healthreform/upload/8021.pdf (accessed March 17, 2013).

Ranji, Usha, Alina Salganicoff, Alexandra M. Stewart, Marisa Cox, and Lauren Doamekpor. "State Medicaid Coverage of Perinatal Services: Summary of State Survey

Findings, November 2009." Kaiser Family Foundation and George Washington University School of Public Health and Health Services. Accessed March 17, 2013. www.kff.org/womenshealth/upload/8014.pdf.

Reid, T. R. *The Healing of America*. New York: Penguin, 2009.

"Report Cards." National Committee for Quality Assurance. Accessed March 12, 2013. www.ncqa.org/tabid/60/Default.aspx.

Rice, Elizabeth, and Denise Betcher. "Evidence Base for Developing a Palliative Care Service." *MedSurg Nursing* 16, no. 3 (June 2007): 143–48.

Rietjens, J. A., et al. "Terminal Sedation and Euthanasia: A Comparison of Clinical Practices." *Archives of Internal Medicine* 166, no. 7 (April 2006): 749–53.

"Safe Practices for Better Healthcare—2009 Update." National Quality Forum, March 2009. Accessed March 12, 2013. www.qualityforum.org/Publications/2009/03/Safe_Practices_for_Better_Healthcare%e2%80%932009_Update.aspx.

Scroggins, Matt. "COBRA Enrollment Rises after Subsidy Enacted: Hewitt." Business Insurance, December 23, 2009. Accessed April 18, 2013. www.businessinsurance.com/article/20091223/NEWS/912239997.

Search results for "trauma center, level 1." Medical University of South Carolina Health. Accessed March 12, 2013. www.muschealth.com/GSASearch/?q=trauma+center%2C+level+I&SearchGo=Search.

"Self-Described Religious Identification of Adult Population: 1990 to 2008." U.S. Census Bureau. Accessed March 17, 2013. www.census.gov/compendia/statab/2010/tables/10s0075.pdf.

"Senate Bill 1001." Arizona State Legislature, 50th Legislature, 1st special session, 2011. Available online at www.azleg.gov/legtext/50leg/1s/bills/sb1001s.pdf (accessed April 19, 2013).

"Senate Bill 1305." Arizona State Legislature, 49th Legislature, 2nd regular session, 2010. Available online at www.arkleg.state.ar.us/healthcare/Insurance/Documents/AZ%20SB%201305.pdf (accessed April 19, 2013).

"Senate Bill 3214." Mississippi State Legislature, 2010 regular session. Accessed March 17, 2013. http://billstatus.ls.state.ms.us/2010/pdf/history/SB/SB3214.xml.

Simek, S., et al. "How Does Time to Treatment Affect the Long-Term Prognosis for Patients with Acute Myocardial Infarction Treated with Primary Coronary Angioplasty." *European Center for Medical Informatics, Statistics, and Epidemiology* 61, no. 8 (August 2004): 91–100.

Social Security Administration. "Medicare." Available online at www.ssa.gov/pubs/media/pdf/EN-05-10043.pdf (accessed April 19, 2013).

"Social Security and Medicare Tax Rates; Maximum Taxable Earnings." U.S. Social Security Administration. Accessed April 17, 2013. http://ssa-custhelp.ssa.gov/app/answers/detail/a_id/240/~/social-security-and-medicare-tax-rates%3B-maximum-taxable-earnings.

Sonfield, A., J. J. Frost, R. B. Gold. "U.S. Insurance Coverage of Contraceptives and the Impact of Contraceptive Coverage Mandates, 2002." *Perspectives on Sexual and Reproductive Health* 236, no. 2 (2004): 1.

"South Dakota: Public and Private Policy Medical Errors and Patient Safety." Quality and Patient Safety. Accessed March 12, 2013. http://qups.org/med_errors.php?c=individual_state&s=42&t=1.

Stanton, Mark. "The High Concentration of U.S. Health Care Expenditures." *AHRQ Research in Action* 19 (June 2006).

"State Decisions for Creating Health Insurance Exchanges, as of April 1, 2013." Statehealthfacts.org. Accessed April 18, 2013. www.statehealthfacts.org/compare maptable.jsp?ind=962&cat=17.

"State Funding of Abortion under Medicaid." Guttmacher Institute, State Policies in Brief, April 1, 2013. Available online at www.guttmacher.org/statecenter/spibs/spib_SFAM.pdf (accessed April 19, 2013).

"State Governments." NARAL Pro-Choice America. Accessed March 17, 2013. www .prochoiceamerica.org/government-and-you/state-governments.

"Statewide Initiative to Help Identify and Prevent Infections." Indiana State Department of Health. Accessed March 12, 2013. www.in.gov/portal/news_events/58592.htm.

"Statistics and Surveillance: 2008 Table Data." Centers for Disease Control and Prevention. Accessed March 17, 2013. www.cdc.gov/vaccines/stats-surv/nis/data/tables_2008.htm.

"Statistics and Surveillance: 2010 Table Data." Centers for Disease Control and Prevention. Accessed April 17, 2013. www.cdc.gov/vaccines/stats-surv/nis/data/tables_2010.htm.

"Statutes and Regulations: Naturopaths." Alaska Department of Commerce, Community, and Economic Development, March 2008. Available online at www.dced .state.ak.us/occ/pub/NaturopathyStatutes.pdf (accessed April 18, 2013).

"Support Licensure of Naturopathic Doctors in Maryland." Maryland Association of Naturopathic Physicians. Accessed April 18, 2013. www.ndaccess.com/MDANP/Page.asp?PageID=5.

"Supreme Court Upholds the Affordable Care Act: What the Experts Are Saying." Rand Health, June 28, 2012. Accessed April 18, 2013. www.rand.org/health/feature/aca_ruling.html.

"A Survey of Medical Tourism Providers," Christina Peters and Katherine Sauer, *Journal of Marketing Development and Competitiveness*, vol. 5 (3), 2011, Accessed April 10, 2013. http://www.na-businesspress.com/JMDC/SauerWeb.pdf.

"Table XV: Immigrant Visas Issued by Issuing Office, Fiscal Years 2003–2012." Travel.state.gov. Accessed April 18, 2013. www.travel.state.gov/pdf/FY12AnnualReport-TableXV.pdf.

"Table XVI(B): Nonimmigrant Visas Issued by Classification, Fiscal Years 2008–2012." Travel.state.gov. Accessed April 18, 2013. www.travel.state.gov/pdf/FY12AnnualReport-TableXVIB.pdf.

Tandon, Ajay, Christopher J. L. Murray, Jeremy A. Lauer, and David B. Evans. "Measuring Overall Health System Performance for 191 Countries." GPE Discussion Paper Series no. 30. Available online at www.who.int/healthinfo/paper30.pdf (accessed April 19, 2013).

"Top 25 Health Insurance Companies." U.S. News and World Report. Accessed March 13, 2013. http://health.usnews.com/health-plans/national-insurance-companies.

"The Top 50 Heart Care US Hospitals." Cardiac Health. Accessed April 18, 2013. www.cardiachealth.org/heart-disease-treatment/top-us-heart-care-hospitals.

"Traditional Naturopathy Licensing." The License Commission of the Americas. Accessed March 15, 2013. www.tlcta.com/naturopathy.

"Trauma Care." Centers for Disease Control. Accessed March 12, 2013. www.cdc .gov/traumacare/index.html.

"Trauma Services at HUP." Penn Medicine. Accessed April 18, 2013. www.uphs .upenn.edu/em/clinserv/hup-trauma.htm.

"Trauma System." Washington State Department of Health. Accessed April 18, 2013. www.doh.wa.gov/PublicHealthandHealthcareProviders/EmergencyMedical ServicesEMSSystems/TraumaSystem.aspx.

Treiguts, Edgar. "State Adds Fifth Level-1 Trauma Center." GPB News, June 8, 2011. Available online at www.gpb.org/news/2011/06/08/state-adds-fifth-level-1-trauma-center (accessed April 18, 2013).

"Uninsured Rates for the Nonelderly by Gender, States (2010–2011), U.S. (2011)." Statehealthfacts.org. Accessed March 17, 2013. www.statehealthfacts.org/compa-retable.jsp?ind=142&cat=3.

"United States 2012 Federal Budget." Wikipedia. Accessed March 11, 2013. http:// en.wikipedia.org/wiki/2012_United_States_federal_budget#Total_revenues_and_ spending.

"United States Cancer Statistics, 1999–2006 Mortality Archive Request." CDC Won-der. Accessed April 19, 2013. http://wonder.cdc.gov/CancerMort-v2006.html.

"United States Cancer Statistics (USCS): 2009 State vs. National Comparisons." Centers for Disease Control and Prevention. Accessed March 17, 2013. http:// apps.nccd.cdc.gov/uscs/statevsnational.aspx.

"United States: Medicaid Beneficiaries." Statehealthfacts.org, Kaiser Family Founda-tion. Accessed April 19, 2013. www.statehealthfacts.org/profileind.jsp?cmprgn=4 5&cat=4&rgn=1&sub=52.

Unti, James A. "Medical and Surgical Tourism: The New World of Health Care Globalization and What It Means for the Practicing Surgeon." American College of Surgeons, June 8, 2009. Accessed April 18, 2013. www.surgicalpatientsafety .facs.org/news/medicaltourism0609.html.

"UPMC Global Care." UPMC. Accessed March 15, 2013. www.upmc.com/abou-tupmc/icsd/Pages/global-care.aspx.

U.S. Bureau of the Census. "Income Alternative Poverty Estimates in the United States: 2003." Report P60, n. 227, tables B-1 and B-3, pp. 18, 20.

———. "Table 74. Population in Group Quarters by State: 2000 to 2010." In *U.S. Census Bureau, Statistical Abstract of the United States: 2012*. Washington, DC: U.S. Census Bureau, 2012. Available online at www.census.gov/compendia/ statab/2012/tables/12s0075.pdf (accessed April 19, 2013).

U.S. Congress. H. R. 1, 108th Congress, 1st session, January 7, 2003. Available online at www.gpo.gov/fdsys/pkg/BILLS-108hr1enr/pdf/BILLS-108hr1enr.pdf (accessed April 18, 2013).

"U.S. and World Population Clock." U.S. Census Bureau. Accessed April 18, 2013. www.census.gov/population/www/popclockus.html.

Vanderbilt University Medical Center, Certifications & Facilities, Accessed April 12, 2013. www.mc.vanderbilt.edu/about

Vequist IV, David G., and Erika Valdez. "Economic Report: Inbound Medical Tourism in the United States." *Medical Tourism Magazine*, August 4, 2009. Available online at www.medicaltourismmag.com/article/economic-report-inbound.html (accessed March 14, 2013).

"Verified Trauma Centers FAQ." American College of Surgeons. Accessed March 12, 2013. www.facs.org/trauma/verifiedfaq.html.

"Verified Trauma Centers." American College of Surgeons. Accessed March 12, 2013. www.facs.org/trauma/verified.html.

"Visa Waiver Program." Travel.State.Gov. Accessed March 15, 2013. http://travel.state.gov/visa/temp/without/without_1990.html.

"Visiting UC San Diego Health System." UC San Diego Health System. Accessed April 18, 2013. http://health.ucsd.edu/specialties/international/visiting/Pages/default.aspx.

"Visitors Medical Insurance Summary", American Visitor Insurance.com, Accessed March 25, 2013. http://www.americanvisitorinsurance.com/insurance/visitors-medical-summary.asp.

"Washington State Credentialing Requirements." Washington State Department of Health. Accessed March 15, 2013. www.doh.wa.gov/Portals/1/Documents/2600/630112Naturopath.pdf.

Washington State Department of Health. "Washington State Trauma Services." Office of Community Health Systems, February 2013. Available online at www.doh.wa.gov/Portals/1/Documents/Pubs/530101.pdf (accessed April 18, 2013).

"What Does Medicare Part A Cover?" Medicare.gov. Accessed April 19, 2013. www.medicare.gov/what-medicare-covers/part-a/what-part-a-covers.html.

"What Does Medicare Part B Cover?" Medicare.gov. Accessed April 19, 2013. www.medicare.gov/what-medicare-covers/part-b/what-medicare-part-b-covers.html.

"What Is Assisted Reproductive Technology?" Centers for Disease Control and Prevention, February 12, 2013. Accessed March 14, 2013. www.cdc.gov/art.

Women's Issues, Reproductive Rights, Hyde Amendments, About.com, Accessed March 25, 2013 http://womensissues.about.com/od/reproductiverights/f/Hyde Amendment.htm

World Health Organization. *The World Health Report, 2000*. Geneva, Switzerland: World Health Organization, 2000. Available online at www.who.int/whr/2000/en/whr00_en.pdf (accessed March 11, 2013).

"World's Top Ten Tourism Earners, 2006." Infoplease, 2007. Accessed March 14, 2013. www.infoplease.com/ipa/A0922054.html.

Writing, Alexis. "The Average Cost for Medical Malpractice Insurance." EHow.com. Accessed April 17, 2013. www.ehow.com/about_5514154_average-cost-medical-malpractice-insurance.html.

Yardley, William. "Report Finds 36 Died under Assisted Suicide Law." *New York Times*, March 4, 2010. Available online at www.nytimes.com/2010/03/05/us/05suicide.html (accessed March 16, 2013).

"Your Medicare Costs-Part A Costs," Medicare.gov, Accessed April 5, 2013. http://www.medicare.gov/your-medicare-costs/part-a-costs/part-a-costs.html.

Ziran, Bruce H., Mary-Kate Barrette-Grischow, and Barbara Hileman. "United States Level I Trauma Centers Are Not Created Equal—a Concern for Patient Safety." *Patient Safety in Surgery* 2 (2008): 18. Available online at www.ncbi.nlm .nih.gov/pmc/articles/PMC2515286 (accessed March 12, 2013).

Zuckerman, I. H., S. R. Weiss, D. McNally, B. Layne, C. D. Mullins, and J. Wang. "Impact on Education Intervention for Secondary Prevention of Myocardial Infarction on Medicaid Drug Use and Cost." *The American Journal of Managed Care* 10, no. 7, part 2 (2004): 493–500.

Index